EPICURUS AND THE PLEASANT LIFE

Author-Publisher © Haris Dimitriadis, 2017

Text editors: Terry MacCallum & Jennifer Nelson

Cover designer: Edward Bettison

Production supervisor: Platon Malliagkas - www.mediterrabooks.com

ISBN 978-960-93-8456-8

*

Visit the site
epicurusphilosophy.com
for a free download of brand new songs
dedicated to Epicurus and his philosophy.

Haris Dimitriadis

EPICURUS

AND THE PLEASANT LIFE

A Philosophy of Nature

To my granddaughter Cleo

Next page: Marble head of the philosopher Epicurus, Roman copy of a Greek original of the late 3rd or 2nd c. BC, British Museum

"Pleasure is our first and kindred good. It is the starting-point of every choice and of every aversion, and to it we come back, inasmuch as we make feeling the rule by which to judge of every good thing. And since pleasure is our first and native good, for that reason we do not choose every pleasure whatsoever, but often pass over many pleasures when a greater annoyance ensues from them."

Epicurus, *Letter to Menoeceus*

ACKNOWLEDGEMENTS

I would like to thank my wife Maria, my daughter Vera and my son Evdokimos for their psychological support and encouragement in the course of the writing of this book.

ೞ ೩

This book has been based on the ancient Epicurean sources as well as on the works of the modern scholars: Haralambos Theodoridis, *The True Face of the Ancient World,* Cyril Bailey, *Epicurus–The Extant Remains*, Norman Dewitt, *Epicurus and His Philosophy*, and Mihaly Csikszentmihalyi, *Flow, the Psychology of Optimal Experience*.

PREFACE

Welcome, seekers of truth!

Now is the time to reject sales pitches and heed the knowledge with which we were gifted upon birth. The legendary and elusive secret to happiness does exist, though you won't find it gleaming on a store shelf, sold in a book store or printed on a t-shirt. This so-called secret has been in your possession and within reach your entire life. In fact, it is not a secret at all.

This book seeks to reintroduce pleasure as our innate guide to living a healthy and happy life. A simple yet powerful assertion based on empirical data which stands up to the strictest scrutiny. Along this journey, we will explore evidence throughout the historical evolution of philosophy up to the time of Epicurus, the ancient Greek philosopher who laid the foundations for a philosophy of Nature. More specifically, the only philosophy which distinguishes pleasure as the inherent human guide to a healthy and happy life.

Our multi-screen, one-click modern society is often accused of hedonism yet this perception is contradicted by a widespread obsession with pain. Of course, pain relief and pain control are noteworthy themes, yet it remains remarkable that a minority seeks to understand pleasure and its role in life. Despite its significance, very few have endeavored to recognize, and present guidelines based on scientific evidence, that pleasure promotes health and happiness.

Contemporary society is characterized by a denial and fear of pleasure. This behavior is usually subconscious and always difficult to overcome. In many ways, we are all influenced and sometimes even consciously trained to resist pleasure. This is done by parents, medical professionals, educators, religious leaders and other authority figures. Furthermore, the enemy is also often found within. Most of us harbor self-destructive tendencies, which lead us to deny ourselves pleasure for a variety of reasons.

For many, healthy living hinges on deprivation. Aspirations of a healthy body, for example, often lead to rigorous, rigid diets, which are only effective for the moment they are followed. Meals become a source of measured pain, in anticipation of a successful outcome that can never be extricated from denial and deficit. Contrasted with a life guided by pleasure, little (if any) resemblance is perceived. When motivated by pleasure, satisfaction and fulfillment are emphasized rather than abstinence and deprivation.

Paradoxically, electronic communication has brought us closer than ever and simultaneously pushed us further apart. A shared sense of isolation emerges out of a growing lack of physical and emotional connection, in parallel with the escalating role of technology in our daily lives. Propelled by discontent and an intense desire for self-actualization and meaning, we have sought solutions in all the wrong places. Certainly industry has been quick to capitalize on this weakness and misguided search to fulfill this enigmatic need. We are encouraged to chase pseudo pleasures, such as overindulgence, gluttony and consumerism. Yet these substitutes pale in comparison to the true pleasures in life, such as making love, intimacy and sharing, creating, moving, learning, laughing. In short, living. And yet above this din, there is a growing appreciation of the critical role pleasure plays in physical and emotional health, creativity, happiness, vitality and even longevity.

The challenge at hand is to embrace pleasure despite the enculturation and conditioning that motivates us to focus on avoidance of bad habits and the like. Ineffective coping mechanisms such as smoking, over-eating and self-medication can be replaced with healthy enjoyment. Natural pleasures, informed by an organic *joie de vivre*, promote vitality and a self-perpetuating zest for life.

Guided by an innate desire for pleasure, every activity is an opportunity to experience joy and delight. In turn, this pleasure is accompanied by the promise of health and happiness.

Haris Dimitriadis
June 2017

A PERSONAL NOTE

Dear reader,

It is with a joyful heart and deep sense of responsibility that I offer the learnings in this book. I propose that you can live the pleasant life if you so choose. Furthermore, I submit to you that the insights of Epicurus are neither less relevant today than they were 23 centuries ago nor are they more suitable to young than old. As the philosopher himself reminds us, it is "...neither too early nor too late, when it comes to ensuring the health of soul."

Born and bred in a conservative family, I was raised in tradition, based on a religious worldview. I was instructed to value material success through status, wealth and the accumulation of stuff. I worked hard and long to climb the corporate ladder and got caught up in the rat race. By all accounts, I had made it. And yet achievement came with a heavy cost, and each success was less fulfilling than the last. When I reached my fifties, I had the profound realization that I no longer recognized myself; I was distressed, anxious, asking for more and more. With the knowledge that this life no longer suited me, I sought a new path to avoid the cognitive dissonance my work life promoted.

Seeking an alternative philosophy of life, I turned to the scholars whose teachings have stood the test of time.

Vague, conceptual and idealistic in nature, I became frustrated with these ideologies as they had no practical application in my life. At last, I stumbled upon a letter written by Epicurus to his friend Menoeceus. That moment, when I first discovered his philosophy of Nature, forever changed the course of my life. I was immediately struck by the fact that this was more than simply another philosophy, but rather the intersection of two mainstream philosophies that traverse human culture; that of finding happiness by pursuing pleasure, and living by the guidance of Nature. This philosophy was incredibly comprehensive and yet exceptionally simple.

Hungry for more, I was disappointed to find that the remains of this philosophy are few: two more letters, some fragments, a poem, and indirect sources. Even so, the suggestions contained therein had an instantaneous, positive impact on the quality of my life, inspiring me to learn more. Leaving no stone unturned, I found crucial aspects of this philosophy could not be explained and others were missing altogether. This mystery only served to further drive me in search of answers. Having exhausted qualitative resources, I turned to the scientific discipline, wondering if and how this might shed light on the subject. I would soon discover that what once seemed mysterious about this ancient Epicurean Philosophy is explained by modern science.

My relationship with Epicurus and his teachings has evolved over the course of the last twelve years. Through diligent study, I became familiar with Epicurus and his philosophy—not only in mind but also in soul. Epicurus' promotion of agency inspired me to accept accountability for all aspects of my life. By my own volition, energy is now channeled into the activities I enjoy and the people I love. With the knowledge that chance resides out of our purview by nature, I consciously let go of thoughts of worry and conjecture, freeing up valuable energy better spent enjoying life. With great effort, I have become less analytical and much more aware of my senses and feelings. Today, I employ reason in decision making only, focusing on the qualitative with a lens of optimism and an appreciation of inherent beauty. I devote my time carefully, enjoying the company of my wife, children, grandchild and friends without watching the clock, savoring each moment whether of great import or of the mundane variety. I find flow in sports, music and dancing. Through radical, conscious changes in perceptions and thinking, my quality of my life has improved dramatically.

This book is a labor of love, a vehicle by which to share my personal experience with you. Despite its technocratic nature, it is undeniably a deposition of my soul, brimming with emotion, pleasure and pain throughout my quest for joy. I am pleased to present an empirically sound, well documented philosophy of life, which serves as a refreshing alternative to the prevailing idealistic culture.

And now, the caveat: happiness is indeed a choice.

Dear reader,
There are no excuses to anyone from this page forward. Neither fate nor fortune cast a shadow upon your life

without your permission. But worry not as you are inherently well equipped for this journey to the joyful life. With determination and perseverance, you too will find the happiness to which you are entitled. You need only take the first step. Open your mind and activate your will to take your life in your hands by pursuing pleasure.

Haris Dimitriadis
June 2017

Contents

PART FIVE: IMPLEMENTATION

PART SIX: APPENDICES

PART ONE: BASIC CONCEPTS

CHAPTER 1

OVERVIEW

"The secret of happiness is in the diathesis (disposition) *of which we are sole arbiters."*

Epicurean follower, Diogenes of Oenoanda

Of all the philosophers to ever walk the golden grounds of ancient Greece, there was one man particularly worthy of notice. So notable was his work that even now, two thousand three hundred years later, his philosophy is one that lingers in the social fabric of man. It is safe to say that it will continue to do so. His name was Epicurus, son of Neocles and Chaerestrate. His philosophy was that of a happy life based on the search for simple natural pleasures. One devoid of the help of religions, god, politics, consumerism, wealth, power, or fame. Epicurus argued that any man can acquire and maintain bodily health and peace of mind by using only his own natural powers.

In as much as this is true, the pursuit of happiness has

no chance of success if it is lonely. It is vital that we have an environment of security that friends and like-minded people create. To live the most pleasant life, one must possess the ability to obtain security, in relationships of mutual benefit with people of like minds, for they are all the solid support needed for life to be pleasant. Friendship establishes an environment of trust and security, overflowing with all valuable practical and emotional support to build our character. Our views of life and of society are shaped by the tenets of friendship. If we are to evaluate the quality of our life, participate in joint activities, and achieve common goals, then friendship, true friendship is a must.

The friendship Epicurus referred to is that between people who share explicit trust, those who seek to forward the affairs of those they call friends. Those for whom friendship is not an unhealthy competition. A Principal Doctrine says that friendship is by far the most important means of wisdom to ensure happiness throughout our lives. Epicurus' most important innovation to friendship was his urging that it should be cultivated systematically. Friendship, he supported, has such an importance to safety and happiness that it should not be left to chance, but cultivated in a planned manner.

The purity of the Epicurean social model of life is highlighted by these words: "If you want to save your peace of mind and your humanity ... carry out your own state of affairs, which will give you what the official cannot." This model is nothing more than a small society of friends united by ties of trust, honesty, kindness and mutual aid, in combination with the values and the perceptions of the Epicurean Philosophy.

The Epicurean Philosophy expresses the Natural Philosophy of life, because it follows the route of the natural functions of the mind. These functions start from the automatic subconscious mind and end up in the volitional conscious. The philosophy assumes that the norm of truth in life is disclosed by nature and not by thoughts. This becomes obvious by observing the behavior of animals and babies who react in response to their instincts and emotions. It is glaring from their reactions that all animals, lower and higher alike, seek pleasure and avoid pain. This means that the search for pleasure and the avoidance of pain are innate attributes which human beings have. They are neither secondary nor incidental and cannot be added or deducted at will.

Pleasure and pain were born together, long before logic was developed. Therefore Epicurus wrote: "We recognize pleasure as the first good innate thing." As life passes and the baby becomes a child, an adolescent, a young and mature man, he always remains attached to the pursuit of pleasure and the avoidance of pain.

At no stage of life or human culture is this relationship questioned. Epicurus explained this wonderfully when he described pleasure as being the beginning and the end to a happy life. He said humans resort to this as a rule in order to judge anything good by the way we feel. To avoid misunderstandings, he also added that pleasure does not mean prodigal and sensual pleasure only, as some might think. By pleasure, Epicurus referred to the natural pleasure–bodily, psychological, and spiritual–that are necessary to bring about a state devoid of any physical pain and the absence of a troubled soul.

The guide to life in the Epicurean Philosophy is the pursuit of pleasure and avoidance of pain that brings about ataraxia–the pleasant state in which we enjoy bodily health and peace of mind. Joy and pain are the start and stop signals of everyday life. Both are green and red lights respectively. That is why our talks in the Epicurean Philosophy start with the word "feel" rather than "think."

Pleasures are prioritized in the Epicurean Philosophy according to their significance in the pursuit of happiness because "other desires are natural and necessary; others are natural but not necessary. And yet others are neither natural nor necessary, but are born from empty ideas." This suggests that we do not satisfy all our wishes. All we satisfy are natural desires that are absolutely necessary and the unnecessary natural desires that do not harm us. The harmful ones are strictly restrained.

Natural human desires are expressed by the physical characteristics of the mind that are in direct contact with the inner and the outer world, that is, the senses, the emotions, and the anticipations (instincts, innate inclinations, and experiences).

Choice and decision are the most frequent activities of daily life. The potential pleasures are numerous; the cost of many of these is prohibitive, and the problems that some of them induce are often superior to the benefits. Therefore, we must evaluate them by comparing one to the other, and by carefully examining what is worth pursuing and what is not. The doctrine below summarizes this in the most apt manner possible: "We do not indiscriminately choose any form of enjoyment, but sometimes we happen to turn our back to different forms of pleasure, when the problems that they might cause outweigh the benefits." It is conspicuous that the avoidance of pain is not always the best choice, for there are, on the other hand, different forms of pain that we may prefer to pleasure. For such pain, the enjoyment that follows after enduring it, at least for some time, will be greater.

The mind's capacity to judge and decide is based on logic. When logic is coupled with valuable experience, it attains an elevation into something greater; it gets upgraded to "phronesis," a virtue equivalent to wisdom. This virtue was picked by Epicurus as the most effective criterion for decision making. Why? You might wonder. It is because by its very nature, phronesis produces a realistic thought. It investigates, to the basis, the reasons for every choice and avoidance. It also eliminates wrong opinions, which are the main source of chaos and disorder in people's souls.

Epicurus challenged and redefined the traditional role of reason that had been assigned by Plato and religions. These schools of thought attribute the ability to exhibit the authentic desires of human nature to logic. They also specified that logic simultaneously evaluates and decides which of the desires should be satisfied. Epicurus argued that the natural functions of logic are only the acts of evaluation and decision, as is done, for example, by a judge in a court. A judge accepts the evidence submitted to it by the physical human features that communicate with the inner and outer world. These physical features are the senses, the emotions and the anticipations. Logic evaluates the evidence placed before it, rejects the false ones, and accepts the true ones. It also requests for more evidence for any testimonies that it has doubts about. At the end of the evidentiary process, logic makes the right decision.

The problems with logic arise when we assign the double role of the judge and the one to be judged by it. That is, to say that logic will on one hand express the desires of human nature and on the other hand, evaluate and decide what it will accommodate is to create a conflict of interests that cannot be resolved.

We live in a real world, not in a world of thoughts and ideas. Hence, logical thoughts are not appropriate in feeding the mind with truthful information without the presence and the mediation of Nature. Thoughts, musings and plans are not true, if they are not based on direct, real and obvious evidence, such as those that carry our physical characteristics, namely the senses, emotions and anticipations. This clearly describes a Principal Doctrine: "... and such evidence must come from the five senses, the feelings of pain and joy, and the impressions of the mind that arise from anticipation..."

Logic is a very useful tool if we can use it effectively. Still, all that it is is a tool of thought, and it is our choice to use it effectively to manage the data sent to us by nature.

The Epicurean way of searching for the truth unveils the Epicurean art of life. In simple terms, this means that to live well we have to follow the instructions of our nature as they are disclosed through the feelings of joy and pain. How we feel is, in fact, the compass of our life. Logic is malleable; it can readily distort reality and interpret the data according to expediency or the fashion of the time. Thus, for example, logic led Plato to the thought that the earthly world is but a flickering shadow and that the true reality is in another dimension, achievable only through mysterious ways of contact with the otherworldly. In religion, logic is displayed by the arguments of faith, of mystery, the metaphysical fear and the divine punishment. For Aristotle and the Stoics, logic suggests that truth is possible through a virtuous life. For the status quo, reason is disguised as power. For the social elite, it is transformed into prestige. For the political reformers, it is social justice. The representatives of materialism see it as consumer welfare, and for the defenders of nationalism, it is in their excessive love for the Homeland.

We could adopt some of the above logical concepts in our lives if they brought about joy and did not serve as a means of accomplishing other purposes. No matter how valuable something good may be, it is desirable only if it contributes to happiness. An Epicurean maxim stresses this point in a dramatic tone: "The good and the virtues and the like are worthy of honor when they bring joy. If they do not bring joy, let it go."

Epicurus argues that our nature advises us to seek happiness. If instead we accept that Logic concedes a higher goal than happiness, then we should be prepared to face the consequences of our choice. Because, regardless of what views we have about the world, about how unjust or hard it is, this is the only real world we have. Our existence is not eternal, we have not been here before, nor will we be here again. Neither are we puppets in god's hands where we are rewarded if we are obedient and punished otherwise.

From the observation of Nature we find that there are things we are able to change while there are others that remain static. We cannot overcome the fact that we will eventually die, or that what is non-existent cannot yield anything. Things do not change because we would like them to. Nature existed before us, and it is necessary to comply to its laws and not to seek the opposite.

There is no doubt that there is a lot of pain around us,

but there is also joy, and it is up to us what to pay attention to. We can isolate ourselves in our rooms, where we might ponder on the mistakes we made or perhaps cry for the loved ones we lost. However, in this manner we are opposing the laws of Nature, which we do not have the ability to impose upon. Epicurus advises us to avoid the unpleasant side of life, to live not in fear of death, god's punishment or to pay attention to religions, the consumerist and other false philosophies; to not hope, and to not seek the impossible. We must look for the truth in the messages Nature sends us through our feelings instead of listening to the advice of others.

Modern science confirms the Epicurean view that our mental state is a product of the unconscious functions of our brain. We know now that biologically programmed instincts use our genes to perpetuate our natural features and culture. Traditional education uses habits to support its ideas and to influence our decisions. Our belief about ourselves, the world and its impact on the reality that we experienced in life are decisive and ingrained in the unconscious depths of our minds. If we have accumulated false beliefs therefore, we will experience them as negative realities in our lives through the unconscious operating pendent of our mind. Our conscious decisions are nothing more than a refinement of our unconscious desires.

This means that the reality we experience is by and large in harmony with the subconscious image we have of ourselves and the environment. Epicurus yielded that the misperceptions are the cause of stress and anxiety in our lives. Through his philosophy, he tried to propagate healthy perceptions that contribute to the tranquility of the mind.

You might wonder how can we intervene in the unconscious functions of the mind and transform the old false perceptions to the correct new ones?

The answer is simple. Nature, in its infinite wisdom, has made arrangements for this. It has allowed for a small part of our mind to be controlled by our will, the conscious. It is through our will, that we are able to perceive our inner and outer world, and that we can perform certain functions, such as talking or walking, as well as thinking, learning, planning, and deciding. We can penetrate into the unconscious, dark paths of our mind with the aid of our consciousness, which connects its neurons to those of the unconscious mind.

So, despite its contained size, consciousness is able to influence and significantly re-programme larger portions of the unconscious mind, where our perceptions and feelings are stored. To affect them, we must use the classic way of learning through repetition. If we can transform the deeply rooted negative beliefs and habits into positive ones through learning, the reality which we will experience will be adjusted accordingly. This hidden power of the mind is the means by which the Epicurean Philosophy remedies the turmoil of the soul.

This view was forwarded by William James, the father of

psychology when he said: "The greatest revolution of our generation is the discovery that human beings can change the outer aspects of their lives by changing the internal perceptions." Indeed James was right; we may gain control of our experience and of the quality of our life by selecting, learning and practicing the suitable perceptions.

You might ask this ultimate question: "How can this be done when we do not have money to make it through the month, when we are struck by illness and the adversities that do not allow us to control our life?"

Control of the conscience and the adoption of the right perceptions are the answers to this question. No matter how fortunate we are, if we do not know how to control our mental energy and experiences, we will never be happy. For how is it possible for some people to enjoy their lives even when they have suffered the worst hardships while others who have health, beauty and wealth are unsatisfied? It is, of course, simplistic to support the view that no matter what, someone who controls his conscience will be happy. There are limits as to how much pain, hunger or deprivation a body can tolerate. To ignore this is to have the same fortune as the one who does not put a barrier to his wishes.

That the mind controls the body is the most fundamental fact of life that we know. Those who can turn a setback into a new opportunity are the ones that survive. The most important requirement for survival and the improvement of the quality of life, therefore, is the ability to turn a misfortune into a pleasant experience. Life is full of examples of people who sought happiness in wealth, strength, reputation and beauty, only to find out in the end that the quality of life depends on how you feel rather than on what you hold.

How shall we utilize the power to control our consciousness in the search for happiness? The first step is to have a clear image of ourself, i.e. our weaknesses and strengths. We must understand our desires and our avoidances, know what actually is or is not valuable to us. The next step is to discover those personal objectives of ours that are in harmony with our physical traits, thoughts, and desires. Such a goal is set forth by the Epicurean Philosophy, where peace of mind is gained by following the feeling of pleasure and avoiding that of pain. Last but not least, we must move into the implementation of our plans without flinching when we realize the responsibilities that they create.

Human consciousness is such that any changes in perceptions and feelings necessarily pass through its control and its training into the favored direction. But even our consciousness is under the influence of habits. Our lives, and the way we live, have for the most part been scheduled for us. We have learned about what to see, what to remember, what to feel, and why to fight. Over time, our experiences will follow the dictates of Nature and society to a large extent.

In order to pave our own path to happiness, we need

to activate our capacity for free will and break what is pre-scribed by heritage as well as the habits in our way of liv-ing. This effort leads to the acquisition of autonomy, not only over the external forces but also over our genetic im-pulses and habits.

The simple truth that mind control is linked to the qual-ity of life has long been known. For thousands of years, the people of the East have used meditation techniques to gain control of their consciousness, conquering happi-ness in the process. The sages of the Epicurean Philosophy used the technique of controlling consciousness in educat-ing their students, thus passing on to future generations, the Epicurean art of life. However, the forcible interruption of its teaching after the 4th century AD brought about the disappearance of this technique. The aim of this book is to ensure the restoration of the Epicurean art in modern life.

In the modern era, the idea of liberation of the indi-vidual from his instincts and the social environment had been identified in the Freudian psychoanalytic approach. According to this approach, the two tyrants who fight to gain control over consciousness are instincts and the en-vironment. Faced with this battle is the ego, desperately struggling to appease the inclinations of the person him-self in the specific environment.

The capacity of free will to dominate the influence of the environment and the demands of our inner world lays the foundation for the optimistic contemplation of life.

Optimism is the final "all is well" message that consciousness sends into the unconscious centers of the brain so as to transfer its energy into the search for pleasure and joy without distractions. For as long as fear and pessimism dominate consciousness, all the attention of the brain is focused on addressing the real or imaginary risks. The optimistic outlook of life is intertwined with the pursuit of happiness, as an Epicurean text illustrates by arguing that for those capable of figuring out what the problem is, the most exquisite and infallible of joys is the stable condition of well-being in the flesh, as well as a confident hope that this well-being will continue.

Negative thoughts are the classical source of pessimism and misery in modern societies. They are based on the experiences of doubt and depreciation from childhood. These are subsequently fed and exacerbated by the erroneous perceptions of achieving high goals instead of pursuing pleasures.

Epicurus suggests an easy strategy in the pursuit of happiness. It is easy to follow and quite straightforward. All we need do is follow our feeling of pleasure. However while doing this, we must learn to limit our desires to the natural and necessary. It is, perhaps, natural for humans to desire the acquisition of wealth, power and fame. But it is vital that we reject the excessive desires for these by intelligently selecting which desires to satisfy. In addition, irrational fears about death, god and natural disasters must become null and void.

The pursuit of happiness cannot be left to chance. It is neither a product that money can buy nor is it one that can be acquired by power. It is the result of the effective and systematic effort to control and orient our consciousness into achieving our goals. We do not have the luxury of waiting for others to help us. We must discover how to do it ourselves. But in this effort, we need valuable assets, such as a strong will, determination and discipline; qualities which are rare in any period of time.

CHAPTER 2

MYSELF OR WHO AM I?

*"That nature of mind and soul corporeal is:
for when it is seen to drive the members on, to
snatch from sleep the body, and to change the
countenance, and the whole state of man."*

Lucretius, Epicurean poet

"Know Thy Self." This saying was inscribed in the forecourt of the Temple of Apollo at Delphi as a means of urging the believers calling the oracle to discover their advantages and disadvantages. It suggested that by knowing their Selves, they could correctly explain to the oracle so they could benefit from it. In a similar manner, we can assert that through self-knowledge we can find out the meaning of life that is suitable for us.

In life, we do not come prefabricated. We are always formed by our genes and experiences. Whenever a new experience is added, a new Self is created. The most interesting thing is not that we are a combination of genes and experiences, but that both genes and experiences speak the same language. Also, they both reshape our Self by affecting the organization of the synapses of the brain. These connections of the neurons of the brain largely define who we are. Our genes shape the outline of our spiritual and behavioral functions. Their involvement in the final image of ourself amounts to 50%. While our genes push us in a certain direction, our upbringing plays its own important role by contributing to the development of the other half of the mind. All studies find that both nature and nurture function in a parallel manner in the formation of Self through their effects on the synapses of the neurons of the brain. Whether or not the influence is direct, as in the case of genes, or indirect, as with experiences, is less important since both eventually have the same effect.

Learning and growth are two sides of the same coin, but the latter precedes the former. We cannot learn before the neurons have been created. However, just as we grow according to our inherent internal directives, we are also influenced by our experiences. Our genes, environment, choices, learning, and experiences wholly contribute to the wiring of the brain and to the shaping of the Self. This then begs the question, "Who am I?"

Myself

In order to explore our Self, it is necessary to define some introductory concepts like: Being, Self, Consciousness, Ego, and Attention.

Our Being is the synthesis of our nature and nurture. Our nature consists of our body and mind. Out of the multiple functions of the mind, three of them play an important role in the pursuit of happiness: the emotional, which processes the internal or external stimuli with regard to safety or risk to create emotions, the volitional, which elaborates on the stimuli with regard to willingness and expresses will. And then there is the logical, which works out the stimuli with regard to achieving results, and generating thoughts. Our nurture on the other hand, consists of knowledge, events, perceptions, habits, and our emotions. All the neuronal structures of the mind, genetic and acquired alike, form our character, the anticipations, or prolepses in the Epicurean jargon.

The concept of Being takes different meanings in the various schools of thought. As long as idealism denies the reality of matter in favor of the hypothesis of the immaterial mind, Being remains abstract. In contrast, Being has physical existence in materialism. Materialism holds that the only things that exist are matter and energy, that all things are composed of material, that all actions require energy, and that all phenomena (including the conscientious) are the result of material interactions.

In *Being and Time*, the contemporary philosopher Heidegger expressed Being as an existentialist phenomenon. The Epicurean position is materialistic, and the meaning attached to Being is closer to that expressed by Heidegger. In this approach, Being is meaningful only when it is engaged in the world. That is, when it is in a never-ending process of involvement with its environment. This Being is called "Being in the world" (Dasein).

Our Self or self-perception refers to our Being in relation to other people; it is defined by our self-concept, self-knowledge, self-esteem, and the social Self. In other words, the Self is considered as that Being which is the source of consciousness, and is responsible for our thoughts and actions. The Self seen subjectively (by the person himself) is referred to as I, and when seen objectively (as an object) is referred to as Me.

Our mind is in control of our Self, and most of its functions are automatic—leaving a very small part of its functions as voluntary. By controlling and managing these voluntary functions, we walk on the road of life, trying on the one hand to satisfy our desires, and on the other to abide by the requirements of the environment.

It has been discovered by research that there is a strip of gray matter in the pre-frontal part of our mind. It has the ability to perceive and process information from our body, our brain, and the external environment. This volitional part of the brain is called consciousness. Consciousness is thus the capacity and the means to communicate with our inner Self and the external environment in order to satisfy our goals.

Among other things, the contents of consciousness include thoughts, feelings, plans, projects and sounds. They also include our feeling of our own importance and ability, as well what we want the successful image of ourself to look like. This image and the neurons it occupies in the consciousness are called the ego. It is impossible for consciousness to contain only the ego, for humans will then be completely cut off from the environment. Containing only the whole picture of ourselves is also impossible because most of it is unconscious, hence we are not aware that it exists, and even if we were, it would not fit into the contained size of our consciousness.

The capacity of the consciousness to receive and process information is very limited. It can realize and process only a small part of what is happening to us and the environment. In addition to this, it can work on only one function at a time. The contents of consciousness and the activation of its spiritual functions are determined by the ability of attention. That is why attention is often referred to as psychic energy.

The nature of truth in life

The identification of the desires that communicate people's real needs is a critical issue that had been addressed by philosophers in the quest for human happiness. This is necessary in order to harmonize our perceptions and goals with those desires. Two approaches were followed in identifying the nature of truth in life. The first one accepts Nature as the norm of truth while the other accepts Logic.

Epicurus argued in favor of Nature as the norm of truth. He argued that the realities of human nature are identified by the primary functions of the human mind, which come into direct contact with the external environment and our inner world; these include the senses, emotions and anticipations (instincts, innate inclinations, experiences).

For a detailed presentation of the Canon of Truth, see "The Pleasure of Knowledge," chapter 15.

Epicurus excluded reason from the Canon on the ground that it is a secondary capacity of the mind; it does not come into direct contact with reality, and as a matter of necessity, it draws information either from the senses, feelings and anticipations, or from other thoughts, opinions and ideas.

On the contrary, Plato advocated a view opposite to the foregoing. He supported that logic is the only reliable source of truth, while emotions are uncontrollable and fraudulent senses. He argued that the senses neither tell the truth to human needs nor to the nature of the world.

Consciousness and attention

There is a region of the brain referred to as the pre-frontal cortical area. This region is a large one indeed, being the site of the performance of a series of spiritual functions, such as calculations, thoughts, plans, reflections, and decisions. Consciousness is but a part of this larger region, which is the workplace of our mind. It is also known as working memory. The information of the working memory that we perceive is the content of the consciousness while every other information contained in the working memory remains in the dark.

Consciousness has a seemingly important role to play; it must recognize the information it realizes, process it and put it in hierarchy. Without consciousness, we would be aware of what is happening inside and around us, but we would not have the opportunity to evaluate and understand it.

Attention determines the contents and the functions of consciousness. To a certain degree, attention is the mental energy that is under our control, therefore, we can use it as we desire. It can be said that we create our Self based on the way we invest in this energy. This single statement, a culmination of all that has been explained, makes attention the most important tool in the process of improving the quality of our life.

The access of external and internal events into consciousness is not a function of the frequency of their occurrence, but of the possibility that they will be grasped by our attention. Reality exists only when we observe it; otherwise it is nonexistent to us. A cyclist that passes by is present for us if we turn our eyes to look at him; or else, he is nonexistent to us. Reality for everyone is only that which we realize and whatever it is that becomes the content of our consciousness.

The possible effect of any information on our lives is evaluated as it enters the consciousness. Is it endangering our goals? Does it enhance them or leave them intact?

When it is in harmony with our objectives and carries out reassuring messages, we feel appeased. Hence, we stop dealing with the safety of the Self and focus most of our attention on dealing with the external environment. Our consciousness is agitated each time new information invades it, and extended experiences of this kind can cause it to weaken in its ability to devote attention to successfully meeting its objectives. The battle we fight, therefore, is against whatever causes disarray in the consciousness in order to gain control of attention.

Information in the consciousness is not scattered; it is arranged in groups to be used directly for the satisfaction of our desires. There is a specific order that is followed here: the grouping and ranking is done in accordance to our biological needs and perceptions, habits and traditions. This hierarchy is not fixed in that it may be rigid or flexible, making it possible to classify a part of the contents of the consciousness depending on our intentions and goals. The internal conflict within consciousness is the result of competitive forces that fight to attract its attention. To avoid these conflicts there is obviously a need for disentanglement in order to evaluate and to prioritize these forces.

A fundamental attribute of consciousness and attention is the sense of loss of the Self. Under normal circumstances, we waste a lot of time dealing with our Selves. However, an extraordinary activity may absorb attention to such an extent that there is none left to deal with the Self. Thus, the Self is lost from consciousness. This development is usually accompanied by a sense of unity with the activity we are engaged in or the environment, be it a mountain or a group of people.

Dealing with our Self is normally a result of the perception of a particular risk. When in danger, we are forced to bring the image of the Self into consciousness so that we can examine the extent of the risk as well as whether or not the Self is capable of facing the danger. There are several times that we perceive that the Self is in danger during the day. Each time this happens, we waste precious mental energy to bring about peace in the consciousness. On the contrary, when experiences are pleasant, there is no reason to deal with the Self, we are engrossed in our activities and enjoy them to the fullest.

Introspection and selfishness have similar repercussions as danger. They force attention to endlessly keep an eye on the Self to either protect it or satisfy and reward it. Dealing with the Self makes us poorer; valuable psychic energy is wasted, and opportunities to experience pleasures outside the Self are missed.

Learning is yet another critical faculty of attention and consciousness. We are incapable of learning unless we have conscious access and pay attention to what is learned. When a query enters our attention, the working memory of the unconscious mind is automatically activated to solve it. As soon as the answer is found, it is returned back to consciousness.

The capacity to learn is constrained by the size of the

consciousness. Research detected that the information that the consciousness can contain and assess is limited compared to the overall capacity of the mind. It is estimated that the processing capacity of its neurons is 126 bytes per second. This corresponds to the ability to remember a seven digit number, seven figures, do one job at a time or listen to no more than two people at once.

The confined size of the consciousness is one of the most important characteristics of our nature because it means that the information that penetrates our consciousness acquires great importance. It is actually what determines the contents and the quality of our lives.

Tackling stress is also a noteworthy property of attention and consciousness. Focusing our attention on what we are doing here and now or on the environment, and certainly not on the Self, reduces the stress felt. When we realize that we are in an intimidating situation, the usual response is to direct all the available energy to the Self. However, this backfires in that it increases disorder and reduces reaction. In a bid to remove stress, we must avoid thinking and worrying about our strengths and weaknesses. In place of this, we should seek engagement in activities that make us feel like a part of them or like a part of our surroundings.

Attention affects the sense of reality we experience. The more attention we pay to physical pain, economic disaster, or social isolation, the more space we allow for it in our consciousness, and the more real it becomes. Hence, it causes more disorder in our consciousness and becomes more painful. The solution does not lie in denying, repressing or trying to manipulate the effect. This is because no matter how hard we try, the painful information will continue to spontaneously spring to mind, especially in our hours of rest. It is better to look suffering straight in the eye and manage it, or perhaps to even consider other alternatives. Many people with disabilities have been able to transform a tragic situation into a tolerable one, and sometimes even to an enjoyable experience, by taking control of their attention span.

Despite the fact that the ability to concentrate is a natural process, experience has shown that it is hard to succeed in this process. It requires intense effort, discipline, and practice. Additionally, both internal and external obstacles are encountered. Within the person trying to concentrate, self-consciousness and selfishness are the obstacles. In these cases, attention is biased and concentrates almost exclusively on the Self, thus opportunities of enjoyment, learning and development are missed.

The greatest obstacle to concentration arises from the pain of loneliness, especially when it is accompanied by an inability to do anything as it turns out on holidays. During the week, mental energy is directed by outside influences—work, shopping, and pleasant TV shows. Sundays and holidays are entirely different from what we experience mid-week because we have nothing to turn our attention to. As such, it is difficult to put our own thoughts in order, and loneliness can become unbearable. When the external stimuli that we learned to attract our attention are absent, attention lingers on, thoughts become chaotic, and the conscience falls in disarray. Because of this, the television is permanently on, despite the fact that it often causes irritation and frustration. With the unending droning from whatever or whoever is on the screen, the brain is protected from personal concerns, and unpleasant thoughts are kept away. Others resort to more drastic means such as drinking, smoking, substance use and pornography. These solutions are, however, temporary and ineffective.

Childhood experiences exert a diachronic influence on the ability to concentrate and feel pleasure. Indeed, to attempt to give an explanation with respect to why some people have a good time doing boring things, while others are bored even in a fun environment, using hereditary advantage and volition is simply not enough. Environmental influences constitute a very important aspect. Among them, parents' interaction with their children has been shown to have a lasting effect on the ability of children to enjoy the experiences in their lifetime. For children who grow up in a healthy environment, they often have free energy to spend on the activities they like, thereby satisfying and developing themselves. Otherwise, their energy is wasted in discussions, negotiations and conflicts about limits and the rules of the house or on the absurd demands of parents.

In a society such as ours with its conflicting objectives, many powerful agents seek to attract our attention, influence our preferences and determine the meaning of our lives. We have on the one hand, the official institutions, i.e. the schools, churches and banks, trying to make us responsible citizens who work hard and save. On the other hand, there are the entrepreneurs and advertisers who bombard us with thousands of suggestions on what to buy. Finally, there's the underworld game system of drugs and sex. This system is often associated with the official system, and it promises us easy treats, as long as we have enough to pay for them. In trying to convince us to work for their goals, they get the help of human biology which is scheduled to succumb when our survival is at risk. When fear and pain blocks their success, they switch, using pleasures like food, sex, and security as a motive. As long as we can recognize and maintain some control, there is certainly no trouble in following the requirements of Nature. However, this is far from actually being transformed into pawns of suspicious centers of power.

Control of attention is necessary to living happily in the cacophony that surrounds us. However, for most people, attention is an invisible or illusory ability; yet research shows that we can improve it through education and practice. The neurons of the mind are like the muscles of the body with some peculiarities. In a manner similar to the body muscles, the "muscles" of the mind need challenges that extend their limits. This way, the neuronal synapses of attention are developed.

The pioneer psychologist William James proposed an attention strengthening test involving a dot on a piece of paper. Attempt to consistently observe a dot on a piece of paper. As you will realize, one of the following two things will happen: one, you will dazzle the image until you can no longer see anything, or two, you will willingly remove your gaze from the dot and look at something else. However, if you ask yourself successive questions about the dot… How big it is, how far it goes, what shape it takes as seen from different optical angles, etc., you will find that you can keep your eye on it for a longer period of time.

In a similar fashion we can develop the attention capacity of particular functions of the mind, such as vision and hearing. All the attention empowering training includes the motion of removing attention from the object of concentration and returning to it at will. Returning the mind to the present when it wanders is the method of practicing the capacity of attention. The repetition of this exercise in the "spiritual field" of the mind strengthens the neurons of attention, as we observe with the body in conventional gyms. With each exercise of removing and focusing our attention, we strengthen it and reshape our mind. This is the well-known property of the neuro-plasticity of the mind.

The following exercise is a strength training for the attention muscles of the mind. Shall we attempt it together?

Begin by focusing on what you are doing. Start with a

few minutes of full absorption, interrupted by a similar time of rest. Whenever you realize that your attention has been removed, make a conscious effort to bring it back to what you are doing. Continue by gradually increasing the concentration and relaxation times.

Careful watching and listening can be practiced especially when we pour all of our energy into what we are looking at or listening to. During this process, we stop any other activity and remove every other thought.

Our physical reactions should be closely observed and associated with our feelings and thoughts. This way we also realize our emotional reactions. This may be done, for example, while having a meal by eating and chewing slowly, enjoying each bite of the flavor and the texture of the food.

We pay attention to the thoughts that worry us. Whenever we have any hindrance, we avoid it by returning our attention to the thought of interest. When we remember poems, songs or anything else of interest, we exercise our brain. This may also be done by reading long texts and books slowly and carefully such that we may pay attention to the most inconspicuous of details. Research has shown that our ability to isolate harassment and increase concentration is heightened when we exercise our body. Hence, this should be done on a regular basis.

Curiosity and patience is of utmost importance. A notable pioneer in this regard is Charles Darwin. He had a distinct ability in that he could devote entire days to observing animals and plants. His secret was his inexhaustible curiosity and patience in bringing to light the slightest details step by step.

Attention strengthening exercises may be employed to meditate.

A common meditating mode is focusing the attention on a single object during the whole meditation session. This object may be the breath, a mantra, visualization, part of the body, external object, etc. As the practitioner advances, his ability to keep the flow of attention in the chosen object gets stronger, and distractions become less common and short-lived. Both the depth and steadiness of attention are developed.

Let's try it together: bring the image of an object to your imagination. Make this imagination as vivid as possible. Then try to keep this image in your imagination for as long as you can, and with utmost clarity. Automatically remove your attention from thoughts or feelings if they interfere. Immediately return the attention to what you were focusing on. Do this for as long as you deem necessary.

The human mind is indeed a powerful tool. It has such excellent properties that allow us to literally satisfy any of our desires and achieve every one of our goals in life. Suffice it to say that we must discover our mental qualities in order to exercise them, and take responsibility for our choices.

A large majority of the mind's actions happen automatically without our conscious participation. Through consciousness, however, we are able to influence the subconscious functions of the mind and increase our control over it. This ability relies on the power of attention. The energy we have at our disposal to select the contents of our consciousness and activate its functions, such as those of thinking, planning, learning, and deciding, accurately depicts what the power of attention is all about. The only things capable of affecting our life are those that we have paid attention to.

Based on thousands of years of experience of human culture, our happiness can be trusted neither to uncontrolled internal impulses nor to the good intentions of the social environment. Taking responsibility of our lives ourselves is the only way to pursue our happiness. This is done when we acquire control of our conscience and attention. The next step is to adopt a philosophy of life that suits our inclinations and aspirations. A personal philosophy of life may be chosen as long as we can support it with proper perceptions of life, practical tools and selection criteria. One of the known philosophies could also be chosen, like the religious, the consumerist or the political; yet experience and scientific research point out that none of these is conducive to happiness. Instead, they go along with the Epicurean Philosophy; it ensures a safe course devoid of disappointments.

Happiness is a personal choice. We have all been equipped by nature with the necessary skills to assert it. The knowledge to discover, to cultivate and exercise these skills are now free for everyone. We no longer have the excuse of ascribing our unhappiness to the external environment, to chance, or to our primitive origin. None of these factors are responsible for whatever unhappiness we find ourselves saddled with.

The separation of body and soul: Duality

The body is perishable and the soul is immortal, these were the professions of Pythagoras, Socrates and Plato. Life on Earth is but an imperfect imitation of the ideal heavenly one that can be indicated only through knowledge and reason. Their views on the immortality of the soul are found at the heart of Christianity and Islam. As of today, they find considerable acceptance among the faithful in both religions. Christians and Muslims alike believe that life on Earth is temporary, a probationary period for the life that follows in heaven. The immortal souls will be judged by god, after which they will spend eternal life in heaven or in hell. The case of dual human nature, one of a corruptible body and an incorruptible soul, has made the identification of a single meaning of life impossible.

Aristotle did not avoid the temptation of dualism either. He argued that the mind is both immaterial and immortal. He supported this argument with the fact that the mind does not look like the other sense organs of the body, as it captures all stimuli. It does not just capture some, as, for example, the eyes and ears do.

The dualistic views, as will be described in detail in the chapter on "The Pleasure of Knowledge," were considered true and until recently, prevailed.

The uniform nature of body and soul: Monism

Dualism had the side effect of the degradation of Nature and emotions and the concomitant enhancement of logical thought and introspection. Epicurus, however, had a contrary opinion similar to the earlier views of the Ionian philosophers, who professed the physical nature of Beings. He proposed the single physical nature of the body and soul, thereby establishing the dominant theory of monism.

Paraphrasing the words of Epicurus in his *Letter to Menoeceus* in which he developed his views, the soul is a physical substance, albeit a very subtle one, which is spread to all parts of the body. When the body structure is dissolved, the soul is dispersed, and as such, it no longer possesses the strength it had before. In the letter to Herodotus, Epicurus wrote about how the senses and emotions are what we now initially build our base on. He said that the only way for opinion to be true is to base all our thoughts on the feelings and sensations. By this advice, we conclude that Epicurus considered the senses to be for external things and feelings for the internal criteria of truth.

The Epicurean positions were rephrased by Lucretius who stated, "the mind and soul are held tight to each other and constitute a single nature" and "the nature of the mind and soul is physical." Meanwhile, interpreting Epicurus, the philosopher Sextus Empiricus reports: "That which we feel and become aware of, are real and nothing can undo it."

The philosophy of Epicurus is psychosomatic. The human body is composed of the body and the mind, both of which have a physical nature. They are born together; they grow and decline in parallel. They work as a unit and their reactions are psychosomatic. We cannot separate one from the other. They reflect different properties of the same thing. This may be likened to the manner in which smell, taste and color are properties of the same food, while the active skills of the body are limited to touch, taste, hearing, sight and odor. Simultaneously, the body passively shares the feelings of psyche, as shown by the phenomena of shame, pallor, sweating and jitters. However the body can never acquire the capabilities of memory, intelligence and logic that the mind has.

The dualistic idealistic views prevailed for twenty-three centuries. As late as the 20th century, the American philosopher John P. Shirley argued that all mental states, thoughts and feelings are innate biological processes that can cause physical changes in the human body due to their biological texture. However he argued that they can also be caused by physical changes. Later, J.E. LeDoux, a professor of psychiatry at New York University, experimentally proved the single physical nature of body and soul and argued that "the Self, the personality, who you are, lies in the prototype of the connections of your brain cells, the synapses." J. E. LeDoux then made a breakthrough, after which he made a report about the plastic nature of most systems in the brain. This, he said, means they can be modified by experience. The plasticity of the brain is determined by the genes. The Self, however, is not only the genes. This makes everyone unique because the Self is a combination of genes, environment and experience. According to him, learning and memory play an important role in creating a structured personality as we move forward in life. The conclusion from these findings is that the brain is re-programmed to meet our needs. Therefore, we can change ourselves through learning and experiences to set and achieve goals.

The tyranny of reason

Plato and Descartes could not be more wrong when they declared that the mind is completely separate from the body. They described it as an intangible "thinking thing," the content of which is a cold consciousness, uncontaminated by natural elements. Studies in patients with damage in the prefrontal cortex, the center of reason, affirmed that logic, like all mental functions, is integrated in the natural Self of human existence. Emotions are also rooted in our nature and influence what to think as well as how to think. In the absence of them, one of two things will occur, we are either robbed of the ability to make any decision at all, or we get self-defeating ones. First, we exist, and later, we think. Subsequently, we think to the extent that we exist as a preamble of the structures and functions of existence, of which emotions have been an integral part long before the emergence of logic.

Logic as a capacity was added in the last evolutionary stage of human creation. It is responsible for thinking, planning, and decision making. It attaches meaning to experiences and guides our natural inclinations. Logic's exceptional physical feature, combined with the contribution of the social and cultural environment, gave it predominance over the other characteristics of the human nature–senses, feelings, anticipations–a development that established values and patterns of life alien to the pursuit of happiness.

In modern times, the dominance of reason has become so rigid that it can be characterized as tyrannical and a main cause of individual and collective mental imbalance. While logic was meant to supply people with a new survival tool, it gradually gained supremacy over the old properties of man. This development was induced and reinforced by the emergence of language and the transition from a hunting group life into a rural and urban life. The sovereignty of logic was expressed through its ability to control the natural world as well as introduce new values and standards, such as those of property, hierarchy and patriarchy. The emergence of the philosophical concept that introduced the idea of dualism was the next important stage in the process of enhancing the role of logic in human life. This claim has been imposed on social life through religions. It also brought about the slowdown of the scientific revolution, the integration of the individual and the consolidation of human civilization.

By recognizing the oppressive presence of logic in everyday life, we can redefine its role and assign to it the role that Nature prescribed for it. This role is one resembling that of the orchestra conductor. It may also be likened to that of the judge who judges the reliability of the natural needs and reaches a verdict. The problems with logic arise when we accept that the desires expressed by thoughts are true, and we base our decisions on them. These are doubtful because they are cut off from the realities of life. They are fluid, prone to external influences and errors. When we assign its physical role of decision making to logic as the Epicurean Philosophy suggests, we establish balance and harmony in our life.

The emotional Self

The emotions are elements of the primitive nature of man. They are rooted in the emotional center of the brain and, as mentioned earlier, they are identified by their physical manifestations (laughter, sadness, palpitations, and so on). This is the objective, foolproof expression of emotions. Their narration constitutes our feelings and represents the subjective interpretation of them. The emotions are of a dual nature in that they can be one of two things; they are either positive and attractive or negative and repellent. This feature of emotions renders them a straightforward means of choice and avoidance, making them the "start, stop" signals of everyday life. With the creation of the rational brain, the manifestations of emotions are perceived by the consciousness.

The decisive effect of emotions on decision making is now experimentally confirmed by Antonio Damazio, a renowned professor of neurobiology who argues that even when we believe that our judgments are reasonable, the choice is always based on feelings. Wrong logical decisions can often be felt, he maintained, and the emotions are, perhaps, signals from the subconscious that warn us about the consequences of our choice. In another series of studies, Damazio found that the view of conscious choice is probably an illusion as the subconscious is responsible for our lives. He further supported the position that our decisions have a strong emotional impact because feelings come from the subconscious.

Consciously or unconsciously, our experiences are recorded in our memory. Those memories that are initiated in the conscious mind are accessible by nature and we can remember them. On the other hand, emotional experiences are often unconscious, and we are unaware of their presence in our memories.

On top of this, our narrations are fluid by nature. A number of external factors influence the way we tell the stories of our lives, and every narrative of a memory has a different complexion and content.

One reason for this is the way we feel at the time of storytelling. If we are sad or happy will influence the way we describe the same event.

Another factor is the time lag between the narrative and the occurrence of the emotion. At the time of narration, we would have acquired new knowledge and experiences that affect our emotional approach to past events. This is due to the biological function of the memory. As scientific research shows, memories are not stored in our brain in comprehensive, independent sections but as constructions assembled once they are remembered. The memories associated with a particular event are all stored in the same physical space. New memories that align with any past experience or knowledge are added, one on top of the other. When we make an attempt to remember this event, the mind takes into account, processes, and combines all of the memories stored in this area, and at last the overall impression of the event is expressed through words. Each time we add a new piece of knowledge or experience, our comprehensive approach influences this event.

An additional factor that affects our stories has to do with our personal capacity to express our emotions in words. Most people express their emotional world as accurately as they can, due to the fact that the words and expressions they use are influenced by their culture and their talent in expression. However, even if we have the ability to choose the right words, the French philosopher Jacques Derrida argues that there are serious difficulties in the definition of the meaning of words. We can never define the meaning of words accurately. The meaning of each word is always "in waiting" or postponed, in an endless chain of words that define it. To define a word, we need others and to define the new, we need even more and so on… the cycle continues, therefore, without an end in sight.

Fear is an emotional function that originated in mammals. The amygdala plays a central role in the emotion of fear. All information entering the Self is processed by the amygdala in parallel to other centers of the brain. The processing is done with the view to detect any signs of risk to the Self. If a risk is found, the autonomic nervous system is triggered to face the risk. The physical manifestations of this mechanism are the result of the emotion of fear produced and stored in the amygdala.

By its nature, the fear experienced is stored in the memory unconsciously for a long-term period of time, often to the end of life. These physical properties of fear served the purpose of helping in the man-hunter's need for survival. It is known that in the forest, the man-hunter's opportunities to escape from a stronger animal were limited. Therefore, if he escaped once, Nature had the good sense to utilize this experience to the fullest extent by storing as much information about the event as possible and for the longest possible time. This was done based on the knowledge that a powerful animal would always be stronger, and it would always be dangerous. Nowadays, there are no direct or constant risks, and this is why we are lacking in the functioning of this mechanism. It is impossible to avoid the activation of this mechanism in usual stressful situations. It is also possible that we continue to fear when the conditions have changed and we are no longer at risk. This explains why the fear that we have experienced in the past often reappears during the course of our life.

The autonomic nervous system is activated by anxiety and fear in a bid to address the risks that generate them. This reaction, known as the fight or flight response, is indicated by a series of normal, albeit unpleasant, physical symptoms. Examples of such symptoms include seizures of panic, tachycardia (increased heart rate), increased pulse, shortness of breath, wheezing, chest tightness, sweating, a feeling of choking, headaches, insomnia, irritability, uncontrolled muscle tension, spasms, trembling, faintness, tingling, tightness in the throat, a dry mouth, problems of speech, fear of death, a sense of madness and loss of control. The fight or flight response is based on adrenaline, the hormone of fear. Adrenaline acts to ensure that increased amounts of oxygenated blood will be available in the body, hence supplying enough oxygen to the muscles of the hands and feet to support whatever decision the individual makes, whether to fight or to flee in the face of danger. The oxygenated blood is also made abundantly available to the brain in order to make decisions in a fraction of a second. This blood is transferred from the low priority functions such as the stomach, genitals, the emotional function and the immune system.

The body's reactions to the tensions of daily life are often exaggerated, and adrenaline production can start for a trivial reason, in response to a small stressor. We start sweating, feeling sick, suffering from tachycardia; symptoms that mark the start of the reaction to stress. Then we worry about how we feel, and this further inflates the stress level. Hence, a chain reaction is initiated causing secondary fears known as "a fear of fear." These secondary physical sensations of anxiety cause panic, the symptoms of which may be the same or perhaps even more intimidating than the original ones that were caused by the stress response. Ideally, the stress response should start and stop automatically. The sympathetic arm of the autonomic nervous system responds to fear and anxiety by triggering the body's defense mechanism. This is followed by an intervention from the parasympathetic arm to restore the balance by allowing the body to return to a calm state. However, the sympathetic nervous system may malfunction under the influence of ongoing anxiety, leaving the body in a state of constant red alert. This puts the mind and body in an alarmed state which can lead to exhaustion and gradually to depression if sustained for a long time. In such a situation, the only way out is to break the vicious cycle by adopting an effective stress management method, as well as by introducing the natural model of life.

How to change Myself

Our character, which incorporates the state of our mood, is a synthesis of our nature and nurture; it is biologically expressed through the neurons and synapses of our brain. In the Epicurean terminology it is known as "anticipations" or

"prolepses," reflecting the view that our character anticipates, to a great extent, our future experiences. In addition
to our character, the automatic functions of the senses and
emotions will manifest, in the course of time, the realities
of our life. Therefore, anticipations, senses and emotions
prescribe the realities of our life. Thoughts, on the other hand, are volitional acts stimulated at a second stage,
when the messages sent by anticipations, senses and emotions are realized by consciousness. It is after this has occurred that logic becomes aware of what has been affected
in the depths of the mind in its absence. Only then is it able
to either approve and follow through with the desires of
the inner mind, or reject and revise them.

Logic is the evaluation and decision making part of our brain.
It is also the means of learning. It is the invaluable human
capacity by which we can change the functions and the
structure of the inner mind that prescribe our character.

But how can we affect these changes?

Epicurus proposes three ways by which the illnesses of
the body and the turmoil of the mind may be cured.

The first is that we radically change the environment we
live or work in when it becomes unbearable. Epicurus proposed that the best way to do this is by quitting instead of
submitting to it or by fighting to change it. This is the path
Epicurus himself followed by running away when chased by
the crowd in Mitylene and by refraining from teaching in
an open space in Athens itself.

Another strategy is that we take control of our consciousness and direct our attention where we will it to ensure that our best interests are served. Attention is the only energy of the mind that is, by nature, in our control, and we are able to use it to meet our ends. The world we perceive and live in is the world we pay attention to. Attention is a resource, and a scarce one at that. As such, we are solely responsible for choosing where to channel it. Attention may be channeled either in pursuing joy or by wasting it in chasing after illusionary ends.

The last strategy is to change the way we interpret the experiences of our life. While we cannot change the experiences per se, our mighty and generous Nature allows us to influence not only our present experiences but our past and future as well. This is brought about by the astonishing power of the perceptions; by changing our perceptions, we can change the quality of our life. This is the major innovation of Epicurus and the legacy he left to the world. Modern psychotherapy is, as a matter of fact, completely based on this premise.

Changes in our character take time to materialize. A new memory that is to become a part of our nature should be strengthened through repetition. As it is repeated, it interfaces with earlier experiences, and it is either recognized and saved or rejected. In this way our memories help to form our Self in the course of time. The new memories are directly associated to organic changes in the synapses of the brain. The entire process of education from birth to death works by learning through repetition.

Early in life, at home and at school, we learn concepts to which we attach meanings, and these meanings are stored in our memory. By repetition, these concepts become part of ourselves and are passed on to future generations through language, traditions, myths and legends. It is through this way that we are able to define who we are and the society in which we live in. This process highlights the importance of education and culture in the creation of the Self. We can only begin to actively question the validity of our values after we understand the way our Self grows. Only then can we attempt to change them if they are harmful, or strengthen them if they are useful.

From this chapter, we can derive that the Self is a synthesis of nature and nurture, while consciousness is the means by which we come into contact with the environment and our inner Self. By employing its competencies, we strive to accomplish our goals in life. Information we perceive, both from the internal and external world, are part of the contents of consciousness. The contents of consciousness are determined by the ability of attention. We know and understand only what we pay attention to. The Epicurean Philosophy admits that our biological characteristics, senses, emotions, and anticipations convey the truths of our lives and show the way to happiness. The body and the soul are material; they are born together, they also die together. Plato's idealistic philosophy and the philosophies that stem from it claim that the norm of truth is provided by logic.

Plato also supported the view that the body is corruptible and the soul, imperishable. Medical research has shown that our nature, physical and mental, is single and organic. This is a confirmation of the Epicurean views. The disclosure of the Self, especially of its emotional part, presents physical difficulties that take persistence and extra effort to realize. We can influence the characteristics of our Self and pursue happiness through learning and experience.

CHAPTER 3

THE BIOLOGY OF HAPPINESS

*"Again, the living powers of body and
mind prevail by union, one with the other,
and so enjoy life; for neither without body
can the nature of mind by itself alone
produce the motions of life, nor yet bereft of
soul can body last on and feel sensation."*

Lucretius, Epicurean poet

The functional unit of the nervous system is the neuron.
It has the main features of the common cell, with an elon-
gated shape that facilitates the transmission of messages.
It consists of four parts: the body, the axon, the dendrites
and the synapses. Communication between the neurons
is an electrochemical process wherein the message starts
with an electrical impulse along the axon. It then results in
a chemical transportation to the next meta-synaptic neuron through chemicals called neurotransmitters.

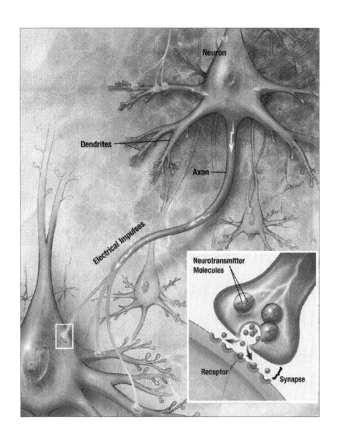

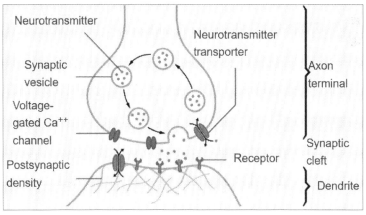

When a stimulus such as light, sound, heat or thought is received, it is decoded and transferred to the corresponding brain centers for identification and processing via the neural circuit. The sensation is then realized by the brain. A new message delivered to the consciousness for example, for assessment and decision making is the result of this process. Such neural circuits are for all kinds of stimuli, such as visual, auditory, emotional and other.

The transmission of messages to the brain

Major cognitive or emotional disorders owe to stumbling blocks in the smooth transmission of messages into the neural circuits of the brain.

A common obstacle has to do with the strength of the message. It is essential for the message to be strong enough in order to induce significant voltage difference between the potassium and sodium ions surrounding the axon for an "action potential" to develop. Then an electrical signal is fired that conveys the message with the information contained therein along the axon up to the ends of the dendrites in the synapse area. However, the neurons are not physically linked. They are separated by an infinitesimal empty space called the synapse. This explains why the continuation of the transmission in the gap between the pro-synaptic and meta-synaptic neurons is made through chemical entities called neurotransmitters. They may be likened to chemical "postmen" that cross the synapse space and convey the message to the next meta-synaptic neuron. When the electric signal reaches the end of the axon near the synapse, it stimulates the special pockets responsible for producing the neurotransmitters associated with this message.

The neurotransmitters are released, and then they flow into the area of the synapse where they enter specific receptors at the ends of the post-synaptic neuron. It is here that they supply their chemical message. If the number of neurotransmitters exceeds a critical level, a potential voltage difference is caused in the post-synaptic neuron. This is capable of triggering a new electrical impulse to transmit the message to the next neuron. This process is repeated from neuron to neuron until the message completes its biologically programmed path. The change in the operating state of the neuron from tranquility to stimulation and back is made within a minimum period of time. Thus, the body is enabled to react quickly to stimuli of the external or internal environment.

You might wonder what happens when the stimulus is so weak that it does not cause a significant voltage difference in the pre-synaptic neuron in order to create an action potential. The answer is simple; the message is simply not transmitted, and there is no conscious or unconscious reaction to the stimulus. In addition to this, a transmission process may be triggered if the signal is not strong enough, but this process may fail to run its course by stopping after a few repetitions. Indeed, if the electrical pulse into the pre-synaptic neuron is weak, the amount of neurotransmitters released is insufficient to carry the volume of information that makes up the message; therefore the post-synaptic neuron remains idle, and the message transmission ends.

Repetition is another factor with a significant impact on the smooth transmission of messages in the brain. It may also be referred to as habit. Each type of message received by the brain follows its own path in the processing centers of the brain. That is why the mind has the elusive number of almost one hundred trillion synapses.

The first time the mind receives a stimulus, it opens up a communication path using hereditary neurons. If the message is repeated many times, the brain responds positively by generating new dendrites or neurons. Through this process, it opens new paths or expands the already existing ones.

The aim of Nature is for the common messages to be transmitted quickly and automatically without any thought. This is the way learning functions. Through repetition it becomes knowledge and is stored in the synapses of the brain. This way it is transferred from the consciousness and logic into the unconscious mind, which then performs automatically all the tasks associated to it. A biological circuit that prefers unscrupulous forms of action is programmed by nature, as the forms of consciousness have other priorities. Hence, if we want to make a change in our Self, we have to repeat it as many times as is necessary for this change to acquire the power of habit. For only then can it function without the intervention of the conscious mind. Any interference of thought is a clear indication that the mind has not assimilated the change, and the Self cannot enjoy its positive effects.

The time required for learning depends on many factors. Of these, age is decisive because the birth of new neurons and dendrites is reduced over time, and the old synapses are not enough to carry new messages with ease. This does not mean, of course, that we cannot change. If it did, it would mean that we could not learn, which contradicts science and experience. As we age, we acquire experience, perseverance and composure. These traits make us enjoy our activities as well as improve our performance when the experiences are pleasant and interesting. In any case, a necessary condition for us to learn something is to be authentic.

If we are to establish new habits or to change the old ones, we need a strong will, perseverance and discipline. Many people assume that changes occur as soon as they realize the need to make them. Hence, they easily get disappointed. What we must realize is that the brain's biological wiring follows its own learning pace, which we have to abide to.

Perceptions and habits make up the third factor that has significant influence on the smooth communication of messages in the brain. Perceptions acquire the strength of habits with time. Thereby, acquiring the ability to automatically distinguish the good from the bad, the important from the unimportant, and what to pay attention to from what not to pay attention to. The more we are certain about the credibility of our perceptions, the higher the priority the mind attaches to the messages associated to them in relation to others, and the more energy resources it disposes for their quick transmission. This property of perceptions is related to "faith," the trust in the truthfulness and the effectiveness of the message embodied in the perceptions. Therefore faith, no matter how absurd, has a beneficial effect on psychology. Epicurus understood the significance of faith to the effectiveness of his doctrines, as the poet Lucretius says: "It is worse to suspect that the legends related to Acheron are true, than the faith in them."

Amongst the most frequent impediments to the undisturbed transmission of messages is the existence or the impression of the existence of risks to life. Danger, no matter if it is real or unreal, is treated biologically by the reaction of anxiety and stress. This is a process that puts the body in a defensive or combative situation in order to deal with the danger. It is known that our physical and biological structure is adapted for life in the woods and not in the cities, based on the fact that ten thousand years ago, humans lived as hunters. The risks in the forests were animals and to defend itself, the body transferred energy resources from low priority functions, like digestion, sex, growth, and emotion, to the strengthening of its physical powers. This ancient defense mechanism is still used by the mind to address the risks of urban life. These risks, unlike physical ones, last for long duration but do not require any extra physical strength. Thus, constant stress keeps the mind in an everlasting defense mode, with tensed muscles and weakened emotional reactions.

Research has shown that stress causes the collapse of the transmission of neurotransmitters in the course of time, due to exhaustion of available energy resources. It causes the activation of pleasant emotions to decrease, and joy becomes rare as we gradually fall into the depths of depression.

Neurotransmitters

Of particular interest is the chemical transmission process that takes place through the neurotransmitters in the synaptic terminals. Brain neurons produce certain chemicals, known as neurotransmitters, which are directly related to mood. Examples include serotonin, GABA, dopamine, norepinephrine and epinephrine. It has been found that these organic substances are produced by the mediation of the hypothalamus, a small organ which is responsible for the emotional function of the brain. When the hypothalamus receives positive or pleasant stimuli, it triggers these neurons to secrete some of the chemicals related to mood.

For every type of message transmitted, a specific neurotransmitter corresponds to it with respect to size and shape suitable for the penetration of corresponding receptors of the post-synaptic neuron. This can be made clearer with the analogy of the lock and key; the neurotransmitters are like keys unlocking the receptors. If there is no perfect fit, the receptors remain locked.

By opening the receptors, the neurotransmitters free the chemical substance they carry and return to their starting point, to be reused next time when a new message needs to be sent. All messages are similarly transmitted to the brain. Despite the seemingly complicated nature of this process, the entire cycle of transmission of information only takes a few seconds. Any hurdle that interrupts the smooth flow of these operations affects the brain and upsets its functions. It has been found that the transmission disorders of pleasurable messages originate from worries, stress and heartache. Simply put, neurotransmitters are brain chemicals that convey information between the brain and the body. Among other functions, the brain uses neurotransmitters to tell the heart to beat, the lungs to breathe, the stomach to digest and so on. Neurotransmitters can also affect mood, concentration, and weight. Generally, they can cause unpleasant symptoms when they lose their balance.

In most people in advanced countries, the level of neurotransmitters is lower than the optimal level. Stress, poor diets, neurotoxins, hereditary predispositions, alcohol, caffeine, and drugs are the main causes of disturbances in the production and transmission of these brain chemicals.

Neurotransmitters are of two types; there are the inhibitory and the excitatory types.

As the name implies, the excitatory neurotransmitters

excite the brain, while the inhibitory calm it down and bring balance. When we are under stress, the hypothalamus perceives the Self in danger and sets off the defensive mechanism of the mind. This is reflected in the release of excitatory neurotransmitters to prepare the body for fight or flight. Normally, when the danger is over, inhibitory neurotransmitters are released through the mediation of the hypothalamus to balance out the excitatory ones, and calm down the body. Though in the case of constant stress, as the one that we, the modern people, experience, the inhibitory neurotransmitters are gradually reduced or eliminated due to the exhaustion of energy reserves, in the endless effort to balance the excitatory ones. This shortage, and finally inability, of the inhibitory neurotransmitters to counteract the excitatory ones is at the heart of the exacerbation of mood disorders experienced nowadays.

Serotonin and GABA are the major inhibitory neurotransmitters. Serotonin is involved in regulating many important bodily functions, some of which are sleep, aggression, eating, sexual behavior and mood. To secure a stable mood, as well as balance any excessive levels of excitatory neurotransmitters bombarding the brain, sufficient levels of serotonin are required. Recreational drugs or caffeine can reduce or eliminate serotonin over time.

GABA (acronym for gamma amino butyric acid), is an inhibitory neurotransmitter. It is, in a manner of speaking, a natural tranquilizer. When it lies outside of normal levels, this is an indication that some excitatory neurotransmitters are overactive. GABA is therefore being produced in excess in an attempt to balance these excitatory neurotransmitters.

Dopamine, norepinephrine and epinephrine are the major excitatory neurotransmitters. Dopamine is a special neurotransmitter because it can be both stimulating and inhibitory. It helps in treating mood disorders, as well as concentration and is linked to the desire for action and creation. This is applicable when, for example, we have low or high concentration problems, like forgetting where we put our keys, what paragraph we stopped reading at, daydreaming, and generally when we are not focused on what we are doing. Stimulants, such as caffeine, push dopamine in the place of the synapse in order to improve concentration. Unfortunately, the constant stimulation eliminates concentration in the end, and the purpose is defeated.

Norepinephrine (aka noradrenaline) is an excitatory neurotransmitter. Disorders of this chemical are linked to symptoms of sluggishness, poor concentration and sleep. Research has shown that norepinephrine helps the body to recognize and respond to stressful situations. People who have a low production of norepinephrine cannot effectively handle the effects of stress, leading to an exacerbation of mental disorders.

Norepinephrine also helps in the production of another major excitatory neurotransmitter, epinephrine (adrenaline). When driven high, this neurotransmitter causes anxiety as well as depressive symptoms. The increase in its production is directly linked to the stimulation of the defense mechanism of fight or flight caused by stress.

Neuroplasticity

The brain is the "control room" of the human body; it has the wonderful ability to detect and respond to the demands of the environment. This property, called "neuroplasticity," provides for the flexibility of the brain to grow and take new shapes, enabling memory and learning.

For example, the nerve cells are adjusted to specific needs by generating new brain synapses and by enhancing the already existing ones. Furthermore, neurons may be re-programmed when circumstances warrant the change. For example, they can change their path to activate a part of the brain that was destroyed by a stroke. Monitoring of the activity of neurotransmitters is an important aspect of neuroplasticity. Neurons have the distinct ability of feeling their environment. They can therefore inactivate or change the function of genes that produce neurotransmitters. For example, in a stressful situation, the brain feels an increase in the stress level and prepares the body for fight or flight. The activation of this defense mechanism requires extra energy, which as a rule is transferred from the emotional functions of the body. The brain is therefore forced to interrupt or reduce the genes that produce neurotransmitters related to pleasure and their receptors—hence disturbing the mood.

Until recently, it was considered that the brain did not

produce new neurons to replace those destroyed. The adult brain was considered to have all the neurons generated during the individual's lifetime. This view proved to be incorrect. Today, we know that new neurons are produced throughout our lifetime. It is also known that the neuronal circuits in certain areas of the brain are actively involved in memory and emotion. A whole lot of medications designed for mood improvement aim to develop new neurons in these areas of the brain in order to counter the effects of chronic stress, which reduces the creation of new neurons.

Endocrinology

The neurotransmitters are not the only important biological messengers of the body. Hormones are used as additional messengers by the body. They are produced in the endocrine system and transfer messages from one organ to another through the bloodstream. The organs that receive the hormonal signals respond to these messages in the same way that the neuron receptors interpret the signals of brain neurotransmitters.

The endocrine and the nervous system are both connected to the hypothalamus, which represents the central "Relay Station" within the brain. The hypothalamus is a very complex part of the brain that controls many bodily functions such as blood pressure, appetite, immunological behavior, temperature, maternal behavior, body rhythms and mood. When the brain detects a potential threat, the hypothalamus tells the endocrine glands to produce a variety of hormones. It is these hormones that give the body the necessary strength to face a dangerous situation.

The major endocrine glands are the thyroid, adrenals, ovaries and testes. The thyroid gland is located in the neck and produces thyroid hormones. Low levels of thyroid hormone (aka hypothyroidism) have often been linked to mood disorders, while happiness is linked with high levels of thyroid hormones or hyperthyroidism. It is possible to relieve mood disorders when hypothyroidism is treated.

Hormones involved in metabolism, in the functions of the immune system, and in stress response are produced by the adrenal gland, an endocrine gland found near the kidney. The main adrenal hormone is cortisol, which is an eminent stress hormone. Like adrenaline (epinephrine), it is released in response to stress. It exerts its effect by making the necessary energy reserves available to the brain. This addresses direct threats or prepares the body for anticipated risks.

Cortisol acts by increasing glucose production in the blood. This enables the brain to fuel the extra energy requirements while simultaneously diverting energy from low priority activities. Prolonged cortisol secretion due to chronic stress, however, disrupts almost all bodily functions and causes many serious health problems like depression, heart disease, insomnia, obesity, and memory disorders.

Estrogen is produced by the ovaries. It is one of the main reasons why women are at a greater risk of developing mood disorders than men. The reduction of the levels of estrogen in the blood reduces the activity of neurotransmitters serotonin and norepinephrine and disrupts the mood.

Estrogen levels are lower than usual during periods like the premenstrual phase, after birth, or around menopause. Women are at increased risk of depressive phenomena when these occur.

Testosterone is a hormone produced by the testes, and it is also connected to mood disorders. The reduction in testosterone production after the age of fifty may be one of the reasons that men of this age are more prone to mood disorders. Unlike estrogen, however, the relationship between testosterone and mood disorders is not as clear.

Light is another factor that may account for changes in mood. It has been found that the amount of light that we receive also affects our mood. This effect stems from the changes caused by light on the circadian and seasonal rhythms of the body.

The circadian rhythms refer to the 24-hour body cycle. They are determined by the amount of light felt by the hypothalamus in the day-night cycle. Brain activity and hormone production are associated with this cycle. When disturbed by varying amounts of light in the 24-hour cycle, circadian rhythms cause mood disorders. Seasonal rhythms function similarly to the circadian rhythms. They are determined by the amount of daylight during each season. People with seasonal affective disorder feel more and more mood disorders as the amount of light decreases with the approach of winter. On the other hand, as spring approaches and daylight increases, their moods improve.

In this chapter we saw that medical research has proven the single physical nature of man and the interdependence of physical and mental functions. Thoughts, perceptions, feelings and choices that constitute the spiritual and emotional parts of the Self are of organic texture and cause organic changes in the Self. When under threat, the brain strengthens its defense functions to the detriment of the emotional functions. If threats are not addressed promptly, the defense mechanism remains in constant alert mode and mood disorders stay put. To feel the positive impact of changes, these should become habits through repetition. The medium of learning is consciousness and reason. Finally, research confirms the intuitive and empirical assumptions of Epicurus that worries and anxiety are the greatest enemies of happiness.

CHAPTER 4

FREE WILL

"Fate, which some introduce as sovereign over all things, he scorns, affirming rather that some things happen of necessity, others by chance, others through our own agency. For he sees that necessity destroys responsibility and that chance is inconstant; whereas our own actions are autonomous, and it is to them that praise and blame naturally attach."

Epicurus, *Letter to Menoeceus*

Will has an important function. This function also happens to be one of the two major functions of the conscious mind, along with logic. Will is that which distinguishes humans from the other living beings. It is a capacity that was added in the last stage of the evolutionary process. Therefore, will is connected to the superior and more advanced of human mental functions.

In simple terms, free will is the ability to do whatever we want. That is, to plan ahead, to make choices and to realize them. Although these traits seem obvious at first glance, in practice it turns out not to be so.

There are challenges to the exercise of one's free will. The extent to which will is exercised is limited by obstacles posed by heredity, the environment, and personal weaknesses.

On top of this, other theories argue that people have no free will at all. One of them is the fatalistic theory that is rooted in superstitions, and the other is a corollary of the atomic theory of Democritus that introduces the idea of absolute determinism. In other words, this theory maintains that the physical laws governing the operation of the universe and human beings define a prescribed future for both Nature and people.

Fatalism and scientific determinism did not leave people much leeway. Epicurus strongly opposed these views by arguing that for unknown reasons, the usual course of things change. He went on to argue that this allows for unexpected new formations and routes in life.

As far as the atoms are concerned, Epicurus assumed that in unknown places and times, atoms deviate from their straight paths so as to cause collisions and unexpected atomic formations. These formations change the natural flow of things in the universe and allow people the freedom of choice.

Modern scientific research has confirmed Epicurus' views. It was discovered that in the universe, the laws of gravity divert micro particles from their straight motion and cause collisions among them. In the same vein, the innate power of will in humans can empower people to deviate from the course that has been programmed by their character and the environment.

Absolute determinism: the future is fixed

This theory argues that each development in the cosmos is determined by previous events; that is, there is a certain specified future for the universe and humans. Leucippus and Democritus argued that all things, including humans, are made up of atoms which move by clearly defined, natural laws. However, despite their initial intention to relieve people of fatalism in this way, they only reinforce the old beliefs, instead of refuting them. The theory of the constant motion of atoms inevitably leads to the logical necessity of determinism. This maintains that there is a certain future for the world that is fully determined by past data. In Leucippus' words: "Nothing happens without a purpose, but always for a reason and necessity."

In the 16th century AD, twenty centuries later, the concept of the prescribed course of things was strengthened by Newton's mathematical theory of classical mechanics. The theory declared that body motion is determined by the starting point, speed and acting forces. In other words, the path of the motion is strictly prescribed.

In the mid-17th century, philosophers like the Englishman Thomas Hobbes argued that the mind works according to established mechanisms, and therefore it cannot show free will.

Immediately after him, other scientists, like the French mathematician and astronomer Laplace, supported the theory of determinism based on mathematical laws. They maintained that the future of the universe is completely specified.

With the advancement of science in the 18th century, the assumption of determinism was entrenched, establishing the view that all human actions are guided by specific laws, and thus, there is no free will.

The philosopher Arthur Schopenhauer had similar views. According to him, humans initially consider themselves absolutely free, even in individual actions. We believe we can start another lifestyle at any time. However through experience, we ultimately discover with surprise that we are not free. Instead, we realize we are subject to necessity, that despite all decisions and thoughts, we are incapable of changing behavior. Schopenhauer concluded that from the beginning of human life until the end, we have the same character, which we condemn.

Relative determinism: there is also free will

While accepting determinism, this theory also accepts that some unforeseen, random events change the set course of things and cause a new chain of events. Therefore the future of the universe and people is not prescribed.

Plato was the first philosopher who advocated the

theory of relative determinism. He said that the body may be subject to the laws of determinism, but the soul has its own degrees of freedom. In the *Republic*, he writes that virtue is not a necessity or a compulsion. It is a free choice that belongs to the person who carries it. Plato argued that anyone who chooses to do evil is solely responsible for his actions.

Aristotle suggested that there are multiple causative reasons behind every event. One of these reasons are the accidents caused by luck. For Aristotle, the specified flow of phenomena is sometimes disturbed by random events, which allows for unexpected developments.

According to the Christian religion, god created Nature, and behind every event, there is the almighty god. At the same time, people have some degree of free choice, especially regarding good or evil. The co-acceptance of the above claims leads to a reasonable deadlock.

How could people have freedom of choice once god is omniscient? Does the omnipotent not control and direct everything?

Faced with this impasse, Christian intellectuals, like St. Augustine in the 5th century AD and Thomas Aquinas in the 13th, compromised by arguing that although people are free, there is also the necessity of divine omniscience. Later, Calvin invented the intelligent approach of separating the divine will into the irresistible and resistible. According to this hypothesis, the irresistible will of god allows for human derogations and options in order for higher goals to be achieved. Questions regarding free will continue to be a source of conflict, with outbreaks among Christian denominations even today.

Emmanuel Kant, a philosopher of the late 18th century, argued in agreement with previous works of the mathematician and philosopher Leibniz that at least some parts of the brain are free. Kant said that people have the freedom of will, but they only use it a few times.

In the late 19th century, the American psychologist and philosopher, William James described a model of free will that operates in two stages. Initially, the mind develops random options for actions and in the second, a determined free will chooses one of them. Later on, other scholars, including Poincare, Popper, Denet, Caine and Heisenberg, perfected James' idea.

The evolutionary theory of Charles Darwin that introduced randomness as a factor that causes the evolution of species, reinforced the theory that randomness can change the course of things.

Quantum mechanics, invented in the mid-20th century by the German physicist Werner Heisenberg, is considered to have put a definitive end to the theory of absolute determinism. According to quantum mechanics, the laws of Newton's classical mechanics that support the concept of absolute determinism apply only in the motion of large objects and not to the individual microcosm. In the collision of atomic particles, only the likelihood of atomic routes can be predicted and not their exact location, a claim which confirms the theory of randomness in the atomic micro-cosm.

During the same period, Karl Popper used quantum mechanics to support the theory of indeterminacy. The economist-philosopher Friedrich Hayek also claimed that human behavior is completely unpredictable because the brain can only explain simpler systems than its own, and it cannot explain the operation of the same.

Sartre, for his part, proclaimed passionately in favor of the existence of free will. He argued that people are free, condemned to freedom. Life is a series of decisions and any decision could be different, he said. When we say that we could not do otherwise, we are deceiving ourself. There were intermediate solutions, Sartre argued.

The freedom of will in the Epicurean Philosophy

The philosophical position of Epicurus on the existence of free will in people led him to the formulation of the atomic theory that refuted some of the aspects of Democritus. Especially he argued that for unforeseen reasons the atoms sometimes deviate from their steady course and cause a new chain of events. In his *Letter to Menoeceus* Epicurus says: "Fate, which some introduce as sovereign over all things, he scorns, affirming rather that some things happen out of necessity, others by chance, others through our own agency. For he sees that necessity destroys responsibility and that chance is inconstant; whereas our own actions are autonomous, and it is to them that praise and blame are naturally attached. It was better, indeed, to accept the legends of the gods than to bow beneath that yoke of destiny which the natural philosophers have imposed. The one holds out some faint hope that we may escape if we honor the gods, while the necessity of the naturalists is deaf to all entreaties."

The Epicurean poet Lucretius in his work *De Rerum Natura* describes the breaking of the causal chain, stating that without deviation nothing could be created: "Then again, if we assume that all motion always goes on in a continuous chain with new motion always arising out of the old in an absolutely determined order; and if the atoms, by means of this swerve, do not initiate a kind of motion that can break through the decrees of fate so that cause may not follow cause to infinity, then how can we explain this free will which we find in living creatures all over the Earth? What, I say, is the origin of this faculty of ours which we have wrested from the fates and by which each of us goes where his pleasure leads him, deviating in our motions just as the atoms do at no fixed times or places, but just as our mind takes us? For it is beyond doubt that in these matters, it is a man's will that provides the initiative, and from it the movements spread through the limbs."

The empirical data on free will

Everyday life shows us that we actually make decisions through our own free will. If there is no free choice, why do we feel so much anxiety when we are faced with choices in our life? Why such political and economic struggles for freedom? Why, in front of the choice between freedom and tyranny, do people almost always choose the first?

Let us remember simple facts from life in order to track free will in action. Suppose that tomorrow is a holiday. We can climb a mountain or read a book. We can ride a bicycle or go out with a friend. Once you read this book, and you hold it in your hands, you are free to continue reading or to stop now. You start this sentence, but you do not have to complete it. In this case, as also in life, we have many options. Nothing forces us to do the one or the other. We are open to choose quite freely. Even in difficult situations we have the freedom of choice. For example, the pilots in an airplane hijacking are usually calm. They choose to comply with the requirements of the hijackers. They are able to react differently from what they do, but they do not choose to do so. They do what they want to do after taking into account the conditions in which they are in and the consequences of their choices. Even someone whose finger is forced to push the trigger can resist. Even someone who is paralyzed is free to choose, as long as he thinks he can. Also while facing dilemmas that cause severe internal conflicts, free will can prevail and lead us into safety and prosperity. In choosing, for example, not to eat contaminated food while dying of hunger, or avoiding a sexual contact that involves risks, or utilizing logic to overcome a fear or anger, we exercise the ability of free will. Of course we cannot do whatever we want. We cannot fly. We cannot house the homeless of Calcutta. Free will is limited by what we can do.

The origin of free will

Some researchers argue that freedom of choice is a result of the evolution of man. They support that evolution promoted those features of human beings that favored their survival and smooth transition from the primitive, to cultural and social life. One of these features is free will, which gives people the ability to meet the needs of society and make complex decisions. Thus, the need for survival has led man to decisions contrary to their primitive roots by making conscious choices and taking risks. This ability of humans coincided with the birth of the rational brain. Animals, plants, engines, and little children up to the age of about three do not have the capacity of free will. Their decisions are reflexive or pre-programmed. There is no doubt today that the ability of animals to learn is a product of their mechanistic brain function. Biology, developmental psychology and the science of computing gave considerable evidence that these mental abilities of animals arise from specific interactions between neurons, molecules and the atoms that constitute them. Furthermore, according to all indications, these interactions are entirely subject to the known laws of physics and chemistry, and the mechanical reactions of the unconscious mind. As the child grows up and develops the conscious mind, he acquires the physical ability to evaluate choices and make decisions.

Understanding. This is the difference between an adult and a baby, an animal, a plant, and a machine. The latter have little or no understanding. A robot knows where to place the final product and an animal where to find food. A flower is aware of the rising sun. However, none of them have conceptual self-knowledge of what they are doing. Understanding requires the integration of new knowledge with other information preexisting in the mind. Until we associate the new knowledge with our understanding of reality, this knowledge is not understood by the mind. All knowledge, including abstract concepts, must be integrated and related to our fundamental experience.

Free will refers only to conscious choices. We choose to think or not, what to think, how much time to focus on a question, how many options to consider, what to choose. We also make higher-level choices, such as of a career, friends, and morality. By definition, free will precludes unconscious choices. However it is not independent of previous factors and causes. The word "free" refers to the ability and the freedom to make smart, informed choices. Surely the available options are made for some reason, and they do not result from unprovoked thought or random factors.

The "free" in free will is not the elimination of the factors that create the available choices, but the unique ability to make the best choice out of them. We can do this because we have the capacity to be aware of ourselves; that is, we have self-consciousness, self-awareness and imagination to process abstract concepts, to project them into the future and to make comparisons. These properties of the conscious mind are the sources of our freedom. These are the sources of self-determination.

The unconscious mind works with given fixed mechanisms so as to produce consistent choices, unaffected by uncertainties, or personal or foreign interference. Otherwise, the available options will be uncontrollable and unpredictable, and therefore, there would be no scope for learning and improving ourselves. Survey results support this hypothesis of the mechanical operation of the mind and thus the assumption that the available options are generated unconsciously, automatically, and mechanically, on the basis of the data in our life at that time juncture. When the data changes through new knowledge or experiences, our unconscious brain functions take into account the changes and create new choices. Through this process, education and experience broaden the available options and improve the quality and effectiveness of our decisions. This is the way free will works.

Could we have chosen otherwise? It is a question that we often ask ourselves in life as we face the effects of previous decisions, often accompanied by feelings of regret and guilt. This attitude does not lead anywhere and is unhelpful for our development in life. When we made the original decision, we took all the available information into account; we set selection criteria and showed preference for one option over another while rejecting others. No matter why we made that choice, it is certain that we made the best choice we could have under those circumstances. So if we could have turned back time and operated rationally, we would again have chosen the best option: the one we had chosen in the first place. Only differences in the external environment and the circumstances might have caused another development. But who knows if it would have been better?

The properties of free will

Without free will, if we had no control over our objectives and choices, if all of our actions were the inevitable result of forces outside ourselves, then for many of us, life would seem a grim reality. If we cannot influence our destiny, then why deal with it? We can comfortably sit in our chair and observe life unfolding before our eyes. We want and need control of our life to give meaning to it, to set goals, to achieve them, and to make decisions that will bring us closer to happiness.

The exercise of free will assumes taking personal responsibility for our decisions and actions. This is an important aspect of human existence. We are beings with an improvised soul, meaning that we can take the responsibility of exercising this capability or of letting our life be swept away into unknown paths by random influences, without taking any action. To the extent that we reject the power of personal choice and assume that our actions are the products of blind forces of nature and nurture, we undermine the effectiveness of free will. This also implies low self-esteem and involuntary determinism, with catalytic negative personal and social consequences.

The recognition and exercise of free will is perhaps the most important factor that determines who we are. In normal conditions, it cannot be imposed by the environment. The individual himself chooses the extent to which he will use it.

So if free will is so great, why do we only sometimes exercise it? Many studies have found that people often avoid coming into the conscious selection process. It is true that the conditions in which we live place restrictions on our choices.

A major impediment to exercising free will is the lack of free time. The evaluation and decision making process that follows the exercise of free will is time consuming; people prefer to make automatic decisions, and only when it is impossible, to enter a conscious selection process. The case of automatic choices is served by habits, traditions, mimicry, and philosophies alike.

The exercise of free will is not only time consuming but it is tiresome as well. Surveys have shown that the self-test, which is an integral part of the exercise of free will, is particularly demanding in energy, and therefore, very tiring. It uses substantial reserves of glucose, and when these are exhausted, the body manifests weakness for retrial. This scientific discovery strengthens the empirical finding that we exercise free will when in good spirits.

The responsibility that follows the exercise of free will acts also as a deterrent for many people. Taking initiatives requires trust in ourselves, mental strength to stand out from the crowd and claim the pleasures we desire. But this action requires a good and strong psychological condition that many lack. People avoid taking responsibilities for fear of failure. They are used to blaming society or the circumstances for whatever happens to them. Others deny any responsibility altogether by accepting the role of victim and by completely repelling it from their minds, as if it does not exist. Those who exercise free will though are obliged to bear the costs of a possible failure; they cannot renounce it by attributing their failure to others. This risk of failure creates fears which paralyze the will and leads to inaction.

A coercive environment also deprives us of the freedom of choice. Free will is significantly limited in authoritarian regimes, autarchic, social and religious structures, a strict family and educational environment, or when we are under psychological pressure and drug addiction.

A daunting environment could serve as a hindrance to free will as well. The family, and often the wider environment, discourage the development of free will. Parents prefer that their children are obedient and follow their instructions without any complaints. They also usually plan their children's future in their absence, without taking their physical and psychological traits, desires and inclinations into account. These behaviors discourage the development of free will in children; they create dependent and passive adults, who even if succeeding to reach the objectives set by their parents, lack in quality and have little satisfaction in life.

From this chapter, we gather that one of the two major functions of the conscious mind is that of the will. The mind expresses desires and the willingness to satisfy them, identifies goals, evaluates the options, and takes decisions and initiatives. Free will is the unique ability of humans to understand who they are and what they want to do, to set goals and to pursue them consistently. It refers to the mind's ability to evaluate automatic thoughts and emotions, to make decisions and re-plan life. The effects of heredity, upbringing, environment and luck can be significantly affected by the exercise of free will. It is a skill that we can learn like any other, and it depends totally on us to what extent and when to exercise its use. The significance of free will has been undermined by the political, religious and social environment because it is the prerequisite for the fulfillment of our desires. Authoritarian societies exercise physical violence to oppress it, while liberal ones use indirect, "civilized" ways, such as psychological violence, brainwashing and the introduction of diseased lifestyles. In the Epicurean Philosophy, freedom of will holds a dominant place. The wise man is responsible for his life. The effects of fate, necessity and luck are considered temporary.

CHAPTER 5

PHILOSOPHY OF LIFE

*"Let no one be slow to seek wisdom
when he is young, nor weary in the
search of it when he has grown old. For
no age is too early or too late for the
health of the soul."*

Epicurus, *Letter to Menoeceus*

In the dawn of civilization at about 700 BC people began
to wonder about the origin of the cosmos, the functions
of the universe, and the meaning of life. The philosophers
who systematically dealt with these questions came up
with diversified answers that cover the whole spectrum of
philosophical thought. By today's standards, some of these
may seem simplistic, others mysterious, but some interesting, ingenious and sophisticated. Due to the time lag, it is
hard for the modern, common man to understand them,

evaluate and possibly adopt them in his life. To overcome this hurdle we will approach the philosophies in relation to their approach in the search for truth. An analysis advances two distinct approaches. The first one uses the truth in observation and experience as a means of searching, while the other, the thoughts of logic. Nowadays, these schools of thought are known as the Natural Philosophy of Epicurus and the idealistic philosophies, respectively, with the singular number denoting the "one" Natural Philosophy, and the plural denoting innumerable idealistic philosophies. Indeed, a man who uses the Natural Philosophy bases his decisions on the true desires of his nature and the real requirements of the external environment, and this is the reason why Epicurus calls his Philosophy the "true philosophy." On the other hand, the idealistic philosophies are as many as thoughts are countless. All philosophies of thought are based on the philosophy that was perfected by Plato. He preceded Pythagoras and Socrates, and Aristotle followed him for most of his life. The pillar of philosophers of the Natural Philosophy are Thales of Miletus, Democritus and Epicurus.

All the ancient Greek philosophies had a violent and abrupt end in the 4th century AD, when Christianity was established as the official religion in the Roman Empire. The last philosophical school, Plato's Academy, was forced to shut down in 529 AD by the Byzantine Emperor Justinian. But although all philosophies had the same sad, official ending, they followed opposite paths in everyday life. Plato's ideas were adopted by Christianity and later on by the Islamic religion, and they have been spreading over societies ever since. On the contrary, the Natural Philosophy of Epicurus and his predecessors was expelled altogether from the face of the Earth, due to its opposition to the Christian ideas of the divinity of god and divine providence. Worst of all, the whole of the 300 rolls of the Epicurean texts vanished around the 4th century AD, depriving the generations to come from studying and implementing them. For this reason, the overwhelming majority of us in the Christian and Islamic world have been raised, educated in and live by following the idealistic approach in the search for truth and happiness.

The Natural Philosophy: Thales, Democritus and Epicurus

Ancient Greek philosophy was simultaneously developed in two separate areas of the wider Greek world, in Asia Minor and Lower Italy, which allowed for the development of two different voltages. The Ionians of Miletus in Asia Minor were engaged mainly in crafts and commerce, which made them people of practice and observation. In science, they focused on studying the nature of the world and weather conditions. Thales is the major philosopher of the Ionian School, followed by his students, Anaximander and Aristomenes. Thales was looking for natural causes to explain the cosmos and ended up with water as the origin of the world. This has been proven to be untrue, but the major contribution of Thales to civilization was his practice of using observation and experience as the norm of truth instead of the interventions of the gods. This Ionian philosophical tradition was broadened and refined over the next few centuries by the atomic theory of Democritus and "the pursuit of happiness" of Epicurus, in order to form the premises of Natural Philosophy, which suggests feelings are a guide for a happy life.

The idealistic philosophies: Plato, Aristotle, the Stoics

The Greeks of Italy were men of intellect and romance. They developed arithmetic and geometry, displacing the interest of knowledge from practice to theory. Plato was enchanted by geometric shapes, in which he found the absolute logic that asserts the absolute truth. He transformed the specific meanings of geometry to morality and politics. But proportionality is illusory when applied to dissimilar things such as triangles and justice or virtue. Despite this glaring shortcoming, Plato's ideas flourished in antiquity for quite some time, supported by dialectic, an intelligent but illusory method of arriving at the truth through questions and answers. The abstract logic and dialectic, in conjunction with the concept of reincarnation that Pythagoras first declared, led to the conclusion that the body is the cell or tomb of the soul, which is the source of logic, and thus the body prevents the perfection of knowledge. What the human mind comprehended was a temporary, incomplete picture of the eternal verities. Since the origin of Plato's ideas was geometry, this led him to astronomy, and then later to the study of celestial bodies. In these, he identified perfection and timelessness of movements, consistent with logic and his ideas. So with Plato, logic acquired a divine entity, and the planets emerged as gods.

The above philosophical fashion dominated the classical period, but after Plato's death it was doubted, even by his successors in the Academy. It suffered an additional, severe blow from Aristotle, who gradually distanced himself from his teacher's ideas, and at a later age he adopted a physical approach in the search of the truth. It is a known fact that his research in botany and zoology led him to claim that in the life of organic beings, nothing happens by chance, and that behind every function of organisms, there are natural causes. The Platonic views in the Hellenistic period were in complete remission.

Aristotle, in contrast to the heavenly ideal world of Plato, praised the earthly world. To him, the goal of human life is living on Earth in "eudaemonia" by combining virtue with reason. This objective, although earthly, is derived through thinking, and therefore it remains idealistic in essence.

Lastly, the Stoics combined both the Natural and the idealistic philosophies, by suggesting a natural life driven by reason.

Religious philosophy

The dominance of the Romans during the Hellenistic period was about to radically change the natural flow of philosophical streams. The Romans needed a strong religion to unite the heterogeneous populations of their Empire in order to reduce uprisings. Christianity was growing fast at that time, and this emerged as an unexpected opportunity to exploit it for their ends. They established it as the official religion of the empire and simultaneously banned the practice and dissemination of other philosophies by the force of the sword. The integration of Christianity in the official state brought Platonic Logic to the fore, and the Epicurean Nature into decline. The dominance of Christianity, and religions in general, has ever since been outright.

Once in the Enlightenment and Renaissance periods, the interest of intellectuals shyly returned to the neglected ancient Greek philosophies. The first interest in the Epicurean Philosophy manifested as late as the 17th century in France by the Catholic priest philosopher Pierre Gassendi. In the homeland of Epicurus, the first interest appeared much later, in the 1950's, when Professor Ch. Theodoridis ventured to write *Epicurus, The True Face of the Ancient World.*

From Epicurus' huge writings of 300 rolls, none survived the targeted religious fury, aimed at the elimination of his philosophy from the face of the Earth. Luckily some original letters and fragments, the extended poem of Lucretius, and the detailed quotes by philosophical and historical sources allow modern scholars to indulge in the reconstitution of the Epicurean Philosophy.

Consumerist philosophy

Religions, with the help of the state, managed to prevail but suffered a severe blow when a new consumerist philosophy appeared in the late 17th century. The industrial revolution that followed it in the 18th century gave a significant boost to consumerism by dramatically increasing the supply of consumer goods at low prices. Rising incomes made consumer goods affordable to the previously impoverished people who were able to improve the quality of their life. This trend led to the formation of a new economic and social environment, with new values and lifestyles. People started to move away from the standards of religious life in search of earthly means to prosperity through consumption, wealth and power. There soon emerged a new class of wealthy entrepreneurs that gradually took over the scepters of financial power and established itself as the new ruling class.

Consumerism had all the characteristics that could turn it into a new philosophy of life for the modern world. Indeed, consumerism satisfies consumer needs, the state's aims for the development of the economy and the entrepreneurs' own interests. It comes, then, as no surprise that entrepreneurs allied with politicians and the clergy to form a new, mighty status quo promoting material welfare as a means to a happy life. This philosophy spread quite rapidly and was supported by the emergence of the economic theory of the free market, which provided the theoretical background for its expansion. Artificial needs and expensive modes of life were created by people's inherent greed, by advertising new potential materialistic values through which the spiritual ones were replaced. People were gradually caught in a vicious cycle chasing success through hard work and indebtedness.

Today most people are overwhelmed by the syndrome of consumerist frenzy. They evaluate others by what they own, by their welfare and social status. Whatever has economic value and glamour is worth trying. All surveys show, however, that consumerism alone does not lead to happiness. When a person's income exceeds a minimum level it hardly contributes to increasing happiness. Psychologists argue that the relationship between wealth and happiness is limited. Although consumerism uses materialistic means to welfare, it possesses an idealistic character. It has been fabricated by the thoughts of logic, regardless of the needs of the people, in order to serve the interests of the "status quo."

Conclusively, philosophical thought was born in ancient Greece. The most influential philosophies that traversed a period of over 2,500 years until today sprang from that region of the world. The Platonic school of thought is heavenly. It accepts logic as the norm of truth. It argues that life on Earth is imperfect and incomplete. The perfect values and truths are based on the heavens, and they can be disclosed by logic empowered by Knowledge. Christianity adopted the Platonic principles for the futility of the earthly life and the perfection of the celestial. It suggests the immortality of the soul and proclaims that the path to god's favour is faith in Christ. The consumerist philosophy is the latest philosophy of life. Its starting point is the industrial revolution, and it advocates the pursuit of happiness through consumerism and success. The Natural Philosophy of Epicurus suggests feelings be the guide for a happy life.

CHAPTER 6

THE MEANING OF LIFE

"Wherefore we call pleasure the alpha and omega of a blessed life. Pleasure is our first and kindred good. It is the starting point of every choice and of every aversion, and to it we come back, inasmuch as we make feeling the rule by which to judge of every good thing."

Epicurus, *Letter to Menoeceus*

In many people's lives, it is difficult to find a connecting link. The absence of a long-term plan makes it hard to maintain harmony in the consciousness and to be able to bear life. Ideally we should turn our whole life into a single experience of happiness topped with the success of a long-term target. At the same time, it is useful to integrate the short term objectives within the wider long term goal so that all efforts in relation to the present, past and future will be meaningful. The available choices for a meaningful life are now numerous. But which is the most suitable? How do we find out what the purpose of life is and what is worth investing our energy in? There is no one to show us. Each of us has to find out by ourselves. Self-knowledge, the Delphic "Know Thyself" is the ancient timeless recipe for discovering the purpose of our life, while the trial and error process is the only way to evaluate it. If we do not bother to ask ourselves what we want from life, and if our attention is so absorbed by external influences that it has no contact with our feelings, we will never be able to design a meaningful life.

The internal conflict in the Self is the result of rival forces claiming to attract attention. Numerous wishes and incompatible objectives seek to be met. The only way to reduce conflict and normalize consciousness is to reject the unnatural and unnecessary desires and prioritize the rest. But while it is relatively feasible to put order in the conscious mind for short periods, it is very difficult to expand it over the whole of life. So it is very important to carefully choose an attractive philosophy in life. If we make the right choice, thoughts, feelings and plans will coexist harmoniously, and unnecessary conflicts can be avoided. But what makes some people have a consistent view of life and others strive in an empty life without meaning? To give a coherent meaning to the chaos of life experiences is a difficult and complex process, related to numerous internal and external factors. It is certainly difficult for someone who is handicapped, poor or oppressed. But this does not mean that we cannot find a meaningful life befitting to our living conditions.

As with philosophies we will examine the meanings of life in connection to the philosophies they are related to.

Modes of meanings of life

The meanings of life are divided into subjective and objective ones. The subjectivists believe that there are no uniform meanings of life for all people. The meaning of life is subjective and depends on the dispositions of each individual, his aims and options. For the subjectivists, something makes sense if the person himself thinks it does. The objectivists instead argue that the meaning of life does not concern the single individual, but society as a whole, or our wider values. Morality and creativity are two cases of collective values which, for the objectivists, give meaning to life. Also the utilitarians, who are considered pure objectivists, argue that the more one benefits his fellows, the more meaning his own life acquires. Another objective source of meaning is the perfectionist conception of Aristotle for a man whose natural aim is the pursuit of virtue and rationality.

The natural meaning of life arises from the biological functions of the mind, such as those that happen mechanically in the unconscious mind. These functions make up our character and mood, without any intervention of logical thoughts. They are related to the senses, the feelings, and the anticipations, as Epicurus claims in the *Canon on Truth*. The natural meaning of life, by definition is related to emotions, which are Nature's guide to life—our inherent natural perception as to what is good or bad in human happiness.

Democritus is known to have suggested the feeling of a good mood or cheer as the natural means to happiness. The sage from Abdera said: "Whoever wants to have his soul calm should not grapple with many, either individual or public, nor do, not to exceed his powers and Nature." The criterion of choice and avoidance according to Democritus are the feelings.

Aristippus of Sinope was an unrepentant sensual hedonist. He emphasized the superiority of sensual pleasures, which he claimed to be more intense than the mental.

The idealistic meanings of life arise from the thoughts of logic, which through repetition become habits and perceptions, and are transferred from the conscious to the unconscious functions of the mind. They originate in Plato, and by definition, they are cut off from the realities of the inner and outer world. The idealistic meanings of life are thoughts of logic which suggest the achievement of goals or living according to certain principles, such as, knowledge, virtue, reason, faith, moral obligation, duty, social justice, success, wealth, and power. Plato was the first philosopher who dealt in depth with the meaning of life, and his views defined the history of human thinking and living. In Platonism, the purpose of human life must be to achieve the highest form of knowledge, from which all good and just things derive utility and value. According to Plato, this knowledge helps us learn about the heavenly ideal world, of which the earthly is an imperfect copy.

For Aristotle, human happiness is pursued through performing our basic functions and activities in the best possible way. This way for Aristotle leads to a virtuous life with rational thinking. The Cynic philosophers, represented by Diogenes of Sinope, claimed that happiness depends on the self-sufficient being and the mastering of our own soul, which is achieved by a virtuous life in harmony with Nature. It is a meaning that combines idealistic and natural features. In the same line, Stoicism through Zeno suggested "to live in agreement with Nature and logic."

The religious conceptions for a meaningful life are rooted in Platonism. They consider the earthly life an indirect purpose not defined by humans. In Christianity, the meaning of life results from the faith in god and the pursuit of salvation through Christ.

In contrast to the idealistic and natural philosophers, there are others who argue that we do not need a meaning of life because it does not exist. Albert Camus argued that the absurdity of human nature is that people are looking for value and meaning in a world that makes no sense and is indifferent to them. He also said that the lack of an afterlife and of a rational, divinely arranged and functioning universe undermines the possibility for a meaning of life. Camus' idea is shared by many nihilists supporting that there is something inherent in human nature that prevents the existence of meaning. The German philosopher of the 20th century, Arthur Schopenhauer, proclaimed that life lacks meaning because we are always unsatisfied, either because we do not get what we are seeking, or we do get it and then get bored of it.

The historic evolution of the meaning of life

The influential philosopher of the 17th century, Rene Descartes, considered the senses an unreliable source of knowledge. He argued that only thought is able to inform the true nature of things. In the same line, Immanuel Kant in his book *Categorical Imperative* argued that the purpose of life lies in the execution of our moral obligation, based on the concept of the implementation of duty.

In the meantime, the earthly meanings of life re-emerged as a consequence of the conflicts between the rising bourgeoisie on the one hand and the established aristocracy and religious authority on the other. The movement of classical liberalism was born from this confrontation, the central concepts of which were labeled by the English philosopher John Locke, the Swiss philosopher Jean-Jacques Rousseau, and the Scottish economist and moral philosopher Adam Smith. They professed that the meaning of life is gained through work, ownership, and the use of social contracts. The philosophical movement of utilitarianism that was created in the 19th century by the British philosopher Jeremy Bentham had appointed as the meaning of life the maximization of happiness to the greatest number of people. This theory, which has its roots in the Epicurean Philosophy, was called the principle of the highest utility.

The current era is characterized by the prevalence of the earthy meanings of life and by the radical changes in the perceived position and purpose of humans in society. Modern science has rewritten the relationship between humans and the world, and the progress of medicine and technology has released people from the limitations and ailments of previous eras. So according to the philosophical and psychological concepts of existentialism, each man and each woman creates the meaning for his or her life. It declares that life is not determined by a supernatural god or an earthly authority because we are free. The main moral values must be freedom, decision and action. In modern times, existentialism was expressed by Kierkegaard, Nietzsche, Kafka, Dostoevsky, Sartre and Simone de Beauvoir.

The Danish philosopher, Soren Kierkegaard, coined the term "leap of faith" in the 19th century. He argued that life is full of absurdity, and everyone should form their own values in an indifferent world. We can live without despair and anxiety, gaining meaning in life with a leap of faith in something specific, unrestricted and free of conditions, even if we know that it has weaknesses. The French philosopher Jean-Paul Sartre argued that it is in the hands of the people to give meaning to their life. The value of life, he argued, is none other than what people choose to give to it. For the German philosopher of the 19th century, Friedrich

Nietzsche, life is worth something only when we have goals that inspire us, and we strive to achieve them.

For Karl Marx, the meaning of human life is to discharge the alienation that exists in the capitalist system. Workers produce in the interest of others, and in this manner, they are converted into a commodity, alienated from the product of their work, as well as from one another. At the same time, all people are alienated from their very nature. Consequently, the elimination of alienation at work can only be achieved by removing private property. The Marxist approach to the analysis of human affairs leads to the inevitable historical trend towards the prevalence of international communism. The ultimate objective and inevitable final form of government for humanity is the establishment of an undisturbed, peaceful, classless society, without state, where justice will be realized by the application of the simple principle, "from each according to his ability, to each according to his needs."

For the modern philosophy of Cosmic Humanism, the purpose of a man's life is the creation of his personality. It claims that happiness is inextricably linked to the prosperity of all mankind because people are social beings who find meaning and value in personal relationships and culture. From the humanitarian, psychotherapeutic perspective, originally expressed by Victor Frankl, the question of the meaning of life should be focused separately for each individual. He argued that people should stop their endless reflections on the meaning of life and, instead, actively participate in activities. The concerns and anxiety caused by the search for meaning evaporates when we participate fully in life, Frankl said. Positive psychologists who claim that the meaning of life comes from a complete involvement and participation in joint activities with other people are on the same wavelength as Frankl. Evolutionary psychology researchers and biologists see things from another perspective. They believe that the ultimate meaning of life is the fulfillment of the reproductive human instincts and the perpetuation of a person's genes.

In human history, countless efforts have been made to discover convincing objectives that would give meaning to people's lives. The means related to legends, religions, politics, patriotism, traditions and social customs are no longer convincing or inspiring for a growing number of people. Currently philosophers and scientists believe that it is naive to believe that there is a single meaning of life, in the sense of a goal which is embedded in our nature or is imposed upon us by a higher power. At the same time, the primary ends in modern societies—consumerism, the pursuit of wealth, fame and power—cause frustration and bring about deceptive feelings in people. While they expect to feel happier than before, they find their expectations defeated.

People react differently to the experience of the weak relationship between material prosperity and happiness. Some try to ignore it and renew their efforts to gain more of the same goods, such as big cars and houses, more power at work, and a luxurious lifestyle. Others choose to deal with its symptoms by dieting and going to health and beauty centers. Some prefer withdrawal and taking care of their garden, or they take up a hobby, or fall into alcohol and substance abuse. Even expensive holidays and exotic delights are not enough to entertain their grief. There is evidence that none of these solutions work. Crime, drugs, alcoholism, divorces, depression, diseases, and suicides have increased over time. These findings show that the root of people's dissatisfaction is internal, and therefore they are forced to find its cause and try to manage it by using their own means.

The Epicurean meaning of life

It is feeling good, living a pleasant life. The introduction of feelings as the criterion of what is good in life makes the Epicurean Philosophy stand out from the rest of the philosophies, which all, in one way or another, give priority to logic and its thoughts. This innovation of Epicurus made him proudly declare that his philosophy is the only true philosophy because it uses the same criterion that Nature does to distinguish the good from the bad. Epicurus says that we make feeling the rule by which to judge every good thing. And later he explains why when he claims that we recognize pleasure as the first innate good within us. Wherefore, we call pleasure the alpha and omega of a blessed life. Pleasure is our first and kindred good. It is the starting point of every choice and of every aversion.

Epicurus also distinguishes himself from the sensualist philosophers who are interested only in the enjoyment of the present moment. He proposes lifelong happiness, and this requires the introduction of a strategy as to which pleasures to pursue and which to avoid. This necessitates the introduction of reason as the tool by which to evaluate our desires and to judge how to match them with the restrictions of the environment as well as with our own capabilities and weaknesses.

We need to exert our free will to assert control of our consciousness so as to use our logic effectively to withstand the pressures imposed on it, both on the part of our inner Self and the environment. This is a hard task for logic to achieve, and that is why Epicurus declares reason as man's highest virtue, making it also inseparable from the pursuit of happiness. Albeit he makes clear, the natural function of reason is the evaluation of the pleasures, not their invention. Our desires are born automatically by the unconscious processes of the inner mind, with no interference from reason, as the *Canon of Truth* suggests.

So to Epicurus, the meaning of life has emotional characteristics, and reason is employed to evaluate them and decide on which to follow throughout life.

The challenges that reason has to face are numerous and painful. It has to decide on which pleasures to give priority to, to what level to pursue each pleasure, and by what criterion to judge the accomplishment of the optimum level of happiness. To handle all these questions, reason needs a yardstick to measure pleasure. At this juncture, Epicurus invents pain, the opposite of pleasure, by which to judge the magnitude of pleasure. By this method, Epicurus proves that each pleasure has limits, and also that all pleasures necessary to happiness are countable and limited too. Epicurus says the obvious, that we need each pleasure up to the degree that we feel no pain from the absence of it. At that level, one enjoys the maximum of pleasure. Once thirsty, we need so much water that no pain from thirst is anymore present. But also, the overall number of necessary pleasures to happiness is limited, and not only that, these pleasures are in abundance, mostly free to use, and that is what makes the overwhelming majority of people able to pursue happiness.

Epicurus urges us to be grateful to the blessed Nature that made all the necessary easily-acquired and the unnecessary difficultly-acquired. He also goes on to advocate that we do not need to endlessly ask for new pleasure because its value is in the quality and not the quantity. Thus he asserts that if you wish to make Pythocles rich, you should not add to his store of money, but subtract from his desires. And he also says that nothing is enough to someone for whom what is enough is little.

For Epicurus, a safe indicator of the level of happiness is the state of the body and mind. The maximum of happiness is reached when the body is healthy and the mind free from worries and fears. He insists that he who has a clear and certain understanding of these things will direct every preference and aversion toward securing the health of body and tranquility of mind, seeing that this is the sum and end of a happy life. To Epicurus, just as to the modern psychologists, body language complemented by the presence or absence of disturbing thoughts is the genuine and truthful way by which to judge the level of our happiness. This optimum level of happiness associated with the health of body and tranquility of mind is called by Epicurus "ataraxia," equanimity, and painlessness. These are the indicators by which we conclude whether we have enjoyed all the necessary pleasures to the maximum degree and have reached the optimum level of happiness. However happiness, along with a maximum, has a lower limit too. According to Epicurus, there is also a limit to simple living, and he who fails to understand this falls into an error as great as that of the man who gives way to extravagance.

We can conclude, therefore, that all the empirical data insinuate that, by nature, man needs a meaning of life. In a disordered world he feels uneasy. He desires a reason for being and wonders how to give meaning to his life in order to endure it. The meaning of life equips us with a plan for life; it paves the way to identify our goals, to opt for the most effective means to fulfill them and to derive mental strength to endure the pains of life. The meaning of life should fit our character in order for us to promptly and gladly pursue it. The meaning of life has been a core issue for philosophies. In the course of centuries, the metaphysical ones that prevailed proclaimed religions. Over the last decades though, the earthly meanings of life are on the rise, proclaiming the joy of consumerism, and the accumulation of wealth and power. Despite their earthly character, they are in essence idealistic because they arise from logic, and ignore the realities of life. In the Epicurean Philosophy the meaning of life is feeling good, living a pleasant life. It is a natural and subjective meaning based on feelings, suggesting a simple physical life along with our friends, free from excessive desires and unsupported fears. As always, and even more so now, the status quo works to impose on us the meaning of life that serves its interest; the only way out for the ordinary man is to gain control of his conscience, set his own meaning in life, and become an autonomous person in charge of his life.

CHAPTER 7

THE PSYCHOLOGICAL APPROACHES
TO HAPPINESS

*"For the end of all our actions is to be
free from pain and fear, and, when once
we have attained all this, the tempest of
the soul is laid."*

Epicurus, *Letter to Menoeceus*

Existential psychology

The existential approach to individual psychology is philosophical. The aim is to understand the position of an individual in the world and to explore what it means to be alive.
Modern existential philosophy emerged in the 19th century
through the work of Kierkegaard and Nietzsche. Both came
into conflict with the dominant ideologies of their time and
focused on the exploration of reality through the personal
way that humans experience it. The historical background

for this approach is from a philosophy that goes back 2,500 years. Its roots are in the Epicurean Philosophy. Epicurus emphasized the adverse effects of existential fears to the pursuit of happiness and for the first time, tried to reaffirm them by using logical and scientific arguments.

It is no coincidence that the doctoral thesis of Marx was on *"the difference between the Democritean and the Epicurean Philosophy of Nature,"* with the central issue being the effects of determinism on the existence of meaning in life and on free will. Nietzsche was also influenced by Epicurus and, in many cases, mentioned his work. He referred to Epicurus as one of the greatest men, an inventor of a heroic-idyllic way of philosophy. He also said: "Wisdom took steps forward with Epicurus, but then it went several thousand steps back. Epicurus would have won. Every respectable mind in the Roman Empire was Epicurean. And this was the completion! But then, Apostle Paul came to the scene."

The Danish philosopher Soren Kierkegaard was a theologian and a religious author. Much of his philosophical work deals with the question of how to live as a single person, giving priority to that specific human reality. It underlines the importance of personal choice and commitment and explores the feelings of individuals when making decisions in their lives. He intensely despised the way people around him lived and believed that the truth could only be found by the individuals themselves, through their life experiences. He stressed that what is lacking in people is the courage, the passion and the determination to make "the leap." He opposed both the Christian doctrine and the so-called objectivity of science.

Nietzsche took Kierkegaard's philosophy a step further. The central point of his theory was that god is dead, and we must rethink ourselves, taking this fact into consideration. He called people to shake off the yoke of moral restriction and discover the power of free will, so as to exalt in unknown heights and learn to live with new intensity. He encouraged people not to remain part of the flock, but to stand out. Nietzsche brought forward the important existential matters of free choice, responsibility and courage.

The German philosopher, Heidegger, believed that philosophy and society were unjustifiably preoccupied with the question of what exists because the world always existed. Instead they had forgotten the basic questions they needed to consider: these are, what does it mean "to be," and what is existence itself? For Heidegger, man is a Being. That is what he is, plus the potential to become something he is not yet. He is a Being in front of himself, a Being in excess of himself that is aiming beyond what he is, seeking to become what he is not yet. The transcendence and the ecstasy that characterizes human existence remains within the limits of the world he is in. Heidegger calls the Being that exceeds himself Dasein.

Jean-Paul Sartre claimed: "Existence precedes Essence." Essence refers to the Aristotelian philosophical idea, defined as the attribute or set of attributes that make an entity or substance what it fundamentally is, which it has by necessity, and without which, it would lose its identity. To Sartre, there is no such predetermined essence to be found in humans. An individual's essence is defined by him or her through how he or she creates and lives his or her life. As Sartre puts it in his *Existentialism is a Humanism* "man first of all exists, encounters himself, surges up in the world and defines himself afterwards." To Sartre, "existence precedes essence" means that a personality is not built over a previously designed model or a precise purpose because it is the human being who chooses to engage in such an enterprise. While not denying the constraining conditions of human existence, he answers to Spinoza, who affirmed that man is determined by what surrounds him. Therefore, to Sartre an oppressive situation is not intolerable in itself, but once regarded as such by those who feel oppressed, the situation becomes intolerable.

When it is said that man defines himself, it is often perceived as stating that man can "wish" to be something–anything, a bird, for instance–and then be it. According to Sartre's account, however, what is meant by the statement is that man is defined only insofar as he acts, and that he is responsible for his actions. To clarify, it can be said that a man who acts cruelly towards other people is, by that act, defined as a cruel man, and in that same instance, he (as opposed to his genes, for instance) is defined as being responsible for being this cruel man. You can choose to act in a different way and to be a good person instead of a cruel person. Here it is also clear that since man can choose to be either cruel or good, he is, in fact, neither of these things in "essence."

In short, to Sartre and the existentialists, man himself gives meaning to his life, value to his actions and has unlimited freedom to achieve his objectives, as long as he wants to. The suggestion that "existence precedes essence" inverts the traditional philosophical view that the substance of a thing is more fundamental than its existence, by claiming that human beings in the beginning of their life hold neither identity nor value; then they create their existence; and through their actions they make their existence more significant than their essence.

This idea was first formulated by Soren Kierkegaard in the 19th century, but it was explicitly expressed by Jean-Paul Sartre in the 20th century. Sartre brought existentialism to the fore and created the French existentialist movement by supporting and illustrating his ideas with a variety of projects. The main points of his theory are the lack of the divine and the individual capacity for free choice. He said that a human is condemned to be free. Sartre brought the individual face to face with his actions and gave him the sole responsibility for them. He believed that regardless of circumstances each one of us is judged only by his acts, which are, moreover, irreversible. In addition, the often nightmarish judgment of others should be based on actions and not on intentions. He considered having freedom in the choice of action and then taking responsibility for it to be the standard by which an individual should be judged. Simone de Beauvoir also uses this concept in her feminist existentialism to express the idea that "you are not born a woman, but you become one."

In 1981, the contemporary psychologist, Irving Yalom identified four absolute existential concerns, that have great importance in psychotherapy: death, freedom, isolation and the lack of meaning in life. Each of these concerns causes internal conflicts in the existential frame of reference, as perceived by Yalom.

Death is the most obvious ultimate concern. It is obvious to all of us that death will come, and that there is no escape from it. It is a formidable truth to which people respond with fear, and they often develop defenses that significantly affect their character. Children are concerned with the subject of death from an early age, and the elimination of the terror of death is an important developmental stage in their lives. Psychopathological symptoms are often caused by a weakness in overcoming the fear of death.

Freedom is usually not something we would consider as a source of concern. It is quite the opposite. Freedom is generally considered a positive concept. The history of Western culture was marked by a longing and a struggle for freedom, but in the existential context, the concept of freedom frightens people. Freedom refers to the fact that a man is solely responsible for his own life, choices and actions. If the fact that we ourselves create our own world is true, this means that we do not stand on solid ground, and that below us there is an abyss. Unlike in our daily experiences, we live a temporary life; we come and go from a universe that is neither coherent nor structured with a great design. The exercise of freedom paves the way for the emergence of responsibility, which is an important source of anxiety for people. People vary considerably in the degree of responsibility that they can take in their life. Some blame others for what happens to them, or the conditions of life, or their bosses and spouses. Others completely deny the existence of responsibility by considering themselves "innocent victims" suffering from external events, possibly disregarding whether they themselves have put these events into motion.

Some do not hesitate to completely deny the existence of their liability, by removing it completely from their mind, as if they were not accountable for their behavior. Another aspect of freedom is will. Will passes from desire to decision, and finally to action. Many people have great difficulty in expressing their desires. Others can be extremely clear about what they want, but they are not able to decide, let alone act. They often experience making decisions in a panic. They may be willing to transfer the right of decision making to someone else, or to act in such a way that the decision is made for them by the circumstances. The passage from freedom to desire, to decision, to action can be a painful process that many people would prefer to avoid.

A third absolute concern is isolation. It is important to distinguish the existential from other types of isolation. Interpersonal isolation refers to the gap between the Self and other people, due to a lack of social skills and psychopathology concerning intimacy. Existential isolation is a term that was first established by Freud and refers to the fact that we are isolated from parts of ourself. Parts of ourself, experiences, feelings and desires, are disconnected from consciousness, and we ignore their existence. They operate underground, however, and agitate our life without our realizing it. The aim of psychotherapy in these cases is to help individuals recover and reunite with the parts of the Self that they were separated from. Many people try to cope with isolation through diffusion. They avoid their personal development and the sense of isolation that accompanies it, preferring to soften the boundaries of the ego to minimize their desires, and to live through the life of another person. Others may be dispersed in a group, a cause, a country, a project. By being like the others, matching in dress, in speech and customs in order not to have our thoughts, feelings and desires, we are preserved from this isolation of our monastic Self. Another common reaction to isolation is obsessive sexuality. Sexually obsessive individuals are not associated with the whole existence of others, but only with the part of it that satisfies their needs. In particular, they are only interested in those parts that serve seduction and sexual intercourse.

The fourth and final concern is the lack of meaning in life. Man seems to require meaning in life. Our neuropsychological function is such that it standardizes random stimuli in shape and substance. When we are confronted with an incomplete circle, we automatically imagine it full. When any state is not shaped, we experience discontent. In a disorderly world we feel unstable and look for design.

The fourth internal conflict arises from this dilemma: how can a Being find meaning in a universe that seems to have no meaning? If we are all alone in an indifferent universe, then what meaning can our life have anyway? Can anyone create a stand-alone sense to endure his life?

The Freudian psychodynamic model

The Freudian model is described by Freud's theory that the soul consists of the id, the ego and the superego. It refers to three theoretical constructs that describe and interpret the activities and the interactions in mental life. The id includes our instinctive tendencies and other primary characteristics; the superego represents our conscience, the limitations of the environment, moralities and musts that counteract the id. The ego stands in between both to balance our primitive needs and our moral–ethical beliefs. A healthy ego provides the ability to adapt to reality and interact with the outside world in a way that accommodates both the id and the superego. When the id is forced to succumb to the superego, the instinctual desires and the feelings created are unconsciously suppressed; that is why we so often suffer from things we do not know. Freud followed Plato in his account of the nature of mental health or psychological well-being, which he saw as the establishment of a harmonious relationship between the three elements that constitute the mind. If the external world offers no scope for the satisfaction of the id's pleasure drives, or, more commonly, if the satisfaction of some or all of these drives would indeed transgress the moral sanctions laid down by the superego, then an inner conflict occurs in the mind between its constituent parts or elements. Failure to resolve this can lead to neurosis.

A key concept introduced by Freud is that the mind creates a number of "defense mechanisms" to prevent conflicts from becoming too acute, such as repression (pushing conflicts back into the unconscious), sublimation (channeling the sexual drives into the achievement of socially acceptable goals in art, science, poetry, and so on), fixation (the failure to progress beyond one of the developmental stages), and regression (return to a behavioral characteristic). Of these, repression is the most important, and Freud's account of this is as follows: when a person experiences an instinctual impulse to behave in a manner that the superego deems to be reprehensible (e.g. a strong erotic impulse on the part of the child towards the parent of the opposite sex), then it is possible for the mind to push it away, to repress it into the unconscious. Repression is thus one of the central defense mechanisms by which the ego seeks to avoid internal conflict and pain, and to reconcile reality with the demands of both id and superego. As such, it is completely normal and an integral part of the developmental process through which every child must pass on the way to adulthood. However, the repressed instinctual drive is not and cannot be destroyed when it is repressed; it continues to exist intact in the unconscious, from where it exerts a determining force upon the conscious mind, and can give rise to the dysfunctional behavior characteristic of neuroses.

The Neo-Freudian psychodynamic model

Many, among them Adler and Jung, criticized Freud's theories for being overly focused on childhood and sexuality. They are referred to as Neo-Freudians, and they generally agreed with Freud that childhood experiences are important, but they lessened his emphasis on sex and sexuality. Instead of taking a strictly biological approach to the development of personality (as Freud did in his focus on individual evolutionary drives), they focused more holistically on how the social environment and culture influence a child's personality development. They argued that children face two equally strong necessities. They desperately need the acceptance and approval of the persons that affect their lives, usually their parents, but they also need sovereignty and autonomy. Their personal voltages are not always compatible with the requirements of their parents, and if the parents are overbearing and neurotic, they cause conflicts between the child's need for safety and personal development. In such a situation the child succumbs for the sake of preserving parental safety. According to new Freudian model, psychosomatic symptoms may be caused later in children's lives due to the allegiance of children's desires to the requirements of the environment.

Cognitive psychology

Cognitive theories are concerned with the development of thought processes and how these thought processes influence our understanding of the world around us. Cognitive psychology revolves around the notion that if we want to know what makes people decide and act in a certain way then we need to understand the internal processes of their mind. In other words, it is interested in the variables that mediate between stimulus-input and response-output, which include perception, attention, language, memory and thinking.

Cognitive psychology is interested in answering questions like: how do we receive information about the outside world? How do we store and process information? How do we solve problems? How does a breakdown in our perceptions cause errors in our thinking? How do errors in our thinking lead to emotional distress and negative behaviors?

Cognitive psychology considers people as dynamic information processing systems, whose mental functions can be described in terms of a computer. The way of thinking and reasoning within mental processes is the software of the brain. Cognitive theories benefited from the flourishing of this research in computing by integrating the achievements of this research with the processes of the mind. The objection to cognitive psychology is derived from dynamic psychologies such as the existential and the Freudian.

Instead of asking how stimuli affect our thoughts they inquire about how these actions emerge from our incentives, that is, from our objectives, needs and instincts.

Positive psychology

Positive psychology is a new branch of psychology that uses scientific methods to explore the factors that influence human happiness. It seeks to extend the scope of research to show that goodness and excellence are both as authentic as diseases, concerns and anxieties; capacities have the same weight as weaknesses; the building of positive traits is worth as much as the treatment of negative; and that the same attention should be given to the satisfaction of desires of healthy people, as to the healing of patients' wounds.

Martin Seligman is considered the founder of positive psychology. He claimed that for half a century clinical psychology consumed itself in a single subject, mental illness, and that it is time to return to its real roots, its original mission, which was the cultivation of human talents and improving the quality of normal life. These views were in line with those of the pioneer in human psychology, Maslow, who stated that the science of psychology is much more successful in its negative, than its positive side. It has tracked down many of the human deficiencies, diseases, sins, but few of its possibilities, virtues, ambitions or psychological power. It is as if it has voluntarily restricted itself to half of its capabilities, and the darker half at that.

New impetus was given to the development of positive psychology and the role of pleasure in the search for happiness by the pioneering research of professor of psychology Mihaly Csikszentmihalyi. This led to the invention and formulation of the "flow theory." The search for the "optimal experience" in the framework of flow theory contributes to enriching the Epicurean positions on pleasure with ideas and applications from modern life. So I will highlight its basic concepts.

The etymology of the word flow comes from people's descriptions, which likened some series of intense experiences to a water stream that took them along its path. In psychological terms, the enjoyment of flow experience is described as the emotional condition in which a person who performs an activity is dominated by a feeling of concentration, full participation and enjoyment of the activity. Its trademark is a spontaneous feeling of joy, even of ecstasy, where we can still lose the sense of ourself or of our emotions. In daily life, similar mental situations are described by the terms: being in the here and now, being in the zone, or being in harmony.

The surveys that detected optimal experiences began in the decade of 1980. In related questions, artists, mostly painters, mentioned that quite often they experienced a state of flow. They described that at times they were so engrossed in their work that they forgot their needs for food, water, and sleep. Similar flow experiences are reported throughout the course of history in all cultures. The

Gurus of Buddhism and Taoism speak of "action of inertia" or "to do without doing," expressions that recall much flow experience. Also Hindu texts, such as the "Yoga of Knowledge," refer to similar absorption modes. Historical sources claim that Michelangelo painted the Sistine Chapel of the Vatican while he was in the highest state of flow. It has been reported that he was painting for days at a time and was so engrossed that he did not stop even to eat or sleep until he reached the point of fainting. After that, he awoke, freshened up and began to paint again, entering full absorption mode. Epicurus, along with his friends, probably experienced a constant state of flow in the Garden.

A flow experience causes interest, develops the Self, cultivates the capabilities to respond to the difficulties of the experience, and has specific goals and clear results. Concentration in the activity is so intense that no attention is left to deal with anything else or to worry about problems. The sense of Self and of time is lost. It is so pleasant that we are ready to do it solely for the pleasure it gives, disregarding anything else. We see how concentrated children are in what they do, and how they enjoy their life. But as they grow up, they are subjected to external pressures to do things they do not want, which results in reduced attention and enjoyment.

The only way to enjoy our life is to use our available energy for the success of our own objectives, gaining control of consciousness and attention. But how do these experiences happen? Some occur incidentally. For example, in a friendly meeting, a theme can attract the attention of all so as to begin talking, making jokes, talking about one's own experiences, and making everyone feel nice internally and also with each other. Although such pleasure can be spontaneous, in most cases it is programmed.

Flow experiences need skill. A drink, a nice view, and a musical piece can be pleasing, but the pleasure that has intensity and duration is the one that requires using our bodily and mental abilities. Reading, for example, is one such enjoyment because it requires the skills to read, to compare, and to imagine. Being with other people is another because it requires the ability of sociability that introverts and the shy lack. Sports, art, literature, and music are the ordinary experiences that can cause such intense pleasure. However, by using our imagination and abilities, we can convert many common, everyday experiences into interesting and enjoyable ones. All of us seek such ways to avoid routine. We chew gum, smoke or drink. Effective, however, are only those activities in which we use our abilities, such as when playing a game.

Flow experiences have clear goals and obvious results: tennis, climbing, and skiing are sports that enable one to exhibit these characteristics. However, sometimes the consequences of our actions are not always so obvious. They take time to materialize, and the results are slow to show, as in painting or writing a book. In these cases, we need to develop a strong sense of objectives and results. Also, the evaluation of the results is different for each person. Those who have fragile personalities need constant confirmation and seek victories in competitive activities. Others have a narcissistic tendency and are more interested in applause and admiration.

Another notable feature of flow experiences is the absorption of attention. In daily activities, consciousness is prey to all forms of thoughts and concerns, resulting in disorder and reduced concentration. Full concentration on an activity, though, causes intense pleasure and leaves no spare room in the mind for irrelevant or unpleasant thoughts.

With flow experiences, we determine the result. Intense pleasure is derived from activities in which we feel in control of the result; our capacities can meet the challenges. If our potential is greater than the challenges of experience, we get bored. If it is lower, we are worried and frustrated. Surgeons, for example, enjoy surgeries because they are confident about their capability to cope with potential risks and that they can control the outcome of the operation. With discipline and systematic preparation, they can avoid the objective risks of surgery and remove the subjective risks, which originate from lack of capacity. The balance of skills and difficulties makes an activity enjoyable, the participants feel in control of the outcome, and therefore, such an activity can become addictive. These activities, while improving the quality of life, impose within our consciousness a specific order of things, making us reluctant to deal with other important aspects of life.

Flow experiences have intrinsic value. Most activities are directed by external factors, and we rarely enjoy the feelings of an authentic activity. Most of what we do daily has no value in itself; we do it out of necessity or because we expect a return in the future. Most people consider the time of work wasted; they are alienated from what they do, and the energy they spend at work does not strengthen their sense of Self. For some people, free time is also wasted; they passively relax by absorbing information without using any capacity. So often life is a chain of stressful or boring experiences over which we have little control. In contrast, authentic experiences raise the Self to a higher level, isolation gives way to participation, boredom to enjoyment, and life acquires value today rather than being a hostage of tomorrow.

Self development is yet another characteristic of flow experiences. All enjoyable activities develop and propel the Self to higher levels. We cannot stagnate. With time our skills either improve and we seek a higher level of challenge or we remain stagnant, get bored and abandon the activity. However as long as we exercise the activity, our skills improve with time, challenges increase and the Self becomes enriched and powerful.

In flow experiences, time does not pass the same way it passed before. We tend to lose sense of time. Hours often seem to last minutes, but sometimes the case is different. Ballet dancers, for example, said that difficult exercises that objectively last for seconds appear to last minutes, in contrast to joyful experiences, where time passes quickly. However in experiences where time plays a decisive role in their success, as in performing surgery, the sense of time is real. There, surgeons are fully aware of time and know how much time has passed at each point of the operation. Although time is not an important parameter of happiness, liberating ourselves from the tyranny of time is relaxing and enjoyable.

Sources of flow experiences are friendship, the body, sports, motion, sex, and senses. See "Pleasure," Part two.

Yoga is another source of flow experiences. When it comes to training for control of the body and mind, Eastern cultures have made significant progress. The most interesting flow activity of the East is Yoga. It is a method for human connection with god, consisting initially in the consolidation of the various parts of the body, and then connecting the body to consciousness to work in harmony as a whole. The similarities between yoga and flow theory are very strong. In fact, we can imagine yoga as a strictly designed flow experience.

However, good things in life do not come only through the body and the senses, but also through the brain. Some of the most exciting experiences arise from the ability to think and read. To enjoy a spiritual activity we need the same conditions that make a physical activity enjoyable, but in particular, concentration. However this is not effortless. In reading our attention eventually decomposes and to continue, we have to force it to turn back to the page.

Memorizing is the oldest spiritual capacity from which all others arise because if we were not able to remember, we could not follow the rules governing intellectual functions. Someone who cannot remember is cut off from the knowledge of past experiences, and he cannot create order in his mind. A mind with some fixed contents is much richer than a mind with fully variable contents. Someone who can remember stories, poems, lyrics, songs, historical dates and wise words, excels over someone who has not cultivated such a capability. He always has the option of amusing himself and of finding meaning in the contents of his mind.

Memorization is not the only tool that can give form to the contents of mind. For thinkers thought is a significant incentive due to the spiritual pleasures it offers. Philosophy, science and the arts feed the pleasure of thinking. By learning a symbolic system, such as of letters, numbers, or musical sounds, we acquire a portable, self-contained world within our mind. One of the most significant pleasures is the art of conversation. When words are well chosen, they create a pleasant experience for the listener. Utility is not the only thing that makes a discussion interesting, but also the range of vocabulary and fluency. Talking enriches relationships. It is a skill that anyone can learn.

Writing is yet another source of flow experiences. Nowadays, electronic devices have led us to neglect the habit of writing. But the main purpose of writing is to create information and not simply to transfer it. Learning and preserving the memory of past events are among the oldest and most effective methods for putting consciousness in order. History liberates us from the tyranny of today and allows our conscious mind to contemplate on days past. It is an enjoyable experience that can serve as a guide for us to have better judgment and make decisions that improve the quality of life. Also, active occupation with science, or simply the study of it, is the best way to bring order to the mind.

Philosophy means love of wisdom. It is this that many brilliant men have dedicated their lives. In contrast to professionals, amateur philosophers do not have to get involved with the historical antagonisms between philosophies and philosophers. They can limit their interest to the basic questions of life: what does it mean to exist? What constitutes a good life? In philosophy, as in other areas, there comes a point in time when someone feels ready to pass from passive learning to action. If we are able to clearly express the important questions that trouble us and can draw out answers that would be helpful to others in understanding our experiences, then we will derive pleasure from one of the toughest and most interesting activities of life.

A man who renounces spiritual development is never free. His thoughts will be directed by the views of his neighbors, publishers of newspapers and television producers. He will be at the mercy of "experts." Ideally, after the end of formal education, lifelong learning, which is motivated exclusively by intrinsic factors, must begin.

If we find enjoyment at work, we can effectively improve the quality of our life. For most people, however, work is an activity that repels them. On the one hand, this may be due to employers' pressure to increase production, and on the other, to trade unions that emphasize remuneration. If instead they both gave emphasis to transforming work into an enjoyable activity, they would enable employees to both increase productivity and remuneration.

Contrary to popular belief, research shows that salary and material benefits in general are not the most important concerns of workers and employees.

Firstly, their common complaint is monotony, lack of variety and challenge. Secondly, it is conflicts with coworkers, and thirdly, excessive pressure and stress. While these are objective problems, they are also influenced by the way they are perceived. Monotony or variety at work depends on the type of work, but also on how we approach work. The same holds for conflicts with colleagues and superiors. Relationships at work can be difficult, but there is always room for improvement. Stress is the most subjective characteristic of work. The same degree of stress can cause disruption in some and interest in others. Some ways to

relieve stress are to better organize work, to share responsibilities with others, to improve communication with colleagues, but also to improve the quality of life at home.
Stress management at work may become part of a comprehensive effort to reduce stress in life. This requires mobili-
zation of attention and dedication to personal goals.

One of the paradoxes in modern societies is that the avail-
ability of leisure time is not translated into pleasure. Compared to people of previous generations, we have many
more opportunities to have a good time, but despite this, we
get bored and worry. While we are looking forward to going
home, we often do not know what to do there. Ironically, it is
easier to enjoy a job than free time because at work, things
are structured. Jobs have targets, results, rules and challenges that encourage dedication of attention and a loss of Self.
Free time, on the contrary, is unstructured and requires far
greater personal effort to fill it. The leisure industry, instead
of driving us into the use of our physical and mental capabilities, offers the passive enjoyment of television–namely,
watching instead of participation. Passive pleasure is para-
sitic; it absorbs more energy for less joy, and it results in
frustration rather than relaxation of the mind. Most jobs and
free time activities are not designed to make us happy. Their
purpose is to generate profits for someone else, but it is up
to us to use them to serve our needs.

We are biologically programmed to live in companionship
with other people. If our relations with people are joyful,

then loneliness can be converted into a pleasurable experience as well. We can enjoy solitude if we find ways to do things we cannot do with others. Most people sulk when left alone. They are terrorized by the idea of isolation from the social environment. Research shows that people are happier with family and friends or simply in the company of others. However, the most negative experiences also come from relationships with people. Bosses and colleagues at work, partners, children, next of kin, are often the main sources of distress. People are very volatile. The same man is wonderful in the morning and disappointing in the afternoon. So we need to learn to behave. The most important test of whether we are able to control our life is the way we pass our time when experiencing loneliness. The less bored we get and the less we look for external stimuli, the more capable we are of enjoying a creative life.

The most intense and complete experience is family life. The family can make someone happy or unhappy. What happens depends on the attention that family members spend on mutual relations and particularly on each other's goals. The weakening of the family institution today is a result of the changes that occurred in the social environment. Rising divorces are not due to less love or morality, but to women's employment, and to household appliances that facilitated housework. The form that the family takes is the result of social conditions. If we are monogamous today, it is because experience has shown us that this is more helpful. The right question is not whether we are monogamous or polygamous, but what we want to be; the answer depends on the consequences of our choice. In either case, if we decide to have a family, it is necessary to make family life enjoyable.

As with family, we may belong to larger groups: a nation, a community, a political party. Participation in public life can be enjoyable if it has the structures of a flow experience. Of course given that mental energy is limited, not everyone can participate in public activities. Some are forced to devote all their attention in order to survive in a hostile environment. Others are so engrossed in their activities that they are not able to devote their attention elsewhere. But life would be hard indeed if some did not enjoy investing their mental energy in common purposes.

How can we improve the quality of our life when things are not going the way we want them to, when fortune treats us unfairly? It would be unrealistic to assert that whatever happens, we will be happy. Indeed, the ability to transform misfortune into opportunity is a very rare gift. However, in almost every situation we face, there is potential for improvement. As we see in everyday life, even awful mishaps can be converted into tolerable or enjoyable experiences. But these transformations require life perceptions that perceive bad luck as an opportunity.

In a nutshell, existential psychology focuses on knowledge, attitudes, and the decisions of the individual in relation to the existential issues of death, meaning, freedom and isolation. In the Freudian psychodynamic model, the person is guided by his internal instinctive forces that, during the development of the psycho-sexual cycle, come into conflict with the requirements of the environment. In these conflicts, instincts are suppressed by the superior powers of the environment and cause psychosomatic symptoms. According to the Neo-Freudian psychodynamic model, the individual is guided by the personal environment in which he grows up. The subjection of the child to the requirements of the environment causes psychosomatic symptoms. Cognitive psychology emphasizes the influence of stimuli, knowledge, and perceptions in thinking and decision making. Positive psychology focuses on the achievement of a pleasurable life, rather than on treating mental illnesses. It emphasizes personal growth, rather than pathology, the importance of knowing our talents and virtues, and participating in joyful flow experiences. The pleasure that comes from experience outweighs the pleasure of material goods. It may often cause the "flow effect," characterized by the loss of a sense of Self and of time. It is so intense that we are willing to do anything for the pleasure it gives us, regardless of anything else.

CHAPTER 8

THE EPICUREAN PHILOSOPHY

"At one and the same time we must philosophize, laugh, and manage our household and other business, while never ceasing to proclaim the words of true philosophy."

Epicurus, *Vatican Saying XLI*

Epicurus, younger than Plato and Aristotle, was able to study their philosophies, but was attracted to neither. The differences he felt with the aims of their philosophy started right away. While they generally admitted that philosophy is designed to meet the needs of people, neither of them transferred it into their life in practical terms. Epicurus, on the contrary, was a pragmatist, indifferent to knowledge that does not lead to action. His priority was knowledge that contributed to people's happiness. That is why he followed the Natural Philosophers of the Ionian school, and especially Democritus who had died thirty years before he was born.

Throughout the seven centuries of its life until the 4th century AD, no other philosophy suffered such harsh criticism as the Epicurean. Epicurus himself was chased by the crowd in his first public appearance in Mitylene, while in Athens, he never dared to teach in an open space. His character and principles were the center of attacks and slander from all philosophical schools: the Platonic, the Aristotelian, the Stoics and lastly, the Christians. The latter, although it accepted his moral teaching, accused him of denying immortality of the soul and the divine nature of god. His discouragement of following a political career provoked the contempt of the ambitious that manned the administration. Finally, his "hedonic" theory caused aversion to those who did not know its true nature. Epicurus' virtues of honesty, kindness, friendliness and charity were only attractive to the anonymous masses.

The pursuit of happiness in the Epicurean Philosophy

Epicurus defined happiness as "feeling good" and "living a pleasant life." He called his philosophy "true philosophy" because it follows the functions and trends of the human mind and Nature. He suggested a simple joyful lifestyle in the company of friends. He attributed the sufferings of people to false perceptions that lead to excessive demands, needless worries and unsupported fears. He called for people to take responsibility for their life by exercising free will and not to be carried away by either their internal impulses, or external influences. To this end, he recommended people take control of their psychic energy so as to channel it to what they aspire.

Some Epicurean fragments seem to have far reaching effects. The secret of happiness is in the diathesis, of which we are sole arbiters, says one of them. Another declares that the cry of the flesh is not to be hungry, thirsty, or cold; for he who is free of these needs and is confident of remaining so, might vie even with Zeus for happiness. Likewise, the wise man who has become accustomed to the bare necessities better knows how to share with others than how to take from them; he has found the great treasure of self-sufficiency, and even when he is suffering, he is eudaemon (happy). Furthermore, he considers pains superior to pleasures when submission to the pains for a short time brings a greater pleasure as a consequence. Again, the wise man is aware that despite being a mortal with a limited time to live, through discussions on Nature, he has seen things that are now and are to become and have been. He should exercise himself in relation to the precepts of Nature day and night, both by himself and with one who is like-minded. In so doing, man will never, either in waking or in his dreams, be disturbed, but will live as a god among men. For man loses all semblance of mortality by living in the midst of immortal blessings.

What should we make of these?

At first we infer that the conquest of happiness depends on the person himself, and so one can be happy even on the edge of survival. The Epicurean sage can withstand all physical pains and still be eudaimon, and when the need arises, he may prefer pain to pleasure. He is capable of directing his attention to where he wishes in order to adapt his experience to the conditions he faces. He can also exceed the boundaries of place and time through "meditation."

In plain words, the Epicurean wise man has the ability to deal with the vicissitudes of life by taking control of his mind without disturbing his happiness. This is a skill that the gurus of the East have been practicing for thousands of years, and one may reasonably suppose that such meditative practices disseminated to Greece during the campaign of Alexander the Great in India which took place over the same period of time—albeit there is no supporting evidence that Epicurus was influenced by the practices of the Oriental philosophies. Epicurean techniques seem more related to the "know thyself" concept of Greek culture than to the relaxation and spiritual growth character of Oriental practices. The Epicurean meditative technique aims at controlling attention, strengthening it, and taking hold of the contents of consciousness. These skills were essential to the students of the Garden to assimilate the doctrines of the Natural Philosophy and free themselves of the precepts of the established culture. Old perceptions stubbornly reproduce the old patterns of thoughts and feelings so willpower, mind control and perseverance are required for any change to take place.

How can we affect a change in ourself?

Let us take the case that we experience the prospect of death with fear and panic. The fear of death is usually due to the perception that there is life after death. To expel the terror of death, therefore, we have to replace this perception with a new one that considers death as the natural end of life, as, for example, the Epicurean principle claims: "We found above all that our spirit is of physical substance, born mortal, and that it is not to remain forever." Through repetition we transform this concept into habit in order to transfer it from the conscious to the unconscious mind. In this manner, the new conception will become a hardwired healthy perception, which will prevail over the old and will redefine the meaning of death, reforming the emotions that used to accompany it. The ability of mind control is exercised in order to keep old thoughts out of the mind.

A strong will and the ability to control our attention enable us to transform any painful reality into a comfortable or enjoyable life. This feature arises from the physical capabilities of the human mind. We can learn and apply it in our daily life to get rid of the "wrong opinions," which for Epicurus is the main cause of turmoil in people's souls. To be successful though, we need the help of sound life perceptions.

The Epicurean perceptions of life

Epicurus recognized that there is an inherent faculty in humans that guides their actions by the emotions they experience. He saw that it operates in a straightforward fashion; it approves whatever is pleasant and rejects the painful. Consequently, he built his philosophy on perceptions and habits that give priority to feelings and abide to, supplement, and support Nature's calls.

His *Principal Doctrines* express the diatheses (dispositions) towards the vital issues of life, such as the attitude towards happiness, pleasure, politics, god, and so on. He claimed that everything else derives meaning through these principles by a series of simple syllogisms. For example, the principle that the universe is composed of empty space (void) and moving matter (atoms) leads us to the conclusion that the nature of the soul is material.

Epicurean principles suggest that we satisfy the natural and necessary needs of the body (food, shelter, health), of the soul (safety, friends), and of the spirit (knowledge), as well as some natural and unnecessary desires, according to our capacities, but not at the expense of the necessary. They also put forward avoiding the unfounded desires for success, wealth and faith, getting rid of the fear of death, god, and disasters, cultivating positive diathesis and positive thinking, and taking control of the internal and external environment by exercising free will and reason. Lastly, Epicurus advises us to have faith in the effectiveness of the doctrines in order to feel their joyful effects, seeing that doubt hinders the mind from absorbing them.

The idealistic perceptions, on the other hand, emphasize ideas, like success, wealth, virtue, and faith which by their essence are not kin to happiness but to reason and well being. One may be successful, wealthy, virtuous, and faithful but still unhappy, and vice versa. A common man may not share all those fancy properties but may be quite happy by simply following his emotions.

The problem with the non-natural philosophies is that they do not aim at happiness, but to other ends, fabricated by logic under the influence of the social environment. This is the reason why Natural Philosophy and the idealistic philosophies of logic are incompatible. They approach the meaning of life by employing different capacities of the mind.

To conclude, the Epicurean Philosophy represents the Natural Philosophy of life, as opposed to the idealistic philosophies. It is the true philosophy because it is the only one that in abiding with the physical functions of the human mind, introduces feelings as a criterion for what is good or bad in life. The rest overemphasize the capacities of logic at the expense of the other human, physical attributes. It introduces a lifestyle based on pursuing natural pleasures in the company of friends. It has been approved by experience and scientific research, and it has been established as a diachronic means for bodily and psychological health.

PART TWO: PLEASURE

CHAPTER 9

PLEASURE

"Stranger, here you will do well to tarry; here our highest good is pleasure."

Inscription at the entrance of the Epicurean Garden

If we were willing to describe the Epicurean Philosophy in a single word, this word would be "pleasure." And if we were willing to use a sentence, it would be this excerpt from the letter of Epicurus to Menoeceus: "Pleasure is the beginning and the end of the happy life." With this, Epicurus establishes pleasure as both the means and the end in the pursuit of happiness in life, in contrast to all other philosophies which introduce logical means and ends like knowledge, reason, virtue, faith, wealth, and so on. All these logical concepts are not related to feelings; that is why we may argue that these later philosophies are not interested in happiness per se but rather in other ends, such as concepts. Righteously, then, did Epicurus name his philosophy the only true philosophy.

"Ataraxia" is a complex feeling consisting of a combination of different types of pleasure related to the body (food, shelter, health), psychology (safety, friends), and spirit (knowledge). By enjoying this kind of pleasure we free our body, soul and intellect from our natural needs (pains) in order to acquire painlessness. This is another way of saying, health of body and peace of mind. This state coincides with a maximum of pleasure since otherwise pain would still exist. Consequently, there would be the potential for a further increase in pleasure to completely eliminate the pain.

Interestingly, Epicurus' claims have been verified by modern research in neurobiology. Indeed, it is well known that all stimuli perceived or created by the mind are accompanied by emotions. This is the biological functioning of the emotional center of the mind. Research has shown that the amygdala, a tiny organ at the back of the brain evaluates every single stimulus to spot any risks or opportunities. Its reactions to these stimuli are emotions that act as signals for the initialization of the defensive or offensive mechanisms of the mind. Emotions relating to pleasure and pain are the inherent natural criteria for choice and avoidance of the unconscious mind. We may call this capacity of the mind the inherent natural "perception" of life. In other words, without any interference of the conscious mind and logic, our mind instinctively follows the stimuli (needs, wants) that create positive feelings, such as pleasure, and avoids those that create negative feelings, such as pain.

The above functions of the mind unfold so that the crucial decisions in our life are taken unconsciously. Logic is ignorant of what goes on in the depths of the brain. We first feel and later think. That is why emotions are related to intuition. In a way, we enjoy or feel sorry beforehand. Logic comes into play later on. Epicurus follows the patterns of Nature to ensure the effectiveness of his philosophy. He offers support to the brain with perceptions that are in harmony with the natural functions of the unconscious mind. Despite being logical constructions, the Epicurean perceptions behave in the same way as Nature's inherent predispositions by using feelings as a guide to what is good or bad. In contrast, the perceptions and criteria of other philosophies are structured exclusively by logic, with no reference whatsoever to emotions and to natural desires. Why, you may ask? Because this is idealism by definition. Both Plato and Rene Descartes denounced senses and emotions as unreliable and concentrated solely on the functions of logic.

Properties of pleasure

Epicurus' declaration of pleasure as the highest good in life held a prominent position. It was investigated so much that even today it remains a point of reference and admiration. Inspired by the behavior of animals and babies, Epicurus highlighted pleasure as the means to happiness. He wrote in his *Letter to Menoeceus:* "Pleasure is the beginning and the end of the happy life, and in this we resort as a rule in order to judge any good by the way we feel." To avoid misunderstandings, however, he adds that when we say that the aim is pleasure, we do not mean the pleasures of the prodigal and sensual pleasures, as some might think, but we mean not to suffer physical pain and not to have a troubled soul.

Then Epicurus put the pleasure of the soul and body on equal footing by introducing the concept of the uniform psychosomatic human composition. So pleasure acquired a dual role by simultaneously contributing to the health of the body and the soul. As with positive psychology, there is a distinction between pleasure of material goods and pleasure of experiences. The first is lacking in substance because people easily get accustomed to it, and it causes boredom, while the latter is a permanent source of joy and personal growth. For Epicurus, pleasure has continuity and duration. Pleasure is not only the satisfaction of a desire, but also the state of relaxation that follows. Every form of pleasure has a limit, as well as all pleasure of life. Furthermore, the use of logic makes for efficient decisions regarding which pleasures to choose.

To determine the "summum bonum" of life, Epicurus resorted to observations of animals and babies who function instinctively and emotionally, and therefore their behavior discloses the real needs of human nature. From these behaviors, he found that animals and babies seek pleasure and avoid pain–that pleasure and joy are inseparable in life. They are nutrients of life, like food. For this reason Epicurus wrote that we recognize pleasure as the first innate good within us. As the baby grows it always remains attached to the search for pleasure and the avoidance of pain. At no stage of life or of culture is this relationship invalid.

The connection between pleasure and health and between pain and illness formed the basis for Epicurus to assert that pleasure is beneficial to both the body and the soul. Namely, each form of pleasure is psychosomatic. The rejection of the immortality of the soul and the confidence in the mortal nature of the body and the soul, their simultaneous birth and growth, their common reactions to joy and pain, raised both body and soul to an equal footing. The body was praised as a vessel carrying the soul and not as a prison or a grave, as Plato supported. The nature of pleasure is twofold because it contributes to the health of body and soul at the same time. The health of the body was identified as the steady state of the absence of pain in the flesh. The health of the soul was referred to as peace of mind named "ataraxia" or equanimity. Its meaning should not be confused with apathy or indifference. The Epicurean wise man is characterized by courtesy of the soul and emotions, by a disposition to help. The concept of ataraxia comes from the sea. Epicurus compared the troubles of the soul to the sea storms that arise from the weakness of logic to recognize that there are limits to pleasure. Moreover, the mind is troubled by excessive fears about death, gods and natural disasters. When knowledge of the true philosophy is acquired, serenity will take over.

Every form of pleasure not only affects the specific body organ which realizes it first, but the whole Self; body and soul. Pleasure is pleasure wherever it may be, no matter what part of the body is directly affected—if it is kinetic or static, moderate or intense.

Although every form of pleasure affects the whole body, they differ in quality (intensity and duration). So while the Epicurean philosophical system supports the material composition of the mind and body, and that bodily and spiritual pleasure are equally essential to health, Epicurus considered that spiritual pleasure supersedes the bodily. This claim was supported by the finding that spiritual pleasure lasts longer. The flesh feels pleasure instantaneously and momentarily. It is blind and unconscious; it looks neither forward nor backward. Spiritual pleasure, on the contrary, has a much longer duration because it can combine the pleasure of the past, the present and the future. For the same reason, the mind can ease or eliminate pain by remembering past pleasure or by anticipating pleasure that will come. Also, the static pleasure of the body, the state of no pain (aponia), cannot last long because it is doomed to be interrupted by the pain of new desires. In contrast, the mind is able to "taste," without interruption, the static pleasure of freedom from concerns and fears. The wise man creatively leverages the capacity of the mind to look backward and forward, but those who look to the past with bitterness and to the future with fear run the danger of transforming this ability into a weakness.

The Epicurean position on the supremacy of spiritual pleasure over the material, as well as of qualitative over quantitative, has been adopted by modern psychology. Positive psychologists argue that all pleasure is not of equal importance to happiness. The simple addition of emotions is not a reliable criterion for the size of actual emotions felt during a period or an activity. The enjoyment of material goods such as smart phones, shopping, sex, drinks, and drugs is pleasant at first, but then we easily get used to them. The worst thing of all is that we soon endlessly ask for more and more of them.

Positive feelings that involve our personal participation in authentic activities are worth our time. The optimal experiences in the "flow model" of Mihaly Csikszentmihalyi have many similarities to the pleasures of the Epicurean Philosophy. The scientific substantiation of Epicurean ideas through research and empirical data provides validity and reliability to the Epicurean Philosophy and confirms the enduring power of its principles. According to the "flow model," people face one of the following four situations during their activities: apathy, boredom, anxiety and flow. The level of skills and the level of challenge to which one is exposed determine which situation will prevail. In particular, a low capacity and a low challenge cause apathy. One can have a low capacity but a high challenge, which creates anxiety. A high capacity and a low challenge, creates boredom. A high capacity with a high challenge creates flow.

A range of emotions, sensations and experiences characterize the state of flow. Specifically, one experiences flow when the activity causes interest and is done exclusively for the enjoyment it offers; when the objectives of the activity are attractive, clear and achievable, and fully harmonized with one's skills and abilities; when we can easily ascertain the progress we make and adapt our behavior accordingly; when we feel in control of the outcome of the activity. When attention and concentration is intense, the sense of Self is lost, concerns or fears disappear, and the perception of time is altered.

The most effective way to find happiness is to discover our abilities in order to gain permanent, instead of momentary, sources of enjoyment. To climb a mountain it is challenging and dangerous, but the joy of it compensates for the difficulties. In contrast, enjoying a drink on a sandy beach under a palm is fun, but it cannot be compared to the joy of the climber. The pleasure that leads to happiness is that which we claim as an achievement through a new experience.

Another thing to note about pleasure is it has limits. The claim that the body and soul are equivalent gave Epicurus the incentive to seek the maximum level of a pleasure. Once again, he resorted to the testimony of Nature, which sets the norm for truth. He found that the extent of hunger and thirst cannot exceed the size of their satisfaction—that is, a plate of food and a glass of water. The same happens with all physical goods. Therefore Epicurus said that simple food brings the same level of satisfaction as luxurious meals, if hunger is satisfied. And even that water and bread give the same pleasure as luxurious meals when the pain caused by their need is removed. These findings describe a Principal Doctrine: "The removal of pain is the maximum limit of pleasure. And when pleasure reaches its maximum it can only be diversified."

As with food and water, the same happens with the natural and necessary desires for clothing and shelter. A shelter provides protection from the cold and rain. That is why it is a basic pleasure—with the maximum pleasure being the acquisition of a home. If it is well decorated, and the furniture is luxurious, it hardly increases pleasure, it may only differentiate it. An Epicurean wrote that it is better to sleep on a couch and be free from fears than sleep, in a luxurious bed and be full of problems. All this is made obvious by a clear mind.

There are some opponents of Epicurus who misunderstand him, confusing the feeling of pleasure with its measurement by supporting that the Epicurean end of life coincides with painlessness, the state of complete inertia or near death. That's an unalloyed falsehood. Both the means and the end of the Epicurean life are pleasure, and the "pain-no pain" scale is employed as a yardstick by which to measure the magnitude of pleasure. Like any feeling, pleasure cannot be measured autonomously, but in relation to its opposite feeling, namely pain. By this, Epicurus proved that contrary to prevailing beliefs, pleasure has a lower and an upper limit, and gradations in between. He showed that pleasure reaches its maximum when pain gets to zero (painlessness) and its minimum at the maximum pain point. With this argument, Epicurus also claimed that happiness is an entirely internal mental process and can be achieved by all humans. This assertion came in contrast to Plato's philosophy, which considers knowledge as the highest good in life, and which, due to its conceptual nature, is indefinite, and limitless. Thoughts can lead us anywhere.

The above syllogisms unveil in a crystal clear way why all the idealistic philosophies old and new, by their nature, have no limits and hence, are prone to anxiety and unhappiness. Indeed, there is no inherent mechanism to stop us from endlessly resetting a higher target when the one initially set has been fulfilled. Nothing can stop logic from asking for more. This natural inability of logic to set limits to thoughts and rational desires is at the roots of the greediness, dissatisfaction, social inequality and unrest we witness in modern societies. All these shortcomings are automatically removed once we introduce the Epicurean Philosophy into our life and set the way we feel as the guide for our life. Once we feel good, we have no reason to ask for more. We are content with what we have.

Our mind, however, is not only interested in our happiness about the present but also about the future as well. This notion introduces "expectations" as a determining factor of our happiness over our entire life. So maximization of overall happiness in life depends not only on our current feelings, but also on those that we expect to come in the future.

Experience shows that over time, pleasure diminishes and pain increases, and there will inevitably come a point when the balance of feelings will turn from positive to negative. This does not mean that we will be completely cut off from pleasure, but that the pain will exceed the pleasure so that the net feeling will be negative. At this point, logic intervenes in order to consider what feelings are to be expected over the rest of our life. If it is estimated that our net feelings will continue to be negative and deteriorate, either due to old age or to a painful uncured illness, then life is not worth living any more. At this point, the accumulative pleasure of our life span has reached its maximum level, and from that point onwards it will decrease.

The above arguments show that not only does each different form of pleasure has a maximum level but that pleasure generally has a maximum too. That is why the prolongation of life or immortality is meaningless. What is important is to enjoy the limited time we have at our disposal to the maximum extent possible. During the normal duration of life, we can feel pleasure at its full capacity so as to leave in a calm and happy state. Unhappy and hooked therein are those who wasted their life on worries and fears. Both unlimited and limited time carry the same quantity of pleasure. The flesh is wary of it, but the mind knows and reassures us that pleasure has limits. As long as we are able to enjoy all pleasures within the normal life span there is no reason to worry or fear death, nor to want to live forever or believe that we will after we die.

Challenging established perceptions that pleasure has a specific duration, peak, and dead intervals, Epicurus argued that pleasure is continuous because pleasure is not only the satisfaction of a desire, but also the joy that follows it. So pleasure was defined in a positive and negative way, which allowed for one to be happy all the time. The testimony of Nature has once again shown the truth of that claim. While emotions affirm that the greatest good in life is to avoid the risk of death, similarly, they also show that the maintenance of health following the passage through danger is also an enjoyment. Consequently, just as the treatment of an illness is a pleasure, so is the maintenance of health after recovery from illness. These two forms of pleasure differ only in intensity. The avoidance of an unpleasant situation, or the enjoyment of a pleasant one is a stronger form of pleasure than those that follow. Epicurus said that the first form of pleasure is in a concentrated, kinetic or an energetic form. The other is sustained, static or katastematic.

Peace of mind and a healthy body, the state at which pleasure reaches its optimum level in the Epicurean Philosophy, is considered static pleasure. The satisfaction of hunger and thirst is active pleasure. The feeling of comfort after their satisfaction is a static pleasure. Watching a theatrical performance or a concert is an active pleasure, while the relaxation following it is a static one. Static is the feeling of having a quiet evening at home, after a feasting binge. Ataraxia is a static pleasure according to Epicurus, who stated that the steady state of wellness and the certain hope that it will last longer, offers more confident joy to those who know how to estimate correctly. Happiness is enjoyed to its fullest only by those who know how to judge correctly because most people, while they usually recognize the kinetic joy of recovering from an illness, they do not attach any value to the fact that they are healthy the rest of the time. Therefore one has to judge correctly.

The necessary pleasures meet those physical desires which if left unfulfilled, would necessarily lead to greater pain. They are bodily, such as food, shelter and health; psychological, like security and friendship; and spiritual, which is knowledge. Under normal conditions, they can be met rather easily. That is why a principal doctrine urges to be grateful to Nature for making necessary things easily acquired.

The optional pleasures are those natural desires that even if not satisfied, do not necessarily lead to greater pain. Such are the desires of the senses, the sensual, activities in Nature, sports, arts, and so on. Expensive meals, drinks, coffees and the like, meet the physical needs of hunger, thirst and entertainment, but they are unnecessary for survival and peace of the soul. We may enjoy them, if they are readily available, but in no case will we get used to them and depend on them for our happiness.

The non-natural and non-necessary pleasures are not easily accessible, require a heavy price to be paid in order to acquire them, and they do not necessarily lead to greater pleasure. Reputation, social status, political power, wealth and other inordinate ambitions to acquire prestige belong to this category. In Seneca's *Letters from a Stoic: Epistulae Morales Ad Lucilium*, Epicurus said that if you live according to Nature, you will never be poor; if you live according to opinion, you will never be rich. Seneca gives an excellent description of the unnecessary pleasures in his *Letters* by saying that Nature's wants are slight; the demands of opinion are boundless. Suppose, he argues, that the property of many millionaires is heaped up in your possession. Assume that fortune carries you far beyond the limits of a private income, decks you with gold, clothes you in purple, and brings you to such a degree of luxury and wealth that you can bury the Earth under your marble floors; that you may not only possess, but tread upon, riches. Add statues, paintings, and whatever art has been devised for luxury; you will only learn from such things to crave still greater ones. Natural desires are limited, but those that spring from false opinion have no stopping point. The false has no limits. When you are travelling on a road, there must be an end, but when astray, your wanderings are limitless. Recall your steps, therefore, from idle things, and when you know whether that which you seek is based upon a natural or upon a misleading desire, consider whether it can stop at any definite point. If you find, after having traveled far, that there is a more distant goal always in view, you may be sure that this condition is contrary to Nature.

Epicurus believed that the acquisition of riches is never an end but only a change of troubles; for the fault is not in the wealth, but in the mind itself–the same mind that made poverty a burden will turn wealth into a burden as well. Furthermore, he suggested avoiding the many riches because they attract false friends, thieves and kidnappers like a magnet. It is no wonder that classic Epicureans followed the saying to "live unnoticed" because happiness is a common experience for all: eminent or obscure, rich or poor, young or elderly, cultured or naive.

With regard to political power, Epicurus believed that we should avoid it because it causes animosities and rivalries, attracting would-be usurpers and sycophants. His views were contrary to the prevailing views in classical Athens, the heart of imperialism, where indifference was considered a major defect. Pericles along with Thucydides condemned the uninterested in public affairs as useless. However in those good days, Athenians were content with their lives. Joyful events, such as celebrations and artistic events, were common, and the market was full of goods coming from all around the world. By contrast, in the years of the Spartan and Macedonian domination that Epicurus lived in, the Athenian society was divided into the "haves and holding" on the one and the poor on the other. Sulky faces, full of envy of the happiness of others, were common. The feeling of resentment grew stronger against the abuse and debauchery of the nouveaux riches.

We saw that for Epicurus, the summum bonum of life is pleasure. Pleasure is inherent in human nature and if removed the very essence foundation of life is destroyed. Lucretius vividly describes the above by asserting that just as we cannot imagine a fire without heat, nor honey without sweet, nor snow nonwhite, so we cannot think of a human being without pleasure. Virtue, on the contrary, is not a pleasure. It is considered valuable to the extent that it is useful in creating or enhancing pleasure. According to Epicurus, logic and the rest of the virtues are valued for their ability to help us make choices because we cannot uncritically satisfy all of our physical desires. Some are expensive, others are unrealistic or excessive or fraudulent. It has been shown that by making use of virtues, we can improve the quality of our choices and achieve better results.

We need few material goods and entertainment. No power, glory, or wealth. We enjoy whatever big or small thing we can do. Our job, family, friends, food, and even loneliness affect us. We are hardly occupied with ourselves, so we have the available energy to devote to the environment. We participate in activities that leverage our strengths and develop ourselves. We are dedicated to what we do here and now. We depend as little as possible on the external environment, on its rewards and punishments. As the *Vatican Sayings* suggests, the study of Nature does not create men who are fond of boasting and chattering or who show off their culture to impress the many, but rather men who are strong and self-sufficient, and who take pride in their own personal qualities, not in those that depend on external circumstances.

Obstacles to the search for pleasure

A barrier to claiming pleasure is introversion. Someone who is worried about how others see him, or is afraid of giving the wrong impression, excludes himself from the possibility of enjoyment. The same thing happens with an egomaniac. He, like the introspective, is concerned most of the time with himself, on how to promote his personal interests. His conscience is completely structured to meet his personal aspirations and nothing else. For him, experiences have value only for their benefit to him and not for their intrinsic value.

Social obstacles are even more difficult to overcome. One of the consequences of slavery, exploitation, and oppression is the elimination of enjoyment. The two social pathologies of lawlessness and alienation are also difficult to treat. Lawlessness usually prevails when the economy collapses, or civilization decays, but also during sharp economic growth, when values are marginalized. The person in this state feels anxiety. Alienation prevails when we are cut off from social events because we are forced to devote all our attention on survival. In this state we feel boredom and frustration.

Along with the subjective pathologies towards pleasure, the whole of modern society seems to have been shaped by an anti-pleasure philosophy. This puritan hostility was reinforced by the rise of a strict work ethic and the mercenary spirit of capitalism.

Strategies to search for pleasure

For each category of desires, Epicurus suggested a particular strategy.

We should first satisfy the necessary desires. The simple and nutritious diet will satisfy hunger and the need for health, modest accommodation offers adequate comfort, friendship covers the need for companionship, support and safety, knowledge ensures faith in the success of our efforts.

The ability to meet the above necessary needs releases the energy to search and meet the natural and non-necessary desires. These, we can choose as we like if they do not prevent the satisfaction of the first. For example, we should not sacrifice health for the sake of amusement and rich meals. If we ever feel such a temptation, it is best to turn to those pleasures which offer the greatest enjoyment with the least cost.

As regards to unnatural desires, Epicurus bluntly advised that we avoid them completely because they are very difficult to acquire and keep. We may, for example, draw headlines for some time, but then we will be anxious to keep ourself in the news.

Epicurus states that mental pleasures are preferable to somatic ones. Unlike the Cyrenaic sensual hedonists, Epicurus evaluated mental pleasure as greater than that of the physical. His position is expressed with clarity and eloquence in his letter to his friend Menoeceus when he stated that by pleasure we mean the absence of pain in the body and of trouble in the soul. It is not an unbroken succession of drinking-bouts and revelry, not sexual lust, not the enjoyment of fish and other delicacies of a luxurious meal which produce a pleasant life; it is sober reasoning, searching out the grounds for every choice and avoidance, and banishing those beliefs through which the greatest tumults take possession of the soul.

And for pleasures with a long-term perspective, the Epicureans suggest avoiding any short-term pleasure that results in long-term discomfort or unease. On the other hand, any long-term pleasure that can be achieved at the cost of a little inconvenience is a proper compromise.

Plainly put, psychologists define happiness just as Epicurus: a calm mind and a healthy body. They also suggest the same means for the pursuit of happiness: pleasure. The desires that contribute to happiness spring out of the functions of our nature, that is the sensations, emotions and anticipations. Each form of pleasure affects the whole-existence, body and soul, no matter which part perceives it first. All pleasure is joyful, though it differs in intensity and duration. Spiritual pleasure excels over the bodily. Modern "flow theory" gives priority to the pleasure gained through experience against the pleasure of material goods, just as the Epicurean Philosophy suggests. In the natural duration of life, we can enjoy all forms of pleasure because each form of pleasure has a maximum level, as does pleasure itself, throughout the span of our lifetime. Prolongation of life and immortality do not increase pleasure. A virtuous life increases happiness, but introversion, lawlessness and alienation are obstacles when we are in search of pleasure. Some forms of pleasure are natural and necessary, others natural and non-necessary, and others non-natural and non-necessary. In pursuing happiness, it is enough to satisfy our natural and necessary desires. Optional natural pleasure does not increase the level of happiness, it simply differentiates it. Unnatural desires are best to avoid.

CHAPTER 10

THE PLEASURE OF FOOD

> *"It is not the stomach that is insatiable, as is generally said, but the false opinion that the stomach needs an unlimited amount to fill it."*
>
> Epicurus, *Vatican Saying LIX*

The ancient frugal diet

The ancient Greek cuisine was characterized by simplicity, reflecting the difficult conditions in agriculture and finances of the time. The most common food on an ancient table was bread, eggs, dairy, fish, meat, lentils, garlic, onions, fruits, vegetables and wine. The Orphic and Pythagorean cults offered an unusual way of life, a form of asceticism based on the idea of purity. Vegetarianism was a central element of their diet. On the other hand, athletes who came to prominence in official games had especially rich diets. It is said that Milo of Croton, champion of Olympic wrestling in the 62nd to 66th Olympics, consumed large amounts of meat, bread and wine every day.

Symposia were a favorite custom of the ancient Greeks. They consisted of two parts, the first of which was dedicated to food and the second to drinking wine. However, wine was usually accompanied by appetizers, the well-known tragimata, such as chestnuts, beans, toasted wheat or honey cake. Symposia were a privilege of the rich. Ordinary people were usually entertained in religious celebrations and family events at home.

The Epicurean diet

For the Epicureans, bodily pleasures played a secondary role in the search for happiness. Their attitude did not imply indifference to the needs of the flesh. On the contrary, the Epicureans were stubbornly opposed to this and were often accused that they were only interested in the enjoyment of bodily pleasures. During the periods of poverty and misery that followed the collapse of the Athenian democracy, living with privations and mortifying the flesh was projected as a high virtue in some quarters. The response of the Epicureans to this hypocritical prudery was overwhelming. They claimed that the beginning and root of any good is the pleasure of the belly, and the wise and superior are associated with that. Metrodorus, a loyal friend of Epicurus in the Garden, wrote to his brother that in the belly lays the greater good. He declared that he neither need to save Greece, nor to require from it wreaths for his wisdom. He said to look instead to eating and drinking wine and pleasing his stomach, without mischief.

Following the clear recognition of the right of every human being to the enjoyment of food and wine, the Epicureans put order and limits to such pleasures. Epicurus wrote to his friend Menoeceus: "Again, we regard independence of outward things as a great good, not so as in all cases to use little, but so as to be contented with little if we have not much, being honestly persuaded that they have the sweetest enjoyment of luxury who stand the least in need of it, and that whatever is natural is easily procured and only the vain and worthless are hard to win. Plain fare gives as much pleasure as a costly diet, when once the pain of want has been removed, while bread and water confer the highest possible pleasure when they are brought to hungry lips. To habituate one's Self, therefore, to a simple and inexpensive diet supplies all that is needful for health, and enables a man to meet the necessary requirements of life without shrinking, and it places us in a better condition when we, at intervals, approach a costly fare, which renders us fearless of fortune."

Healthy diet

According to the World Health Organization, a healthy life is characterized by a balance of nutrients, such as fats, proteins and carbohydrates, and the necessary number of calories needed to support the body. It is important to put healthy food into our diet to protect ourselves from the common diseases of modern times, like obesity, heart disease, diabetes, hypertension and cancer. The recommendations are known and classic: restriction of fatty foods, a shift from the consumption of saturated fats to unsaturated, an increase in the consumption of fruits, vegetables, legumes, whole grain cereals, nuts, and a limitation in the use of sugar and salt.

Today it is difficult to implement a healthy diet because there are many and also tasty, temptations around us. Chocolate, sweets, soft drinks, savory snacks and fast food often bend one's will. Modern lifestyles also push one in this direction. With men and women at work all day long, cooked food is for many a last resort. But all this has increased the frequency in appearance of a number of chronic diseases that endanger life. The World Health Organization estimates that 2.7 million deaths yearly come from a diet low in fruits and vegetables. Globally it is estimated that an unhealthy diet causes about 20% of cancers of the gastrointestinal system, 30% of ischemic heart diseases, and 10% of strokes, all which could have been prevented. A healthy diet and the integration of physical activity in everyday life are the best recommendations to maintain good health and normal weight.

Nutrition and mental health

Diet affects both physical and mental health to the same degree. The human body is an interconnected system in which the brain has the central control. Everything we do is determined by the brain. However, when the rest of the body is not healthy, the ability of the brain to function properly is also affected. Being physically fit is crucial for the proper functioning of the brain. Diet, whether we believe it or not, affects our thoughts, choices, decisions, feelings, and in general, the quality and the way we live our life. Approximately two thirds of the brain consists of fat. The neurons take approximately equal amounts of omega-3 and omega-6 fatty acids to function smoothly, otherwise brain allergies, hyperactivity and mental disorders are caused. In particular, the neuronal membranes consist of fat acids, which together with the amino acids, glucose and minerals, are responsible for their growth, functioning and health.

Also, the axons of neurons are protected by a cover, the myelin, which consists of 30% protein and 70% of fat. But while our daily diet is abundant in omega-6 fatty acids it is deficient in omega-3. Therefore we have to supplement it with food high in omega-3, such as fish, nuts and green vegetables. It is no coincidence that the increase in depression rates in the past 100 years was accompanied by reduced levels of consumption of omega-3 fatty acids. By way of contrast, in countries that consume a lot of fish, such as Taiwan, the depression rate is much lower.

We know that when we experience a stressful situation, the mind is prepared for the classic defensive reaction, known as fight or flight. This process marks the increase in stress hormones, such as adrenaline and cortisol, which causes, among other things, an increase in muscle strength to deal with the threat. Energy and vitamins needed by the body for this purpose are "stolen" from the maintenance and growth functions of the brain cells (the neurons). However, it has been found that even a small deficiency of vitamin B in the body can disrupt the nervous system, increase stress and reduce mood. Extreme anxiety can lead to even greater imbalance. In such cases, the effect of the reaction fight or flight in the body is dramatic. Hundreds of chemical changes occur in the body as stress hormones absorb important nutrients such as magnesium, carbohydrates and vitamins B, C, and D. The reduction in the level of carbohydrates in the body causes a decrease in serotonin production, a hormone that affects peace of mind and mood, leading to a disturbed psychological balance. Then, the attempt to replenish carbohydrates often leads to overeating and increased bodyweight. This justifies the fact that anxious people are usually overweight.

Our diet has changed so much in the last hundred years. Not only have we reduced the variety of food we eat, but also the intake of essential nutrients for the maintenance and growth of the brain has radically been altered. Industrial fats, that are now associated with depression, heart disease and diabetes, first entered food production only 100 years ago. We are full of the wrong calories and malnourished from what the brain needs to grow. Deficiencies in omega-3 fats, in vitamins B12 and D, magnesium and iron, are quite common today. If we add neurotoxins, which modern chemistry utilizes for coloring and preservation of foods, the impact of nutritional deficiencies are even more painful.

Science is linking diet to mood. When Hippocrates said to let food be our medicine and medicine be our food, he was right. Indeed, many food nutrients have the same biochemical functions as modern drugs. Nutrient substances rich in antioxidants have the same properties that drugs do for the treatment of depression and dementia. Indeed, if we also add nutrients from other foods, we can utilize natural antibiotics, antiviral, anti-inflammatory, and substances that fight obesity and diabetes. Research shows that the reduction or avoidance of sugar, caffeine, alcohol, chocolate, and the increase in water consumption, vegetables, fruit, and fish oils have a positive impact on mental health. Also some eating habits, such as eating regular meals and healthy snacks periodically, are useful for a healthy diet.

In most societies, preparing foods and eating meals has been part of a pleasurable and emotional group activity with family and friends. However nowadays, this vital and innately pleasurable activity has become distorted and is actually leading to sickness and obesity. Many people skip meals altogether as they rush off to work, and dine alone at lunch, or on junk food, eaten on the run. Or they have their business lunches and dinners where commerce is king, not pleasure. Few regularly sit down to a relaxing, enjoyable dinner with loved ones or friends. After regularly eating unhealthy foods in an unhealthy manner, many people then try to lose weight with an array of diets. For them, "healthy" living involves deprivation. The diets they follow are rigorous, rigid and relentless. Every meal becomes an ordeal. It is no wonder people cannot stick with these for long. A life guided by pleasure would not resemble this in any way. Enjoyable meals are also healthier meals. People digest their foods more easily and absorb vitamins, minerals and nutrients more effectively when food is eaten in a pleasing environment.

Conclusively, the Epicureans, although accused of being prone to pleasures of the abdomen, supported the simple diet, though they did not refuse rich meals when they were offered.

Today we are able to satisfy our basic nutritional needs, and with a proper, healthy diet, we can ensure our mental and physical health. Diet affects our thoughts, choices, decisions, and mood because about two thirds of the brain consists of fat. But while the brain requires equal amounts of omega-6 and omega-3 fatty acids, our daily diet is deficient in unsaturated oils and omega-3, and it is necessary to supplement it with fish, nuts and green vegetables. Worries affect the nutritional balance of the body as stress hormones absorb important nutrients, such as carbohydrates. The effort to replace carbohydrates usually leads to overeating and weight gain.

CHAPTER 11

THE PLEASURE OF HOUSING

> *"It is better for you to be free of*
> *fear lying upon a pallet, than to have a*
> *golden couch and a rich table and be full*
> *of trouble."*
> Epicurus

Home plays multiple roles in life. It is the personal space in which we feel safe and get the physical and mental powers to take action in society. The house has to provide basic amenities and personal space to each family member in order to develop his personal inclinations and cultivate social relationships. The option of renting or owning a house must be properly thought out, considering the coverage of taxes, maintenance costs, and possibly repayments of mortgages.

The ancient Greek house

Ordinary people in ancient Greece had small and simple houses. The materials used in their construction were trivial, so often the walls collapsed from wear and weather, and burglars pricked home walls and easily entered. Houses had one or two rooms with little basic furniture. Most houses had a back yard, which was the center of activity where children could play safely. It was divided into separate areas for men and women. The andron was the special room for the entertainment of men, with a separate entrance for the visitors so as not to intersect with the women of the house. Often large families had parents, children, grandparents, relatives, unmarried women, and slaves, all under one roof.

We know that at the age of 35, in 306 or 307 BC, Epicurus bought a garden outside Athens with the amount of eighty minae. There, he founded his school, which was the main campus of the Epicurean Philosophy, and built houses inside it, where he and his close friends lived. Cicero described the buildings as not very spacious. When he visited Athens at 51 BC, the main building, which had turned into a ruin, was in the process of relocation.

House ownership: for and against

Housing conditions in modern societies are, in their majority, satisfactory. Both housing size and quality meet the needs of a modern man. But besides being a shelter, the house in modern consumer societies has become a predominant demonstration of wealth. Therefore, when choosing a house, we are often influenced by external factors that lead us to expenses exceeding our financial means. The importance of housing in the pursuit of happiness has eluded the usual contexts, as it is often accompanied by large financial obligations that limit one's sovereignty and cause anxiety. All surveys show that the trend internationally is for home ownership.

What reasons are pushing people to home ownership? What are the advantages and disadvantages?

Home ownership is an essential component of the human psyche. All studies show that most people would like to own their home. The importance of property to the modern perception of a safe and successful life is central. A privately owned residence provides owners a greater sense of freedom and of social upgrading. It leads to higher levels of self-assessment and control of life, as a homeowner can make modifications in his home to meet his needs and preferences. A good living environment and functionality of the house supports our lifestyle and increases our satisfaction from life. Also, a home purchase symbolizes that one has achieved an economic status, reached his objectives in life, and therefore, he is on track.

Ownership also stimulates participation of the owners in local, voluntary and political activities, in order to protect the capital invested in the home, but also because they can identify themselves with the house and the neighborhood. Participation in joint activities, in turn, increases the feeling of satisfaction in life. Research shows that home ownership has positive effects on the physical and mental health of the owners. This may be due to the fact that owners take greater care of their homes, so as to meet the highest health and safety standards, and also that self-sufficiency and self-esteem create a pleasant mood.

Home purchases may not always prove successful. Social upheavals may downgrade neighborhoods, lead to neglect of the local environment and crime. In these cases, homes are undervalued, and the degree of satisfaction of the owners decreases. Moreover, owners are obliged to live in deprived and dangerous regions, which create the feeling that they have lost the possibility of controlling their life. Economic downturn is another factor that can make homeowners insecure. The recent economic downturn has made many owners, who obtained a mortgage, economically, socially and psychologically vulnerable. Finally, in some cases, maintenance costs and tax charges may be so high that the owners' income is not sufficient to meet the costs and, occasionally, they are forced to flee them.

The most common mistake in buying a home is that we spend an exorbitant part of our income to service obligations from mortgages and to pay the other costs of the house. This often leaves inadequate balances to satisfy other essential needs, causing loss of independence and stress.

Wrapping this chapter up, the quality, size and amenities of the house of our dreams depend on our financial means. Home ownership is most people's dream. However, as the cost of purchase is high, it is necessary to take the obligations undertaken in a changing economic environment into serious consideration. We often surpass our financial means in buying a house, causing more pain than joy. It is advisable to invest the proper amount of money in housing so as to leave room for the satisfaction of other basic desires. If our financial means are limited, it is prudent to restrict ourselves to a smaller or older house, or even to rent.

CHAPTER 12

THE PLEASURE OF HEALTH

*"The right understanding of these
facts enables us to refer all choice and
avoidance to the health of the body and
the soul's freedom from disturbance,
since this is the aim of the life of
blessedness."*

Epicurus, *Letter to Menoeceus*

It is a commonplace to emphasize the importance of health
in life. While in theory, we all recognize this necessity, in
practice, we forget it; we become indifferent, and we often expose ourselves to risks. The uncontrollable chase
for success prompts us to do overtime work, and by un-
dertaking heavy responsibilities, cause stress and psychosomatic symptoms. Also, while we usually show excessive
interest in physical health, we often neglect mental health.
The same occurs with state healthcare agencies that rank

psychological services as a second priority. However, physical and mental health is inseparable. The World Health Organization defines health in its broadest sense, as a state of complete physical, mental, and social well-being. The quality of health depends on heredity, the way of life, and on the economic and social conditions. The significant progress over the last decades in medicine, pharmacology and psychology has improved the quality of health and has contributed to longevity. Life expectancy in developed countries has increased by thirty years since 1900 and by six years since 1990.

From Asclepius to Hippocrates

In the Hellenistic period, there was no substantial medical care. Healthcare had been left to the will of the gods, to nostrums and practical therapists. People had learned to endure pain and accepted the ephemeral of life. Death could find them any time, in wars, in disease, hunger and crime. The ancient Greeks believed that the gods determined their health. So when ill, they thought that a god was displeased with them and was punishing them. The usual suspect was the god of healing, Asclepius. During the 4th century BC, knowledge in medicine began to take off. The main representative of the "new medicine" was Hippocrates, who suggested physical medication, independent from the will of gods. At the end of the 4th century BC, the "customers" of the Sanctuary of Asclepius at Epidaurus were diminishing due to the spread of new medicine. The

Romans absorbed most of the Greek knowledge in medicine and gave it new impetus. The most famous doctor in Roman times was Galen. He was a pioneer in surgery. He undertook such risky operations in the brain that no one for two millennia after him dared to do anything like that.

The role of emotions in the Epicurean Philosophy

Epicurus defined health as one of the few essential goods, the lack of which causes pain. Moreover, he gave physical and mental health the same priority by stressing to neither be ill in the body, nor get agitated in the soul. As healthcare was inadequate at that time, Epicurus focused on the mental support of people to withstand pain by saying that all pain can be easily treated because the severe pain is short, and the constant has a low intensity. He used to also give personal psychological advice, as we conclude from his letters that remained after his death. He wrote to his friend Menoeceus that the purpose of all our actions is to be free of pain and fear, and when once we have attained all this, the tempest of the soul will be laid—seeing that the living creature has no need to go in search of something that is lacking, nor to look for anything else by which the good of the soul and the body will be fulfilled. When we are pained because of the absence of pleasure, then, and then only, do we feel the need for pleasure.

The faithful Epicurean follower Diogenes of Oenoanda claimed that the secret of happiness is in our disposition (our perceptions), of which we are sole arbiters. Emotions hold a special status in the Epicurean Philosophy. Epicurus considered them comparable to the senses and to wisdom. He claimed they have two distinct and equally important roles: they determine the degree of life satisfaction, and serve as guides in making fast and reliable decisions.

The birth of emotions

The emergence of emotions in living beings coincides with the creation of the emotional center in the human brain. Emotions are almost non-existent in reptiles, amphibians, and other species of prior periods. The modern American neuroscientist Paul Maclean, who pioneered the discovery of the emotional center used to say that it is very difficult to imagine a lonelier and more emotionally empty being than a crocodile. Although love signs are encountered in birds, the emotional center began to evolve later, after the first mammals. Two such behaviors of mammals, and to a lesser extent of birds, are the strong and long-term care of mothers for their children and their disposition to play. The more sophisticated a mammal is, the more intense these behaviors are. Our hominid ancestor could determine the differences in feelings he felt at distinct circumstances of his life, as in a cave where he polished a stone or a bone, on the run to catch a weaker animal, in flight when he was chased by a stronger animal, or when he was after a female. However, the evolution of man brought an inexhaustible variety and a vast emotional depth, which has nothing to do with what pre-existed.

According to Darwin, the creation of emotions in humans was the result of organic adaptation intended to solve survival issues. Indeed, emotions improved the quality of decision making, and in this sense, they promoted natural selection and survival in the evolutionary process of humans. This happened for three reasons: the first is that emotions can give reliable guidance when we have limited information from the environment. The second is that the decision-making process based on the way we feel is fast. Finally, the participation of emotions in decisions makes them more effective. The modern, pioneer neuropsychiatrist, researcher, Antonio Damazio, who investigated the relationship of emotions to logic and biology, supported that emotions play a crucial role in issues requiring a high spiritual level. He proved that emotions and their biological origins in the emotional center of the brain are involved actively in decision-making, often unconsciously. Later the psychology professor at Berkeley and a pioneer in the study of emotions and anxiety, Richard Lazarus, said that emotions are necessary in order to make a rational decision, and in this sense, they are necessary for survival.

Scientific research has shown that emotions are related to the activation of certain areas of the brain that direct attention, motivate behavior, and assess the importance of what happens around us. In 1937, the American neuroanatomist James Papez formulated the view that emotions are created in a specific brain center, namely in an organ circuit consisting of the hypothalamus, the anterior thalamic nucleus, the cingulate gyrus and hippocampus. This circuit, now known as the "Papez circuit" operates harmoniously and is responsible for the central functions of emotions and their symptoms. Neuroscientist Paul Maclean later discovered new organs and new structures of the emotional center, which he added to the Papez circuit. Thus the present form of the emotional center arose, which is known as the limbic system.

Mental health

Over the centuries, philosophers, doctors and psychologists studied sentiment, questioned its origin, its role in mental life, and its impact on the survival and adaptability of people. Some philosophical and religious schools of thought considered the emotional aspects of personality as inferior, negative or sinful, in need of an ongoing review of reason. However, maintaining good mental health is vital for a healthy and long life. The World Health Organization defines mental health as wellness, a situation in which people are conscious of their abilities, face the usual stresses of life successfully, work productively, and are able to contribute to society.

Ongoing stress is usually behind mental disorders and

symptoms of premature aging that modern people face nowadays. Following a pleasant philosophy of life and psychotherapy can drastically reduce the amount of stress one experiences. One can learn how to effectively manage it when it exceeds personal limits. Relaxation, meditation and acupuncture, which are often used to fight anxiety, only temporarily treat the symptoms, leaving the cause ignored.

According to the World Health Organization, the most common mental illness today is depression. Research in advanced societies has shown that it is the main cause of sluggishness and helplessness in people aged 15-44 years old. Often it coexists with a variety of other diseases such as chronic pain, heart disease and cancer, while it is generally associated with a low quality of health. Despite the discovery of effective treatment, the need for treatment of depression remains high. Emotional diseases are of particular concern in advanced countries, as more than 20% of diseases are related to mental illness. From mental patients, 80% eventually get some form of treatment, but with a considerable delay that exceeds even one decade from the time of its manifestation. Less than one third of those who receive treatment take the necessary care to make it effective.

Emotions are very useful if used correctly. The ability to use emotions wisely is a kind of intelligence. Emotional intelligence is linked to realizing the emotions of other people and managing our own in a practical way. When we succeed in this, we will be able to use emotions wisely and creatively.

Positive emotions

As we have described in the chapter, "Biology of Happiness" the electrochemical processes involved in emotion are a complicated integration of the chemicals of happiness produced in the brain, as well as of the hormones that are produced in the endocrine system. For example, some of the pleasant reactions are due to chemicals released into the emotional center of the brain. These substances are transferred to the nervous system through neurotransmitter molecules, which are the chemical messengers of pleasurable messages. Elevated levels of dopamine, for example, were identified in the experience of happiness. Also, the so-called runner's pleasure accompanying physical exercise was found to be caused by endorphins. We can therefore assume that positive emotions, such as joy and love, are the outcome of the activity of neurotransmitters and hormones.

It is known that some people are more happy and relaxed while others are more prone to stress and anxiety. This is due to hereditary and environmental characteristics, but it is largely attributable to one's perceptions on life. This is supported by a recent theory, that highlights the importance and contribution of positive emotions in survival. Positive emotions push one into action, in search of experiences, creativity and altruism. When we feel good, we are much more active, open, and willing to offer to the people around us. Also, with the help of knowledge and skills we acquire in the course of this process, we enhance adaptability, self-confidence, self-esteem and optimism. Moreover, when we are frustrated and embarrassed, positive emotions act as antidotes to negative feelings and a bad mood.

Positive thinking and attitude

Do we see the glass half-empty or half-full? The answer to this simple question shows our general outlook on life that decisively influences how we feel. It indicates how optimistic or pessimistic we are. The Epicureans call it "diathesis," disposition. The way we perceive a situation can affect our stress level and ability to cope with it. Positive attitude means approaching an unpleasant or stressful situation in a more positive and constructive manner. However, adopting a positive approach to life can be difficult when one feels frustrated or is bombarded by bad news. The benefits of positive thinking and optimism transcends a mere relief from stress. It leads to better health, constructive social relations, and increased performance.

Optimism maintains a dominant role in the Epicurean Philosophy, as it is an inherent attribute in maintaining equanimity. The steady state of wellness and the certain hope that it will last longer offers more confident joy to those who know how to estimate correctly, describes an

Epicurean text. All research confirms this stance. Optimism is the message to the brain that the future is expected to be safe and that it can fearlessly channel energy resources in search of pleasure, creativity and development. As long as pessimistic thoughts predominate, the mind is in a defensive mode, wasting energy resources unnecessarily in enhancing muscle strength to deal with the alleged or actual future risks.

We are provided by nature with a capacity that allows us to be happy. All we need is just to get to know it and be willing to use it to the fullest. As we have pointed out, the mind controls our life, and every change in our life starts the process of change in our brain. However, most of it operates unconsciously, according to genetic instructions and the habits acquired through our experiences. The importance and role of habits in the functioning of the mind manifest the way to change ourselves, which is none other than learning. Each new knowledge or experience, by repetition, creates new neuronal connections in the brain and, over time, an integrated neural circuit that serves the needs of this knowledge or experience. All needs and desires arise from these unconscious functions of the mind. If we are willing to make changes in our life, we have to first "convince" our unconscious mind through learning. If the changes are contrary to our nature, the unconscious mind will do whatever it takes for the failure of our efforts. If we have grown up in an environment dominated by negative thoughts, such as questioning, depreciation and pessimism, it is obvious that strong neural circuits have been created in our minds that function in line with the negative perceptions of the environment, namely for the failure of our goals. The same happens when we ourselves question our abilities–by accepting that we cannot do anything well or that everything will go wrong.

Negative thoughts are probably the most important source of misery in modern societies because they are the cause of long-term stress; they set the body into an extended red alert mode, where there is a depletion of energy reserves and gradually, exhaustion and collapse. One of the most painful consequences of this development is the serious disruption of the emotional functions. How can we deal with the phenomenon of negative thoughts? We can do this by creating neural pathways of positive thoughts through learning and control of attention. With daily training in positive thinking, we can open synaptic pathways at the expense of the negative, which will gradually become new habits, and will join the powerful system of our unconscious mind.

The basic Epicurean Natural Principles are an inexhaustible source of positive thoughts. We fully accept, learn, and imprint them in the synapses of our mind through repetition and experience. We should be patient and insistent. The pace of changes depends on many factors, and it may take some time to actualize. We should not easily get disappointed because our brain, by nature, always responds positively to learning and training. As long as we are aware of the way that our mind works, we can do whatever we like with it. It is a matter of time and effort. Happiness is a choice.

The book *Learned Optimism*, by Martin Seligman, suggests some very helpful exercises to break the habit of pessimism and learn the habit of optimism.

The first step in developing positive thinking is to realize the debate in which we participate with our Self and to identify the negative thoughts it contains. This self-debate affects our emotions and decisions and may become the greatest asset or our worst enemy. It all depends on how it is used. Negative thinking usually appears when we criticize ourself after a mistake. The way by which we react to our faults uncovers the presence or absence of negative thought. If we foresee continuous failures and question our skills, that single negative thought is likely to worsen the already low level of self-confidence and self-esteem, and create a new chain of feelings of frustration and despair.

Negative self-discussion contributes to a pessimistic outlook on life. Certain thought warps could ignite this continuous pessimism, if not consciously checked. There is the rationale of "black-white." Usually for the thinkers of black-white there is no middle ground. The prediction of extreme negative developments exacerbates anxiety, tension and conflicts. Another group of people, known as the over-generalizers, tend to make general assessments of their lives based on isolated adverse developments. When a mishap occurs they usually think that "not a thing goes well with me." The trend of unjustified generalizations implies a negative approach to life, exacerbates the problems and causes stress. Some other people tend to interpret any comment or action from others as a personal attack on their abilities. They are affected by the slightest thing and underestimate themselves without there being any real reason. This negative approach causes undue stress and anxiety in their life.

Paying special attention to incidents and the thoughts that are associated with them that produce mood changes, helps to curb these negative thoughts. Positive self-conversation also promotes positive thinking and can evolve into an optimistic outlook on life. Preparing a list with positive affirmations and thoughts helps plan thinking in advance and gradually promotes automatic positive thinking. Lastly, it is helpful to be surrounded by people who see things optimistically so as to learn the model of positive thinking firsthand and under various circumstances.

From all this, we can draw the conclusion that the high level of healthcare in modern societies enables the treatment of most disease and pain, the improvement in our quality of health, and increasing life expectancy and lifespan. Urbanization of life and increasing material prosperity in recent decades has caused a surge in mental illness and a shift in emphasis from physical to mental health. Health is single and psychosomatic, and so it is wise to expel the prejudices surrounding mental health problems. With the help of a proper philosophy of life, and psychological and medical support, we can effectively address a broad range of mental illnesses. We are aware of the developments and progress in the field of medicine, pharmacy and psychology; we appreciate their contribution to happiness and enjoy their services. We rely on emotions to get to know our internal world and make choices. We are looking for experiences that cause positive emotions; we learn to think positively and to face even the most unpleasant developments in life with optimism.

CHAPTER 13

THE PLEASURE OF SAFETY

*"To secure protection from men
anything is a natural good by which you
may be able to attain this end."*

Epicurus, *Principal Doctrine VII*

Safety is an instinctive human need. All our actions aim at increasing security in our life. It is usually inversely related to return or pleasure. The greater the risk we take the greater the expectation of return or enjoyment. Preference or avoidance of risk differs among people. It depends on innate characteristics and upbringing. Statistically in their vast majority, people avoid risk and seek safety. However, there are some people who become excited by taking risks and seek them.

Apart from the personal tendencies and choices, safety level is significantly affected by external factors, which we can neither influence nor control. We are daily in danger of road accidents, crime, unemployment, poverty, natural disasters, and so on. In order to calm down though, we need a minimum degree of security. In the old days people ran more risks than we do today, due to lack of medical care, frequent wars, authoritarian governments and crime. Economic risks were also serious, but people faced them with resignation as they had learned to be frugal.

Safety in the Epicurean Philosophy

During the Hellenistic period that Epicurus lived in, the governance of Athens and of other Greek cities was carried out by individuals friendly to the Macedonian conquerors. These were usually involved in the consolidation and expansion of their power and were indifferent to public security. People, frightened and hungry, suspected each other, and tried to ensure safety conditions alone or with friends and acquaintances.

At the turn of events in 306 BC, when the appointed ruler of Athens, Falireas, was overthrown, Epicurus found the opportunity he was waiting for to open the Garden. The political change in the city was accompanied by a violent uprising leading Falireas' partners to persecution, exile and execution. Within this highly insecure environment, Epicurus justifiably defined physical safety as a necessary pleasure. The insecurity Athenians experienced was extreme and complex. Crime risks, political authoritarianism, economic misery and existential fears had peaked. Epicurus and his friends barricaded themselves in the Garden in an effort to establish minimum conditions of physical safety and psychological defense through the strengthening of friendship and solidarity. One Principal Doctrine says that while safety is achieved to some degree through the support that one finds in riches, true security is found through a quiet life and removal from the crowd.

The greatest dangers we face today are psychological and economic, while the risks of accidents and substance dependence are on the rise. Also newer risks, from an uncontrolled propensity to over-consumption and investment in capital markets, exacerbate uncertainties.

Psychological security

Psychological security is the ability to feel safe within ourself, to rely on our abilities, to self-protect and to stay away from unpleasant situations. Self-protection has to do with our ability to connect with the world without abusing our powers or enduring the oppression of others. The loss of capacity to self-protection makes us vulnerable to attacks and weak in our ability to defend our personal boundaries. We are all vulnerable to aggressive and degrading behaviors, such as sarcasm, contempt, tantrums, a negative tone of voice, injustice, accusations, and pillorying. However, the psychologically insecure get hurt much more. Memories of negative experiences are recalled, and old hidden feelings of guilt, inadequacy and fear are revived. If we did not developed the skills to face similar situations when they reappear, we always experience them in the same painful way.

Psychological health is considered a natural and necessary pleasure in the Epicurean Philosophy because we need a strong will, confidence and determination to control our thoughts and emotions, and the ability to take decisions and actions. The more secure we feel with ourselves, the easier it is to achieve our goals, and the more we enjoy our life. Conversely, the more content we are with our life, the more secure we feel within ourselves.

Financial risk

In modern times, we run very different risks than in the past, while past risks that continue to exist today have changed in size and composition. Financial risk nowadays takes the form of financial crisis, unemployment, consumerism and investment in stocks.

Financial crises have taken a heavy toll. In situations of sudden economic collapse, some categories of people suffer dramatic reductions in their income while other groups are trapped in large obligations that they are unable to meet. The psychological consequences of any economic crisis are, unfortunately, painful. Surprisingly, the most significant impact it has on peoples' lives has to do with the existential vacuum rather than with the fall of their economic capacity.

Indeed, the gap created by an economic crisis swells excessively in people's minds, due to the great weight they attach to preserving their adequacy as consumers. So as they see their financial means reduced, they feel an irreplaceable vacuum, often accompanied by anxiety and panic attacks. The most appropriate solution for the restoration of their psychological balance is to search for an alternative meaning in their life and lifestyle. The Epicurean Philosophy offers an enjoyable and effective way to overcome any hurdles in life.

Unemployment is, perhaps, the greatest risk for people in modern industrial societies. The necessary expenses for food, housing and utilities raise the bar for the income of minimum survival, and as most people rely on their income from work to meet these costs, they fall into full financial deadlock when they lose their job. An economic crisis is accompanied by a series of stressful situations that may start by restrictions in diet and clothing and end in eviction and seizure. In extreme situations, economic deprivation can lead to divorce, family neglect, violence against children, criminal behavior, traffic accidents and suicide. Work provides status, purpose and meaning in life. Therefore, its loss, and the unemployment that accompanies it, is one of the most stressful things that we can experience.

Beyond its financial implications, unemployment becomes a permanent source of concern and anxiety due to the loss of identity and lack of daily activity. The psychological problems that arise, such as reduced self-esteem and self-confidence, reduction of social relationships, a sense of weakness and insecurity, may prove to be even more painful than the economic ones. Throughout the difficult period of unemployment, it is necessary to look after ourselves and to maintain a positive psychological outlook. It is also appropriate to take stock of our life, review our objectives, and learn from our experiences by taking our life into our own hands and trying all over again. Many successful people have experienced major setbacks in their life, but they did not give up, and managed to turn them into successes.

How to deal with unemployment?

Instead of complaining about the misfortune, or the unfair treatment we had, or how badly we handled something, or blame others, it is preferable to accept the new situation. The sooner we do so, the sooner we will move on to the next phase of our life. Now, more than ever, it is important to take care of ourself. This means taking care of our physical and emotional needs, and learning about effective stress management. It is accommodating to start criticizing or blaming ourself, but what we need now is to maintain our moral flourishing. We need increased confidence as we search for a new job.

Fixation on negative thoughts is the worst thing that can happen to us. Therefore, just as they spring to mind we directly repel and replace them with positive thoughts. If, for example, we start thinking that "it was my fault that I lost my job," we react by rejecting this way of thinking and argue instead: "I lost the job because of the recession and not because I was bad."

Isolation can make us temporarily feel comfortable, but it will not be of help for long. Hence it is better to avoid being isolated. Also, drinking and smoking offer, at best, temporary relief, but they can quickly lead to addiction.

We should try to find ourselves in a positive support-ive family and friendly environment in order to elevate our confidence. We do not try to shoulder the stress of unem-ployment alone. The natural reaction may be to withdraw due to embarrassment, shame or pride, but that will make us feel worse. We say that we have not got a job and that we are looking for one. Even simple words of sympathy and encouragement are a huge boost in this difficult time.

The vast majority of new jobs are not advertised, but spread by word of mouth. That is why networking is the best way to find a job. Unfortunately, we are hesitant so as not to be considered annoying or a self-seeker. Networking though, does not mean using people, but building relation-ships. It can be efficient and enjoyable.

Unemployment affects the whole family, so we keep the lines of communication with the family open and we ask for its participation in important decisions. We inform fam-ily members about our plans, our efforts, and about any positive developments. We give our people the opportu-nity to speak about their concerns and make recommen-dations. On each occasion, we share activities and fun, so as to strengthen existing family ties, to relieve pain, and to face the future with optimism. Children are seriously affected by unemployment, so it is important to be hon-est with them. They have their own way of thinking, and they usually imagine the worst happening. They may even imagine that they themselves are responsible for us being unemployed, or that they burden us financially. We need to reassure them by saying that the loss of work is not the fault of anyone, and to accept their help, if they are old enough and willing, in order to feel part of the team.

The consumer is the most substantial component within the structure of the capitalist system; its behavior has a great significance in the successful operation of it. Overconsumption is a common practice that bears a high risk for the common man. Consumption can be good if we buy what we really do need. But consumerism is bad, adding little to our wellbeing. A particular strand of overconsumption is purchasing things, not to fulfill our basic needs, but to fill voids in our lives and make social statements about ourselves. It turns out, stuff isn't making us any happier. Our obsessive relationship with material things is actually jeopardizing our relationships.

On overconsumption, see chapter 22.

Investing in the stock market bears two significant systemic risks: economic downturn and manipulation of stock prices.

When the economy is growing and business profitability is high, investing in the stock market is generally profitable, and the return on stocks is more attractive than on deposits or real estate. However, in the case that the economy is slow or failing, stock prices follow, and we run the risk of losing our profits and the invested capital as well.

In the advanced economies, a rigorous institutional framework exists to protect small investors from the possibility of price manipulation by institutional investors. In less developed or developing economies, things are different. The Stock market is narrow, the protective official framework loose, and manipulation of stock prices is a common practice. Institutional investors and big stock holders manipulate the market, causing sharp fluctuations in prices and driving the small investors out of the market with a loss.

Overall, investing in stocks may end up in us losing all of our money. Before we buy a stock, we should understand the risks and decide if they are risks we are comfortable taking. If they are not, we prefer to stay away from the stock market.

Other contemporary risks

Dependence on substances is perhaps the greater scourge of modern times. Cigarettes, drinks, and drugs destroy health and suck from the low surpluses of households and the pocket money of young people. The stress of life, consumption patterns, mimicry, and the modern lifestyle lure youth to substance use. Addictive substances containing nicotine, alcohol, and opium gradually make users captives. Over time, artificial pleasure replaces the natural joys of life. Alcohol and drugs are often used for self-treatment for the symptoms of depression and anxiety. Unfortunately, their abuse aggravates the symptoms of depression which seem, initially, to soften, while the interaction with drugs reduces the effectiveness of the treatment. When a mental health problem is not addressed, the substance abuse problem usually gets worse, and when consumption of alcohol or drugs increases, mental problems also rise. So eventually, it becomes difficult to determine if the major problem is substance abuse or mental disorder. The negative attitude shown by the users-patients further complicates the issue. People pretend they are not suffering, and hardly admit that they are afflicted by mental disorders or are dependent on alcohol and drugs. They believe that they will overcome everything on their own and are ashamed or afraid of disclosing what they are going through, lest they be considered weak. The first step for someone is to recognize the problem so as to eventually drive out the demons and enjoy a normal life.

The risk of car accidents has been increasing rapidly nowadays claiming a heavy toll. According to a report by the World Health Organization published in 2004, about 1.2 million people are killed and 50 million are injured each year in motor vehicle crashes around the world. The report also notes that accidents are the leading cause of death for children aged 10 to 19 years, and that with simple prevention measures, the number of deaths could be halved.

To wrap up, people in the Hellenistic times were very insecure. Crime risks lurked everywhere, the economic downturn was at a peak, and health care was nonexistent. Epicurus realized the importance of security to peace of mind and tried to soothe existential fears by using convincing scientific theories and psychological support. Today, the security situation is better than before. However, mental disorders, financial risks, the risk of dependence on substances and the risk of accidents have increased. Moreover, concern and anxiety particularly plague urban populations because they face high living costs coupled with the specter of unemployment.

CHAPTER 14

THE PLEASURE OF FRIENDSHIP

"All friendship is desirable in itself,
though it starts from the need for help."

Epicurus, *Vatican Saying XXIII*

Friendship has a prominent position in the Epicurean Philosophy. It is one of the few natural and necessary desires in the pursuit of happiness. Even if we meet the rest of our needs, it is impossible to achieve peace of mind without friends. Epicurus, being practical and realistic, had placed the starting point for friendship in its utilitarian dimension. However, he added that while, in the beginning, a friendly relationship may be motivated by certain benefits, it has the potential to develop into a deeper relationship, as friends find common perceptions and set common goals.

What happens today in modern societies? While all surveys show that people are happier when they are with friends, in everyday life, few are willing to invest time and mental energy in a friendship. Especially given the time it takes to acquire friends, it can sometimes lose its spontaneous character and we need to cultivate a friendship, as we also do with work or family. Friendly relations can take many forms: for those who cannot tolerate loneliness and have little emotional support at home, it may develop into a relationship of dependency. For others, it may become an enjoyable way to ward off loneliness and chaos in their conscience. For a minority of people, finally, it can acquire depth and become a source of joy and personal growth.

Friendship in antiquity

Aristotle left one of the most remarkable analysis for friendship. He made a distinction between genuine friendship and its other two forms, which have to do with mutual utility and pleasure. Aristotle says that friends are those people who want the best for each other for the sake of friendship because each loves the other for who they are, and not for any temporary capacity. According to Aristotle, the perfect friendship is difficult to develop, and therefore, special conditions are required. There must be some equality or analogy among friends because it is difficult to approach one another if they have an unequal social status. But even among equals in status, there is a need for some similarities in character, in inclinations, and ideas. Friendship, advocated Aristotle, must be based on honesty, unselfishness, and willingness. Another interesting, classic form of friendship is given by the Roman politician and orator Cicero who believed that true friendship is possible only between good people. Friendship, he added, is based on merit; it does not offer material benefits, nor ask for any.

Friendship in the Epicurean Philosophy

In the Hellenistic period, the importance of friendship was established by the social conditions of the time. The Athenians need for security and deliverance from fear was intense because the world around them had become strange and dangerous. One of their principal defenses was to rally people with similar ideas fed by the Greek culture. Therefore, Epicurus proposed that people cultivate friendships where possible; when impossible, to keep neutrality; and when even this was impossible, to completely avoid contact. His attitude towards isolation was influenced by the fate that Anaxagoras, Protagoras, Socrates, and Aristotle had had, who all were either exiled, escaped elsewhere, or were persecuted or killed. Epicurus, himself barely escaped arrest and death by a furious crowd when he taught publicly in Mytilene.

Epicurus first exploited friendship within philosophy. He spread the idea of brotherly love embracing all humanity, and highlighted it as a necessary incentive in the search for happiness. Through the prompting, "if you want to save your peace and humanity stay away from politics; make your own state that will give you what the official cannot," he indicated a Friends' Society as an appropriate social environment for the pursuit of happiness. This, of course, does not suggest having a commune type of life, but rather stresses the importance of being surrounded by likeminded people connected with ties of friendship.

Epicurus' innovation to friendship was the exhortation to cultivate it systematically. Friendship, he has supported, is so important for safety and happiness that it should not be left to chance. Put a smile on as you approach people, he recommended to his friends. But he added, to maintain friendships and enjoy a pleasant life, we must love our friends as we love ourself. The reciprocity of love makes a friend rejoice in the joy of his friends as if this was his own, and suffer in the same degree at their distress. The wise man believes that he should put as much effort into the enjoyment of his friends as he puts into his own. A Principal Doctrine stated that those who are able to achieve, first and foremost, safety in symbiosis with their like-minded, spend the most pleasant life because they have each other as a solid support. Another one complemented by saying that of all the good wisdom offers to ensure the happy life, in every respect, the maximum is making friends.

In Cicero's book *On the Ends of Good and Evil: De Finibus Bonorum et Malorum,* the Epicurean debater expressing his views on friendship, considered friendship as a means first, of pleasure, and then of personal safety. Especially, he argued that as with virtue, so are friendships the most faithful guarantors and generators of pleasure, as much for friends, as for ourselves. Loneliness and life without friends is full of threats and risks and logic itself dictates that we arm ourselves with friendships. When this is acquired, the mind feels secure. But Epicurus advised us to evaluate future friends carefully. He said that those who ask for help all the time, as well as those who do not ask at all, should be rejected from the start.

The characteristics of friendship

Are utilitarian friendships worth trying for? Do they contribute to happiness?

Being a utilitarian means making choices according to their usefulness. But what might be the utilitarian objectives of friendship? If they are unfair or designed to satisfy inordinate ambitions for enrichment and glory, then they are reprehensible. Conversely, if a utilitarian friendship aims to secure my survival and prosperity, and in this effort it benefits my friend as well, it is entirely normal and moral. This is due to the fact that it contributes to my survival and prosperity while, at the same time, helping others. It would be absurd to act regardless of my basic survival needs, or against them. From the start, human contacts have a utilitarian nature. Even voluntary acts and charities satisfy primarily personal needs. However, even utilitarian relationships of interdependence have gradations. In their basic version, they may have an exchange format: "I give to thee, if you give to me." On a second level a friendly relationship could mean, "I give to you without expecting immediate payback, but I hope that if the need arises, you will stand by me." At a more advanced stage, utilitarian friendships could be not physically, but rather emotionally targeted. "I stand by the frustrations of your life, but I expect that you will do the same, if something similar happens to me." The utilitarian friendships then, whether materially or emotionally motivated, contribute to our survival and prosperity while helping others, and for this reason, they are in line with the Epicurean principles.

In a friendship of mutual respect, we can achieve a high degree of spiritual contact and satisfaction, and experience feelings of fullness and joy. A friend stands as a mirror of us. He displays the evolution of our life; he arms us with mental strength to succeed in our goals, to express our innermost thoughts and concerns, and to seek ways out of hardships with his advice. On this highest level of friendship, the utilitarian element is inconspicuous. Friendship is characterized by trust, selflessness, honesty, love for the friend's own good motivated solely by the historical relationship we have with him, as well as for the common ideas, perceptions and joint actions. At this level, one takes altruistic actions in the name of friendship, and highlights and cultivates the deepest and noblest feelings. Friendships based on mutual respect are distinguished by intimacy, mutual care and joint action.

Friendship differs from other forms of interpersonal relationships, even from those characterized by mutual care, such as relationships between colleagues. Friendships are deeper and provide greater intimacy. We can find intimacy in friendship from the degree of mutual self–disclosure-that is, if we tell friends things about ourself that we could not conceive of ever saying to others. Self-disclosure is of particular importance to friendship because bonds of trust are created through this feature. At the same time, it shows the degree of determination we invest in a friendship because by self-revelation, we become vulnerable.

A link in friendship is having common interests, which develop common values and goals. Friends should be involved in common aspirations motivated partly by the friendship itself. The common goals may include discussion, game, and common experiences. However, some of them should have at least the friendship itself as motivation. There cannot only be a personal interest, for example, "I will assist you in building your fence now, if you help me paint my house later." In contrast, the activity must be exercised in order to do something with my friend, and the satisfaction I get is through this joint activity, rather than through a personal gain. Joint action is an essential feature of friendship because it suggests the existence of familiarity and common interests. A weak relationship in terms of intimacy and mutual self-disclosure leaves little room for common action in the name of friendship.

According to all scholars, a prerequisite for friendship are friends who care for each other—that is, they care for each other solely for the sake of friendship. This actually means that friends should love each other. The concept of caring for someone includes both sympathy and action on behalf of the friend. Friends must understand what is happening to their friends and feel the appropriate emotions: joy for their successes and disappointment for their failures. Moreover, as an expression of care for their friends, they should promote the good of a friend for the sake of friendship, rather than for any ulterior motive.

Since the mid-1970s, research has dealt with the relationship between friendship and morality, especially with the reservation made by Kant that friendship creates special commitments for specific people and therefore is biased. Indeed, through friendship we support commitments to our friends which by far exceed those we have with other people, simply because they are our friends, as parents care for their children because they are their own children. So it is clear that friendship is inherently biased in favor of friends, and in this sense one may argue that it is not moral. The attempt to reconcile one with the other leads to contradiction.

In the course of the emotional development of the individual, friendships are prominently placed in priority after the parental relationship, but before the relationship of the couple. In childhood and adolescence, friendships are the most important relationships in the emotional life of teenagers and often the most intense relationships that they will have throughout their life. In one of the first studies on children's friendships, it was found that as the child grows, his expectations about a good friend become more complex. The findings pointed to three stages in the development of the expectations of friendship. At first, friends emphasize geographical proximity; second, shared perceptions and commitments; and third, joint activities, a common way of life, and common interests.

Relationship of friendship to happiness

Conventional wisdom accepts that good friendships enhance the feeling of happiness. In contrast, loneliness, especially when it is accompanied by lack of social support, is associated with increased risk of heart diseases, infections, cancer and higher mortality rates. That is why some researchers call friendships behavioral vaccines that protect physical and mental health. There are important findings that show that social support has a significant impact on happiness, health, and the ability to handle the difficulties of life. However, we need to take care of the quality and nature of the social groups we are involved in, as well of friends, colleagues and relatives.

In his book *The Loss of Happiness in Market Democracies,* Robert Lane, a professor at Yale University, explores why in today's prosperous democracies so many people find themselves unhappy. Relying on extensive research, he concluded that while all the evidence suggests that the main sources of happiness are friendships and a good family life, people give weight to the accumulation of wealth and consumerism. Lane argues that income has little to do with happiness when it surpasses the poverty line. He urges us to change priorities and place companionship, which includes family solidarity, friendship and social support, over income.

One way to ascertain the value of friendship is to ask ourselves: "Why invest time, energy and resources in a friend and not in myself? What makes friendship worthwhile to me?"

Experience and research has shown that the most important, positive aspects of friendship is that it helps us to evaluate the quality of our life, in that a friend acts as an objective mirror of ourself. We establish our outlook on life and the society in which we live, and we build our character. We develop consistent and long-term, moral and spiritual values; we achieve our goals by participating in joint activities. We integrate into public life, draw strength to face extraordinary life events, and we acquire practical and emotional support.

Friendships today

It is generally recognized that over the years, friendships lose the power and importance that they previously had. Everyone admits that apart from a mate and a family, they need some friends, but the kind of relationship they describe as friendship clearly shows that the relationship they are talking about has very little to do with friendship. Studies show that the quality and quantity of friendships in advanced countries has decreased. A large percentage of people say they do not have trusted friends and use family as a safety net during difficult moments. Some attribute the finding that friendships today have eased off to the fact that friendships have lost their relation to social institutions and have taken on a recreational character. Indeed, though we may consider a friendship as a free personal relationship, it is formed under specific social, economic and cultural conditions.

Another theory considers that the feeling of self-sufficiency and economic prosperity leads many people to the superficial conclusion that they have no need for friends. Thus, they isolate themselves behind bars and walls, living with a limited number of peers and often in their immediate family environment. This behavior however, gradually leads to loneliness, introversion, and depression. Other researchers argue that it is not prosperity per se that leads to isolation, but the way we handle it. They support that self-sufficiency, when accompanied by altruism, leads to self-realization, increased satisfaction and happiness.

In summary, the analysis of friendship left by Aristotle is a point of reference and inspiration even today. The main motives for friendship, according to Aristotle, are usefulness and pleasure on the one hand and virtue on the other. Aristotle supports the second, suggesting that a true friendship must be based on trust, kindness, honesty, unselfishness and willingness. To develop a perfect friendship, there should be equality or analogy between friends. But even among equals in social status and similarities in character, inclinations and ideas are also essential. A friendship helps to evaluate the quality of our life because a friend acts as a mirror of ourselves. A friend is also helpful in enabling us to achieve our goals, participate in joint activities, integrate in public life, draw strength in difficult periods of our life, acquire emotional support, and shape our personal identity. The Epicureans suggested usefulness and pleasure as the initial motives for friendship; they added, however, that for friendships to be maintained, friends should cherish their friends as they do their Self. The reciprocity of love makes a friend rejoice in the joy of friends, and suffer to the same degree in their distress. Friendships in modern societies are limited, and this is a reason that many people consider themselves unhappy despite their economic prosperity. Thus, research urges us to change priorities, and place the companionship of family solidarity, friendship, and social support over income.

CHAPTER 15

THE PLEASURE OF KNOWLEDGE

> *"In all other occupations, the fruit comes painfully after completion, but in philosophy pleasure goes hand in hand with knowledge; for enjoyment does not follow comprehension, but comprehension and enjoyment are simultaneous."*
>
> Epicurus, *Vatican Saying XXVII*

The definition of knowledge was a point of intense confrontation between philosophers and the main cause for the formation of the idealistic and realistic philosophical streams, which, by warring one another, penetrated human history. The idealistic philosophy accepts logic as the standard of truth. In contrast, the realistic natural philosophical stream that is expressed by the Epicurean Philosophy accepts human physical characteristics as the criteria of truth in the form of sensations, feelings and anticipations. This latter philosophy came as a revolution to the established philosophies of the time, and even today, it continues to challenge the dominant philosophies. Epicurus valued reason. However, he considered that its role is not to devise reality, desires and needs, but to evaluate the soundness of them.

The outright pervasiveness of the idealistic philosophy through the religions of Christianity and Islam marked the evolution of human civilization and largely identified people's character, mood, and way of life up to now. Life would have been entirely dissimilar to this if the reverse had occurred. In retrospect, when we look into the history of knowledge, we will realize how the problem of knowledge was created and has evolved, and we will form an accurate picture of ourselves and the society we live in.

Knowledge in antiquity

The Greek philosophers of antiquity raised the issue of the reliability of knowledge as a first priority. They tried to establish criteria for the confirmation of knowledge based on logic, experience, feelings, inner search, and science.

Thales of Miletus is considered the creator of the scientific revolution. Before him, people explained the origin and nature of the world through the myths of anthropomorphic gods and heroes. Phenomena such as lightning and earthquakes were actions attributed to gods. Instead, Thales attempted to find natural explanations for the creation and operation of the world without making reference to supernatural forces. For example, with regard to earthquakes he argued that the Earth floats on water that, when shaken by waves, causes earthquakes. His most well known theory is the cosmological, whereby the world was created by water. According to the modern mathematician and Nobel laureate philosopher Bertrand Russell, Western civilization begins with Thales.

Socrates advocated the search for knowledge through reasoning. He assumed that there are three categories of knowledge. The first is sensation. Perceptions of sensations, Socrates said, are true at least for those who have them, as a kind of private knowledge, but they may also be dreams or illusions. The second form of knowledge is belief. It is a perception that for those who have it, is definitely considered to be true. However it can be challenged by others. Socrates claimed that the argument of Protagoras that man is the measure of all things refers to this concept. It means what is true is true for me, but myriad others may consider it a lie. The third form of cognition is knowledge. He defined this as a belief that comes from reason or causes (reasoning). This is reflected in his saying: "True belief supported by reasoning is knowledge."

Plato trusted logic as a means in searching for truth. In the *Timaeus* he argued that the truth of knowledge depends on the manner in which it has been acquired. If it is experiential, then it is just an opinion because the world of the senses is fluid and unreliable. If it comes from non-aesthetic sources, such as logic, it is reliable and robust because it comes from stationary sources of knowledge. Also, in the *Meno* Plato developed a theory for the relation of knowledge to experience by arguing that it is possible to know something that we have never been taught. This faith was based on the idea of reincarnation, that the soul existed in past lives and knowledge was transferred from those lives to the present one. So he accepted that people have a wealth of knowledge even before they acquire any experience, and this, in a nutshell, is known as the pursuit of knowledge in the "heavens."

Aristotle suggested the need to demonstrate knowledge through the discovery of the cause lying behind it. This was the beginning of empirical knowledge; the knowledge acquired through non-subjective experiences, as opposed to personal ones, available through reasoning, perception, intuition or introspection. Although he is considered an empiricist, he accepted that some truths or first principles were obvious and could be accepted without empirical confirmation.

The skeptical philosophers, like Pyrrho, supported the abstention from any judgment about things. The origin of their thought was that nothing can be known, as the human senses do not convey truth or falsehood, and therefore, people do not know the inner essence of things, but only how they appear. The Skeptics added that by blocking reasoning, by being content with events or objects as they appear, without confirming anything regarding reality, we can escape from the complexities of life and achieve calmness and peace of mind. This theory about the weakness to verify knowledge is the first and most comprehensive presentation of non-cognitivism in the history of thought.

Archimedes was one of the first philosophers who sought knowledge through experiment and technology. His discoveries in mathematics, physics, astronomy, hydrostatic, static mechanics and pulleys are well known. His works were forgotten for centuries, but sought again in the Renaissance and contributed significantly to the works of the most important mathematicians and physicians of the time, such as Newton, Kepler, Galileo and Descartes.

The sophist Gorgias argued that the use of speech could present an irrational view as being true and strong. He claimed that convincing words and convincing arguments have the power of gods and Nature. He used the sounds of words and rhythm to mesmerize his audience. His works deal with paradoxes, unpopular, even irrational issues that he defends with rhetorical tricks and witticisms. The lesson we get by Gorgias is that a clever orator can prove anything, just by using verbal tricks.

Knowledge in the Epicurean Philosophy

The end of a happy life in the Epicurean Philosophy is equanimity, the calmness of the mind that stems from the belief in the truth and effectiveness of knowledge. This attitude contrasted with the view of skeptics like Pyrrho, who advocated the weakness in the idea of unveiling truth. Epicurus instead argued that there are opinions about things, awaiting confirmation, while those already confirmed are considered to be true. By relying on the confirmed opinions, he compiled a list of forty Principals, to which he attributed the weight of doctrines, of incontestable truths. These "truths" formed the core of his philosophy. So for the first time in philosophy, documented knowledge was defined as a way to search for happiness.

The importance of the search for knowledge in shaping an integrated happy life is eloquently described by the orator of 2nd century AD Lucian: "This, and this alone is your sure and steady hope, the discovery of truth. Without this, happiness can not be found. Your only hope is in the ability to judge and to distinguish falsehood from truth and, like with money changers, to understand what is worthy and genuine and what is counterfeit. And if you happen to acquire this expertise, then confirm what is said. Or else know that nothing will prevent anyone from dragging you by the nose or making you run like sheep for the sprouting grass that will tend to you. Or more correctly, you will be like a liquid spilled on a table that goes anywhere with the push of a finger. Or, in the name of Jupiter, you will be like a reed that grows in the riverside, tilted by every murmur in the air, and stirring when even the wind is imperceptible."

The view that the standard for truth in life is Nature is consistent with human experience. The baby expresses its desires through instincts and emotions and, much later, acquires and uses logic, which shows us that Nature precedes logic. The criteria for truth in the Epicurean Philosophy are organic. Epicurean perceptions about the search for knowledge caused radical changes in the way people thought. Take the example of justice. In the traditional Platonic conception, justice is a virtue because it is a harmonious composition of the three components of the soul–that is, of logic, passions and desires. In the Epicurean Philosophy, the importance of justice arises instead from its usefulness. The means to verify it has to do with our emotions. From their observation we find that when justice is assigned we feel joy, and when injustice prevails we are sorry. This means that through emotions our nature makes plain that justice is useful, and thus, it is advisable to accept and agree among ourselves not to harm, nor to be hurt. Justice for Epicurus is an agreement based on its usefulness, and this is shown by observing our feelings. There is no need for abstract philosophical thinking in order to see its value.

The Canon of Truth

The Canon of Truth consists of the triad of the senses, feelings and anticipations. Perceptions are anticipations with a special function. They interpret and give meaning to the experiences of our life and our genetic dispositions. They are the means by which we can change our anticipations (character) to improve the quality of our life. This exceptional capacity of perceptions caused Epicurus to declare them as a distinct criterion of truth.

The senses are the first criterion of truth. The direct contact that the five senses have with the outside world makes them the basis for determining what is true. In addition to this, they are naturally capable of receiving and transferring the features of the stimuli they receive to the brain. The senses have no logic or memory. For example, the eyes transmit the color, the shape and the size of the object they see to the brain. This information is true and unambiguous, but the identification of the subject with these features is processed by the brain. Any error is due to logic and not to the fault of the eyes. In a relative manner, when we hear a melody, the ears receive and transmit the characteristics of the melody to the mind. These characteristics are always true, but the mind will decide on which melody it is.

Epicurus argued that the senses record a true relationship between the observer and the object of the senses because they do not use logic, and therefore, they are not subject to refutation. The opinions and thoughts formed in the human mind through the processing of information received from the senses are subject to rebuttal.

Interpreting Epicurus, Sextus Empiricus, a philosopher of the 3rd century AD reports that coming to wrong conclusions is due to the mind and not to the scams of the senses because the senses do no wrong. According to him, every sense should be accepted as none of them can be denied. Anything we are aware of and feel is real, nothing can undo it, nor can anything else be used to cancel it. The senses bring out reality, they do not raise doubt and discussion, for neither do they understand what irritates, nor do they remove, add or change anything because they lack reason and always indicate the real.

Also Lucretius, the Roman poet of the 1st century BC, wrote about the senses in his poem *De Rerum Natura*. His poem communicated that the eyes are not deceived because their job is to see where the light is and where the shade is. He went on to say that whether or not the light or the shade is the same as that which has just been is not a concern of the eyes. Rather, it is something that should be cleared by the calculus of logic because the eyes cannot know the nature of things. Therefore, the error of the mind cannot be passed onto the eyes.

The mind is prone to mistakes and errors, due to the addition and subtraction of data transmitted by the senses. For an observer, for example, the moon may appear to move while the moving clouds remain constant. Or it may seem that the coast moves and the moving boat remains still. In both cases, it is the spontaneous mind and not the senses that erred by adding movement to the fixed objects and depriving the ones that were truly moving of their motion.

Epicurus called this mistake the "addition of opinion." To avoid the possibility of incorrect judgment, logic should not make hasty judgments. It should follow a sequential approach by initially giving faith to nearby direct stimuli because distance alters the characteristics of the stimuli

that are sent to the senses. However, even the nearby testimonies may be wrong, as in the case of a straight rod
which appears to be broken when viewed in water. It is for
this reason that the laws of physics, the testimony of the
senses, and other people should be taken into account.

Emotions are the second criterion of truth. According to
Diogenes Laertius, a biographer of ancient philosophers,
the Epicureans considered there to be two emotions. One
is joy and the other is pain. The first is familiar to us while
the other is foreign.

For Epicurus and the Epicurean Philosophy, to live according to Nature means to live according to the laws of
human existence. Emotions are an integral part of these
laws, and they demand respect and trust. According to
Epicurus, the soul and the body come to and leave life
together.

In the search for happiness, it is appropriate to submit
every decision to the test of emotions. We must ask ourselves: how would I feel if I made this decision compared to
if I made another? For example, in deciding the career we
want to pursue, we take competitive jobs that are stressful
into account, while being aware of the fact that the pursuit
of wealth and fame bears a heavy responsibility, worries
and anxiety.

It has been concluded by research over the past decades
that to interpret the state of our soul correctly and effectively in everyday life, it is useful to differentiate the physical manifestation of it, the emotions, from its narration,

feelings. Emotions are the result of biological functions within the emotional center of the brain that are perceived by their physical manifestations (laughter, sadness, palpitations, shivering, sweating, face color, and so on). Emotions are signs of how we feel and they cannot be mistaken for what they are not. They are brought about just as a stimulus is grasped by the emotional center of the brain. This is the direct method. Another method arises indirectly from the thoughts produced by reason, as the initial emotions are realized by the conscience. The sources of emotions in the course of human life vary. In infancy, they are mainly caused by the instincts, in childhood by the senses, and in maturity by thoughts, perceptions and decisions.

Feelings are the narrated emotions. They are an expression of biological emotions put into words. Due to the fact that logic is involved in the narratives of how we feel, the risk of misinterpretation is very likely. For instance, minor emotions can be seen as significant. Logic may sometimes be unable to unravel mixed feelings; it may also be affected by judgments from past experiences, misconceptions and influences.

Emotions which are in reality neutral or negative are often cunningly described by our logic as fun. This erroneous description is, hence, capable of misleading people. A possible explanation for this is that logic ignores their physical manifestations. Another is that it unconsciously interferes with them by arbitrarily adding to and subtracting from the messages they send (the addition of opinion). It may be, therefore, that what we consider to be a true feeling of joy is actually a feeling of sadness translated as pleasant by the intervention of logic. The conclusion that can be derived from the above is this: as far as we are concerned, it is better to trust the physical manifestations of our psyche, and in relation to others, it is better to look at what they do rather than at what they say.

Finally, research has shown that the emotions and their biological roots in the emotional center of the brain are actively involved in decision-making, albeit often unconsciously. This means that even when we believe that our decisions are based on logic, they are actually indirectly determined by emotions. We will also note that when our rational decisions are wrong, we are often able to feel it. The emotions, researchers say, are probably unconscious signals that warn us about the consequences of our choices. Practical problems encountered in the management and utilization of the capabilities of emotions are due to a number of reasons. The difficulty in recognizing their bodily manifestations is one of them. Another is our shyness in disclosing them to third parties, and the last is the lack of trusted friends.

The anticipations (prolepses) are the third criterion of truth. Epicurus was the first to use the word prolepsis (anticipation) in philosophy; therefore the interpretation of the word became a subject of broad discussions that led to disagreement among scholars. There are two prevailing versions.

The first one is attributed to Cicero; he interpreted the

prolepses as innate ideas. In modern terms, they correspond to the instructions embedded in our DNA by nature. It is according to these instructions that the genetic part of our brain is built. The inherent capacities and functions of our existence are located in our genes, and they reflect our "innate" needs and inclinations.

The second interpretation, attributed to Diogenes Laertius, considers prolepses to be real experiences stored in our memory. They are said to act as a template in recognizing new experiences whenever they appear in the future. These memories refer to things or ideas with a clear meaning that cannot be disputed or misinterpreted, as for example an orange or a man, love or hatred. Whenever these things or meanings appear in the future, the mind automatically compares them to the stored memories, effectively recognizing them without any conscious effort. If we have, for instance, the prolepsis of an orange in our memory, every time we see an orange in the future we can automatically recognize it without thinking. Also, with the experience of love which is already stored in our minds, we are able to recognize it without the intervention of reason when it appears in the future. Therefore, it may be said that the prolepses of things and ideas become the criteria by which we determine what is true within our new experiences.

The genetic and the acquired parts of our brain both have a biological base in our mind and therefore, they each constitute different criteria to determine what is true. Indeed, research has shown that repeated experiences acquire physical presence in our minds and in reality, it is impossible to separate them from the genetic properties of the mind (instincts, innate inclinations). Every time we acquire a new experience, a new Self possessing new neuronal connections is also created. Thus, instincts, innate inclinations, and experiences operate in the same manner and have the same impact in the shaping of our Self. The only difference between them is that instincts and innate inclinations exist before experiences.

The use of anticipations of abstract ideas, vague concepts or complex emotional states as criteria for truth requires particular attention because they have vague characteristics by nature. They cannot, therefore, serve as reliable identification standards for similar situations in the future. Despite this, our mind still goes ahead and uses them unconsciously as prototypes to address similar states in the future. It does this simply because doing so is convenient, leading it to reach incorrect conclusions. What comes to mind after this explanation? It is the concept of ''spontaneous'' decisions, and this is one of the reasons why such decisions may be wrong.

Perceptions constitute the fourth criterion of truth. Their interpretation has been a cause of concern and disagreement among scholars because Epicurus used to call them "the fantastic apprehensions of the mind." Nevertheless, by evaluating the ancient and modern bibliography we come to the conclusion that the above expression is another way to denote "the perceptions of the mind."

The purpose the perceptions serve is to automatically

interpret the stimuli that the senses, the emotions and the anticipations send before logic intervenes. In doing this, they adhere their own meaning of reality onto the stimuli. Perceptions have both genetic and acquired characteristics. As the name suggests, the latter are formed indelibly through the repetition of our experiences. It is through these experiences that we learn to interpret the general issues of life in a certain way–a way we become used to calling our perceptions about our life.

Our perceptions, being hardwired into our brain, give meaning to the events of our life as soon as they occur. In this sense, they are part of anticipations. However, Epicurus seems to give a special importance to them and prefers to declare them as a distinct criterion of truth. There is a solid truth to this for, indeed, the perceptions are the only hard wired part of our brain that can be changed through repetition and learning. The whole of the Epicurean Philosophy is based on this attribute of the mind.

Perceptions are the means by which the Epicurean Philosophy tries to change the wiring of our mind and improve the quality of our life.

The four criteria of truth acknowledge the realities of our life. How is this so, you ask?

The anticipations give an instant image of our state of mind. On one hand, this includes our genetic capacities and functions while on the other, it incorporates the memories of our experiences in life. The anticipations are as real as anything can possibly be because they have a biological base in our mind that makes up our character. The latter "anticipates" our path in life.

Our perceptions, both of a genetic and acquired nature, give instantaneous meaning to the anticipations. They are hard wired in our brain and are distinguished from anticipations because of their special features and importance in the pursuit of happiness.

Along with the anticipations and perceptions, the functions of the senses and emotions are also hardwired in our brain and constitute criteria for truth. Epicurus argued that anticipations, perceptions, senses and feelings bring to light the realities of our life. Epicurus excluded logic from the Canon of Truth because such thoughts are volitional, short-lived acts and are prone to errors. It is more than possible to think of anything and forget it after a while. As a matter of fact, this is what most of us do. Thoughts may disregard the realities of life and anything can be imagined. Epicurus suggests that the role prescribed to logic by nature is planning, evaluating, and decision making, as we shall see next.

The reliability of the triad of the Epicurean Canon of Truth— senses, feelings, anticipations—was challenged by the opponents of Epicurus mainly with regard to the validity of the senses. The senses were often accused of not transmitting reality and of being misleading. But Epicurus never argued that the senses are always reliable. He said that they disclose what they perceive, but their reliability is affected by the prevailing conditions. For example, the image of an object located a kilometer away is true but different from the equally true image of the same object when we get closer. The image transmitted by the eyes depends on distance. This is not something that the eyes should know because they have no reason; logic has to prevail and take into account that size depends on distance and that the actual size is perceived when we are near, by clarity. Epicurus says in the Canon that, although in general sensory impressions are real, external factors can affect their reliability, so they need to be tested by logic. Also, distant or small objects are not perceived by the senses, and the views of such phenomena are necessarily based on estimates. Therefore, whether sensible or not, it is useful to examine the reliability of the senses according to the principles of confirmation and non-refutation.

Testing the Canon of Truth

The confirmation of the truth of an opinion can be implemented in two ways. It can be confirmed either through the senses, if we are able to use them, or by induction, if we cannot. Let us suppose we see a man coming from far away, and we think he is Epicurus. The confirmation of the truth of our view can be perceived by the senses. We expect the man to approach to see that, indeed, he is Epicurus. The initial position is confirmed by the eyes. The phenomena that we can confirm through the senses are called vivid. Many times though, we are not able to confirm our opinion through the senses. The assumption, for example, that the inner and outer world consists of atoms and void cannot be proved by the senses. Atoms are too small for us to see, and the vacuum is invisible. In this case, the verification is performed in a conclusive manner, making use of proportionality for a property of the phenomenon to be examined. Suppose we express the view that human skin allows the outflow of sweat. We cannot confirm this assumption through the senses, so we use a property of the skin that confirms it. We know that the human skin has pores and that all porous bodies allow the outflow of liquids. Therefore by analogy it is confirmed that the skin allows the outflow of sweat.

The mode of reasoning in testing non-refutation is the "reductio ad absurdum." Consider again the earlier mentioned example where we expressed the view that the person we see coming from afar is Epicurus. This view is not refuted because if it is, and we assume that he is not Epicurus, then the person we see with our own eyes who has now closely approached us would not have the characteristics of Epicurus, which is not true because we see that, indeed, he does have them.

Likewise, the concept that human skin allows the flow of sweat is not disputed. Because if it is and we assume that the skin does not allow sweat to pass through it, then we must accept that liquids cannot pass from porous bodies, such as a sieve. But we know that a sieve allows the flow of liquid, and thus the skin also allows the outflow of sweat. In a similar way, we can conclude that the proposal that the void exists is not disputed. Because if it were, and we assumed there is no void, then we should accept that there is no motion since all space would be complete and compact and a moving body would find no room to move. But motion exists, which is obvious. The non-acceptance of the proposal that there is a vacuum leads to a false conclusion, so therefore the proposal that the vacuum exists is not disputed.

As we said, Epicurus accepted that the senses are the basis and the starting point for every effort to reach the truth and also that inductive reasoning is not always reliable, so we should be cautious in its use. Therefore he demanded more evidence in cases of no direct aesthetic perception, such as comparisons to the perceptions of people from other places and in various time periods. Such investigations may come closer to the truth, but it has been proven that they do not bear scientific certainty. For example, throughout time and in all places, people see the sun moving across the sky, and in accordance with the Canon, we should conclude that the sun orbits around the Earth, which has been disproved. How then can we move from relative certainty to complete certainty? In modern times, technology and scientific research gives us this opportunity. And most importantly, we can easily and inexpensively acquire it over the Internet. So we can use the Epicurean rule for the practical aspects of everyday life, but when we are looking for expertise, it is best to resort to science.

How do knowledge and experiences form anticipations? The primary ideas that words express are stored in our memory, and there is no need to prove their validity each time. They have value because they are common to all people and can be used as a yardstick to draw conclusions. Similar forms displayed in front of our eyes, similar sounds in our ears, similar flavors and scents that stimulate the palate and our noses, all these standards are strengthened in our brain through memory, creating mental representations, which Epicurus called "anticipations." These representations are expressed with symbols and are the benchmark for the new sensory impressions, so as to recognize shapes, sizes, colors, tastes, smells, textures, and so on.

Epicurus loathed generalities and controversial language. Every word for him was a symbol depicting an intellectual image and responded to the image of an existing anticipation. Epicurus was asking: can the idea that the word expresses be perceived as an image? If yes, it is safe and can be accepted. Otherwise it must be rejected. With regard to the clear meaning of words, Epicurus wrote to his friend Herodotus that the precise meaning of words must be assumed, so that no one is confused in endless interpretations.

Knowledge in the Christian tradition

In Christianity, knowledge is considered a supernatural revelation, a spiritual gift from god to people provided through the power of the Holy Spirit. The Old Testament refers to the tree of Knowledge of Good and Evil from which Eve ate the forbidden fruit. Her act was the cardinal sin and resulted in the punishment of the first people with their fall from grace. Since then all people are guilty and should believe in god in order to be forgiven.

Let us see the rest of the story in action: from the 4th century AD, that is, since the Christian religion was imposed as the official religion of the Byzantine Empire and took part in the exercise of power, the level of science, knowledge and education began to decline. The father of the Church, Augustine, formulated the basic principles of the Church saying that since there are the Holy Gospels, there is no need for science. He declared that all a man needs could be found in the Bible, and if something is missing from it, it is potentially bad and harmful. The knowledge of the Greek language, which was the foundation and the prerequisite for any science, was restricted. During the first six centuries of Christianity, the old public education and the sciences of antiquity were replaced by theology. A science was considered useful only if it could support the preaching and doctrines of the Church. In the early 7th century, public education was virtually eliminated. The dissemination of the ancient Greek writings was limited to the social elite, in churches and monasteries.

In science, all discoveries and theories that were not based on the Bible were discarded. The natural sciences, which flourished in antiquity, were called absolute nonsense and were treated as an attack on the majesty of god. Soon sciences such as biology, zoology and geography degenerated. Even progress in medicine was effectively blocked for nearly a thousand years. This attitude stemmed from the old Jewish belief that diseases were god's punishment for the sins of the people. The treatment of a disease was considered an unwarranted interference in god's will. Typical was the attitude of the Catholic Church towards Galileo, whose discoveries rejected the Ptolemaic view of a geocentric universe. He was sentenced to house arrest because his views conflicted with the book of Genesis, were considered as dealing with magic and astrology, and brought disruption to the socio-political order that supported the Church. It took many centuries before the Church officially rescinded the condemnation of Galileo.

Scientists and philosophers in the 18th and 19th centuries challenged the Christian beliefs, supporting the idea that god could be a simple projection of psychological impulse. The philosopher Hobbes argued that religion was created out of fear and prejudice. Sigmund Freud argued that religious faith was the result of a projection of a protective fatherly figure in the difficult phases of life.

The most important development that called into question Christian belief was the theory, formulated by the British naturalist Charles Darwin in the late 19th century, of the natural selection of species. Darwin explained everything related to human development on the basis of progressive adaptation of the organisms in their natural environment. According to Darwin, no mind or any divine intention is required to explain any human behavior.

The scientific positions of Darwin's natural selection and the projective views of Freud on god continued to have a significant impact on many aspects of the philosophy of religion in the twentieth century, intensifying the conflict between science and religion. Religious positions received new harsh criticism from Karl Marx who argued that god is simply a psychological projection that aims to soothe feelings of human suffering. For Marx, religion was an "opiate" that held the masses at rest.

Another direct challenge of religious belief came from the modern astrophysicist Stephen Hawking who claimed that because there is a law such as gravity, the universe can be created from nothing. Also, in his book *A Brief History of time,* he argued that the existence of god is not necessary to explain the origin of the universe. Later in *The Grand Design,* he stated that the question is whether the method of the Big Bang was selected by god to create the universe for reasons we cannot understand, or if it was established by the laws of science. He also stated that he believed the second. He argued as well that the concept of heaven is a myth. There is no heaven or afterlife, and such a perception is a tale for people who are afraid of the dark.

The search for knowledge through introspection

The philosopher of the 17th century, Rene Descartes, considered the senses an unreliable source of knowledge. He argued that it is only thought that unfolds the true nature of things, essentially repeating the Platonic and Christian views. To prove it, he used the example of wax. He took a candle and stated that his senses told him that it had certain characteristics, such as shape, texture, size, color, odor, and so on. Then he brought the candle near a flame and found that its characteristics changed completely. However it was the same piece of wax as before, of which the senses still informed him, now that all its features had changed. He concluded by saying that something that he thought was perceived by the eye was, in fact, only perceived by the mind.

On this ground, Rene Descartes created a system of knowledge that rejected the senses as unreliable and instead admitted only to logical reasoning and the inductive method of knowledge acquisition. Descartes was the main representative of the "introvert" philosophers. He shifted the emphasis of knowledge from observation of the outside world into thinking through introspection, and embarked on a quest to find conclusive truths. With his views, he adversely affected the development of knowledge and culture.

The modern quest for knowledge

The English philosopher of the 18th century, David Hume, was skeptical on anything that proved to be true by induction.

Along with the empirical philosophers Locke and Berkeley, he opposed any knowledge that was based on perceptions that are not confirmed by the reality of experiences. Hume accepted as knowledge only the analytical, mathematical logical thinking confirmed by empirical data. Also, the German philosopher of the 18th century, Emmanuel Kant, in his famous work *The Critique of Pure Reason,* sought to connect logic to experience. He expressed the hope of ending the era where objects outside experience are used as evidence to support futile theories. He said that it remained a scandal of philosophy and of universal human reason that things outside us had to be accepted simply by faith. He argued that experience is purely subjective if it is not treated by pure reason, and also that the use of logic without confirmation by experience leads to theoretical illusions.

The contemporary American philosopher Willard Van Orman Quine added that even the proof of mathematical theorems should be subject to empirical verification. The basic idea of empiricism, according to Quine, is the denial of the existence of any knowledge in advance. He added that nothing is logically and necessarily true of the natural world, and logical truths do not say anything about the physical world, unless they are applicable and verified empirically. The Austrian philosopher Karl Popper, in the early 1930's, argued that science is erroneous and has no validity. He argued that the most reliable method for finding the truth is the empiricism of trial and error.

In the book *Belief, Truth and Knowledge,* the contemporary Australian philosopher David Armstrong addressed the issue of uncertainty of knowledge that was first raised by Plato in *Theaetetus,* suggesting the search for evidence in outward causes. Armstrong sought credible explanations as evidence of true opinion, and not inductive thoughts as did Plato. He argued that not only must we believe in the true opinion, but also to know the causes behind it. For example, if I feel hot, I cannot draw the conclusion that the room is hot. My true opinion on the existence of heat is not knowledge that the room is hot. I must look for external evidence that would convince me that, indeed, the room is hot. The problem of knowledge for Armstrong arises when we accept as knowledge another thought or idea or concept, rather than an experience of the senses that is not challenged, as proof (realism versus idealism).

The modern scientific method was crystallized in the 17th and 18th centuries. In his work *Novum Organum,* which referred to Aristotle's "Organon," the philosopher Francis Bacon outlined a new system of logic that improved the old philosophical process of syllogism.

Nowadays the discovery of knowledge has come under the jurisdiction of the scientific community. Scientific study and research spread through universities and research centers. The discovery of new knowledge has boosted technological progress. Modern man can easily access reliable knowledge through science. The assumptions and the predictions that scientific researchers make to interpret various phenomena are tested repeatedly until the conclusion is confirmed or denied. Scientific research seeks objectivity and avoids a one-sided interpretation of the results. A key feature of scientific knowledge is the disclosure of the data and the methodology used, so that they can be tested and verified by other scientists. When research study is confirmed, only then is it accepted by the scientific community. Scientific methodology requires intelligence, imagination and creativity. It is not a static set of standards and procedures, but a continuous process of adjustments and improvements aimed at the configuration of consistent and comprehensive models and methods.

The growth of the Internet in the last decade has changed the usual method of searching for knowledge. Knowledge that was previously disseminated in print form is currently published only in electronic form or parallel to printed material. Today, students, professionals and ordinary people are turning to the Internet to obtain information about research. Within a few moments search engines provide endless sources of information–charts, studies, opinions, news, files and anything else of interest. The Internet is now an inexhaustible source of knowledge. But there are also serious risks for deception. Knowledge sources must be reliable and have to be checked and cross checked for their reliability.

The paradigm of Gorgias regarding his ability to manipulate truth and hypnotize his audience using verbal tricks has had a dynamic resurgence in modern times. It has become more effective through being enriched by the provisions of technology, and especially through the daily presence of television in our homes. Two forms of manipulated information aim at the formation and control of perceptions and opinions: advertisements of consumerist marketing, and political and economic misinformation.

What can we conclude from all this? The search for knowledge is of particular importance in the pursuit of happiness because knowledge shapes our thoughts, perceptions, emotions, choices, decisions, and our way of life. The true sources of knowledge, according to the Epicurean Canon of Truth, are the senses, emotions and anticipations. All knowledge, though, should be tested by logic for confirmation and non-contradiction. In complex cases, it is appropriate to resort to scientific knowledge and statistical data. The Internet is an important source of knowledge, but we need to cross-reference the reliability of the information. In religions, the source of knowledge is logic. Modern people's perceptions have been shaped by the idealistic Platonic ideas incorporated into religions. The progress of science and the improvement of living and cultural standards have brought Epicurean principles back to the forefront in our search for knowledge. People today resort more often to scientific knowledge in order to discover the truth. The new risks of distortion and manipulation of knowledge come from the established political and economic status, pushing people to unbridled consumerism. This creates excessive desires, disappointments, guilt, anxiety and unhappiness.

CHAPTER 16

THE PLEASURE OF THE SENSES

"I do not know how I can conceive of the good, if I withdraw the pleasures of taste, withdraw the pleasures of love, withdraw the pleasures of hearing, and withdraw the pleasurable emotions caused by the sight of a beautiful form."

Epicurus

The requirements of financial resources in the Epicurean Philosophy are minimal. But in conditions of economic crisis, even these low financial resources are scarce for some people, limiting their desires to what is strictly necessary for survival. In contrast, other groups of people can taste not only the natural and necessary forms of pleasure, but many more. These extra forms of pleasure are considered optional in the Epicurean Philosophy. They give way to leisure and people's interests; they offer a variety of emotions, but they do not increase the maximum level of happiness. Among others things, the senses, the body, Nature, and culture can offer endless pleasures and bring harmony to the consciousness.

Vision

What we see are not the objects, but the light waves reflected by the objects. Once the light waves reach the retina at the back of the eye, the rods and cones convert it into nerve impulses and pass them on to the optic nerve to create the corresponding image. This in turn is compared to the anticipations stored in our memory. In order to see, the mind has to recognize the new image. There are many times when the eyes see something, but the brain does not recognize it because there is no experience concerning it in its memory. As we wander into an area, we can see new things, gain new experiences and feel pleasant things. A walk in the garden and the park allows us to enjoy colorful flowers and plants. The smile of a loved one can give us joy. The world around us is full of nice things to see, to listen to, to touch, and to smell. It is worth devoting a little of our time to becoming beware of what is happening around us. There are many things that can give us joy, but we do not notice them.

What is beautiful or ugly is subjective. It does not relate to our eyes, but to our experiences and culture that give us their own interpretation of what our eyes see. Images have a significant effect on our emotional world.

For example, bright colors, creepy eyes and strict portrait expressions were found to increase pressure and stress, while the delightful views of scenes and landscapes reduce stress, improve attention, contribute to a faster recovery from illnesses, and improve mood and the general feeling of satisfaction in life.

Taste

When eating, the chemicals of the food are dissolved by the saliva and induce the sensation of taste. The taste receptors contain thousands of taste buds, which send impulses to the brain. This, in turn, recognizes the kind of taste, whether sweet, sour, salty or bitter. As with image and sound, flavor depends to a large extent on odor. If we have congestion of the sinuses and cannot smell, food seems tasteless. Generally, to identify a taste the brain uses signals from the eyes, the nose and the mouth. If one of these signals is corrupted or missing, it is difficult for the brain to distinguish the taste of food, and the appetite is disrupted. Food, like sex, is embedded in our nervous system. Research shows that people feel happier and comfortable during meals. A risk with food is that it can be converted into addiction. Therefore the torque to the pleasures of the stomach is often treated as misconduct and a risk to health. The sense of taste is significantly influenced by stress. Stress and depression alter the thresholds of bitter and sweet tastes in the body, resulting in a disturbed appetite and possible weight mismanagement. In our hectic life, we sometimes forget how much fun food is. We are fortunate today to have the opportunity to enjoy foods from around the world to gain experiences of flavors that our parents and grandparents could not imagine. Let us spend some time at dinner tonight to cook something that excites us, and let us enjoy the taste of each bite. If this is not possible, let us schedule a special meal that we like once a week. It will make us anticipate something pleasant and will fill us with optimism.

Hearing

Sound waves travel through the ear to the cochlea, where 16,000 hairs, and cell receptors, send the messages to the encephalon. As with the eyes, the brain interprets the frequency of the vibration, compares it to its memories, and recognizes those sounds that are similar to the ones it has already experienced. The ears receive thousands of sounds, but the brain chooses only the ones relevant to its experiences. Hearing depends largely on vision. Even people with normal hearing can hear more easily by looking at the face of the speaker. Image creates familiarity with the style of speech that the brain transforms into listening mode. It has been found that by blindfolding the eyes for 90 minutes we can enhance our hearing. Even a short-term light deprivation seems to be enough to set the hearing circuits that are dormant in the visual cortex into motion. Our ears can bring many joys. The sounds of laughter or our favorite music. The chirping of birds on waking can bring a smile to our face and cheer us up.

Smell

When we breathe through the nose, the olfactory receptors are stimulated by chemical molecules present in the air, and they send the messages received in the olfactory bulb to the base of the brain. The brain, in turn, identifies the type of each scent. Unlike the experiences of other senses, smells are recorded in our memory in permanent storage. Therefore we easily remember smells we experienced in our life, no matter how old they are. We all have smells that remind us of pleasant moments of the past and make us smile with satisfaction. For example, the smell of a freshly baked apple pie, homemade bread, and freshly cut grass. Pleasant scents, beyond the enjoyment of smell, awaken pleasant feelings from the past.

Touch

The three layers forming the skin, the epidermis, the chorion and the hypodermis, have millions of sense receptors. When stimulated by touch, these receptors activate nerves that communicate with the somatosensory cortex and through them, transmit information concerning the temperature and pressure at the time and point of contact. The brain processes the messages that carry the stimuli, and analyzes and attaches to them a meaning based on the feeling of joy or pain. If they are interpreted as pleasant, the brain activates the pleasure-producing hormones, which I describe as the Biology of Happiness. Otherwise, it activates the body's defense mechanisms.

The sense of touch is so important that its absence can lead to physical and behavioral problems, disruption of the normal development of the brain, and even death. Massage has beneficial effects on physical and mental health. For example, it has been proven that anorexic women who underwent massage therapy discovered that there was a reduction of anxiety, depression and stress hormones. Studies have also shown that 30 minutes of massage is sufficient to overcome pain, boost confidence and remove feelings of anxiety. Just by holding our partner's hand in the presence of a potential threat, the brain calms down. The higher the quality of the relationship, the more positive the signs of relief from touch will be.

Touch is critical to the newborn, infants and children. Babies who are held regularly grow faster and are healthier than those who are not touched frequently. There is evidence that even people who are in a coma respond positively to being touched. Deep emotions are expressed silently through touching. There is great pleasure in certain forms of touching and great solace in others. Touch also helps relieve physical pain and emotional distress. Touch improves the circulatory and lymphatic function, helps fight fatigue, and enhances the body's immune system. A cascade of the body's pleasure chemicals are stimulated simply through touch. In addition to the healing and health-promoting aspects of touch, the pure sensuality of a loving touch between partners is essential to a fulfilling life. Loving touch deepens intimacy and heightens sexual gratification.

Our senses connect us to the environment. The messages they receive from the world are sent to the brain, which processes and interprets them, creating the experiences of our life, our memories, thoughts, perceptions, emotions. Of the thousands of stimuli our senses get from the world, we perceive only those that are connected to our experiences, beliefs and culture. The majority of them are never recognized by the brain. Our five senses are some of the most powerful weapons we have available to increase our satisfaction in life. Let us use them to absorb the beauty of the world and enjoy pleasant experiences.

CHAPTER 17

THE PLEASURE OF SEX

"You tell me that the stimulus of the flesh makes you too prone to the pleasures of love. Provided that you do not break laws or good customs and do not distress any of your neighbors nor do harm to your body nor squander your pittance, you may indulge your inclination as you please. Yet it is impossible not to come up against one or another of these barriers, for the pleasures of love never profited a man, and he is lucky if they do him no harm."

Epicurus, *Vatican Saying LI*

Sex is an issue that people avoid discussing, especially in the close family circle. The idea that sex is embarrassing was caused by our parents' attitude when they avoided answering or gave us some strange and vague answers, when we, as children, asked them how we were born. Nowadays, parents once again avoid informing their children and wait for their sex education to come from school.

Like any pleasure, too much sex is harmful to our health. In ancient China, the Chinese emperors had a shorter lifespan than common men because they kept thousands of women in the harem.

The positive effects of sex

The same sexual contact can be pleasant, rapturous, or neutral, or painful and intimidating. Overall it is a pleasant experience, but over time it can turn into a routine. Fortunately there are ways to transform it into a permanently enjoyable experience. We can, for example, give it variety, interest and challenge. But sexuality really grows if it takes on a psychological dimension through romance, and the sharing of emotions and promises. A new dimension opens up when, along with the physical pleasure and romance, there is also an interest between the sexual partners for the success of their personal goals. By adding this dimension, sex becomes a thoroughly enjoyable experience. However, in order for it to remain fresh, it needs to be updated and reinforced through joint activities, such as traveling, reading, art, and sports. There are no fixed criteria as to how often we should have sex, but if we have safe sex with stable partners, sex can benefit our health immensely.

Sex can benefit our health in many ways. It acts as an effective pain reliever, through oxytocin, a chemical substance released during orgasm. So if we have a headache, sex is a sure way to relieve it. Also the endorphins released during sexual contact have been shown to improve mood. Besides, we can strengthen our relationship by having sex. This helps to establish stable relationships that tend to make us happier, healthier, and live longer. That is why we observe that the married, especially men, usually have a longer life span than the unmarried.

Planned sex can improve cardiovascular function. Regular sex with a stable partner reduces the risk of heart attack. Sex with unknown partners can overstimulate the heart and cause the opposite effect on men with a weak heart. Also, regular sex can increase our tolerance to colds and the flu. Few people have realized that sex is a pleasant alternative to taking a flu injection.

In fact, sex serves to relieve stress, lower blood pressure and facilitate sleep. After sex, we usually feel relaxed and can sleep better. We can lose weight by having sex because we burn about 85 calories in 30 minutes of sexual activity. And the more sex we have, the better we feel about ourselves. Sex improves emotional health and memory and reduces the risk of prostate cancer in men. The appearance of sexual problems in the performance of men may be an early warning signal of other diseases. Specifically, coronary disease may first appear as impotence because the penis is fed from the same blood vessel system as the heart.

Sex, money, happiness

More money does not mean more sex, but more sex can make us feel richer. The good news is for those whose bedrooms have more activity than their bank accounts. Research on the relationship between sexual activity and happiness find that sex vigorously and positively enters the equations of happiness. The findings show that sex contributes to happiness more than money. This is not to say, of course, that being poor but sexually active is the secret to a happy life. Contrary to established beliefs, more money does not bring more sex, say researchers of the economics of happiness. The findings of the surveys also show that a long marriage has a positive effect on happiness, as opposed to a short one followed by divorce. Moreover, it has been found that married people have 30% more sex than single people and that the higher the educational level of partners, the more positive the effect of sex is to their happiness. Other econometric calculations confirm what psychologists have long known, which is that people who consider themselves happy are usually richer in sexual activity. Sex is an antidepressant. Many studies confirm that people suffering from depression have less sex and that the involuntarily celibate are often possessed by unpleasant feelings–anger, frustration, self-questioning, and depression–for the missed opportunities of life without sex.

Sex and love

Love is essential to happiness and health. Studies consistently show that loving people are healthier overall, experience less illness in life and live longer. They have stronger immune systems and experience less heart disease, stress, chronic pain and other conditions.

Loving people also experience a more intense sexual life. This is due in part to their better state of health but also because loving people are better able to give and receive pleasure. In general, they are more in touch with their emotions and more aware of the emotions of their partners. Loving people are frequently more physically active, and physical activity has been shown to improve one's sex life greatly. Sex is a crucial part of loving and pleasure in life. But a healthy sex life has additional benefits beyond the pleasure of the moment. Studies demonstrate the healing powers of the pleasures and passions of love: first from falling in love, then through growing physical delight, onto a deepening intimacy between partners. There is evidence that love increases creativity, sharpens the intellect, enhances intuition and makes life worth living. In a life guided by pleasure, the healing force we call love is the foundation.

Sex and Epicurus

Sexual desire belongs to the category of natural and non-necessary desires. Although it stems from the hormonal activity of the body, one can live without it and therefore it is not a necessary pleasure. Orgasms are undeniably pleasant, but we must be careful and selective in order to maintain our equanimity. Epicurus advised caution towards sex because it creates passions that usually cause problems. That's why he advised a friend of his to follow the strong drive he allegedly had for sex, if he could avoid all side effects. He understood from him that his friend's natural disposition was too greatly inclined toward sexual passion. He said to follow his inclination as he willed, provided that he neither violated the laws, disturbed well-established customs, harmed any one of his neighbors, injured his own body, nor wasted his possessions. He also advised his friend to take care so that he is not found doing so and punished; for a man never receives any good from sexual passion, and is fortunate if he is unharmed.

Lucretius agreed with free sex, but not with passionate love affairs because they cause traumas not easily treated. He argued that feelings accompanying sexual relationships bring much evil, such as agitation in the mind, indifference to obligations, guilt, insecurity, loss of social reputation, expenses for gifts and entertainment. This process is unstoppable and endless; it does not meet physical needs and leads away from peace of mind.

Sexuality is certainly the most enjoyable experience, after water and food. The desire for sex is so powerful that it can absorb all the psychic energy from the other necessary human needs. Like every other aspect of life, it can be enjoyable if we are willing to take control of it, to cultivate it, and to give it depth and complexity.

CHAPTER 18

THE PLEASURE OF NATURE

"The wealth demanded by nature is both limited and easily procured; that demanded by idle imaginings stretches on to infinity."

Epicurus, *Principal Doctrine XV*

The positive relation between Nature and health

Many psychological studies support the view that activities in Nature lead to increased physical and mental health. This positive link between Nature and health is so strong, that it is considered an effective strategy for better public health. Indeed, many studies have shown that the symptoms of anxiety disappear faster through contact with Nature than with other standardized treatments.

Another parameter of experience with Nature can be its

social aspect. While many activities in Nature are solitary, others have a pronounced social character. The natural environment offers opportunities for contact, social support, intimacy and bonding in an exotic environment. The challenges that activities in Nature include offer many opportunities for the development of culture, comradeship and altruism. Contact with Nature has positive effects on the syndromes of attention deficit and hyper-mobility of children. Several studies confirm that it improves children's ability to focus their attention and manage their impulses. Contact with pets also has similar positive effects on children. It introduces them to the physical world, it calms them down, and it makes them responsible. It also teaches them how to develop healthy relationships.

Direct contact with wildlife

The majority of people who have experiences in the wilderness evaluate them as among the most important in their lives. Experiences in the wild create the sense that the world is enchanted, alive, united and meaningful. For example, a sociological analysis of the mountain experience argues that while climbing it feels as if one belongs to a single comprehensive cosmos. The awareness of ourself as a part of Nature feels charmed, and being alive has meaning. Nature nurtures the sense that everyone is unique, and at the same time, a part of the whole. Some go as far as to claim that man and Nature are a single being, of which the one aspect is man and the other Nature.

According to the famous psychologist Maslow, Nature offers peak experiences, classified as optimal mental health experiences, as well as lower intensity experiences with an often longer duration, characterized by a sense of calmness and serenity.

Carl Gustav Jung saw Nature as a canvas where the archetypes of the collective unconscious mind are projected. Jung wrote that in the wild we have the opportunity to directly meet the archetypes of our subconscious because the natural environment removes the veil that covers them, exposing the contents of the soul. Indeed, many spiritual mystics, including Moses, Jesus, Buddha and Mohammed, sought similar experiences in the wilderness before starting their teaching. In Nature we feel more familiar with our thoughts and feelings. We are calm, as we understand the impermanence and insignificance of our daily concerns within the immense eternity of natural phenomena. We deepen our insight in spiritual concepts and eternal processes; we raise our awareness of human values and spiritual meanings.

The benefits of working in Nature

Working in Nature improves well-being. A new field of clinical treatment practice based on the benefits offered by working in Nature claims that horticulture, agriculture and forestry increase the body's resistance to diseases, improves self-confidence and self-esteem and enhances mental health. They even attribute to it the rehabilitation of patients who have had a stroke. Working in Nature stimulates the senses. It is not only the sounds and the smells around us that cause euphoria, it also comes from touching the soil.

Working in Nature provides an opportunity to showcase our creativity and ingenuity. It reassures the conscious mind and gives our unconscious the comfort of discovering solutions to problems and avoiding the patterns of negative thoughts. Also, the growth of plants and the expectation of a satisfactory harvest create a sense of optimism, a feeling of satisfaction and pride.

Activities in Nature develop positive creative thinking in order to tackle the problems of disease control, watering, harvesting and storage. We spontaneously accept the naturalness of birth and death, as we see that all seeds do not germinate. That perfection is a myth is proven in practice. Interaction with the environment pleases the soul as we observe that we can influence the environment, and therefore, we can do the same with ourselves and our future. Work in Nature alleviates pains, and emphasizes ability. It is the key that unlocks possibilities and opens the way to physical, emotional, and intellectual development and prosperity.

Activities in Nature offer a series of intense psychosomatic pleasures, combining the benefits of exercise and contact with Nature. This complementary combination of pleasure fills the mind with a wide variety of emotions, ranging from peace to enthusiasm.

CHAPTER 19

THE PLEASURE OF EXERCISE

*"I take the liberty of observing that you are not
a true disciple of our master Epicurus, in indulging
the indolence to which you say you are yielding. One
of his canons, you know, was that 'the indulgence
which prevents a greater pleasure, or produces a
greater pain, is to be avoided.' Your love of repose
will lead, in its progress, to a suspension of healthy
exercise, a relaxation of mind, an indifference to
everything around you, and finally to a debility
of body, and hebetude of mind, the farthest of all
things from the happiness which the well-regulated
indulgences of Epicurus ensure;"*

Thomas Jefferson to William Short, 1819

The benefits of exercise have been known since antiquity.
Cicero, around 65 BC, said that it is only exercise that supports the spirit and keeps the mind acute. However, the

relationship between physical health and exercise was only recently discovered. Researchers found that exercise and sports are important in obtaining and maintaining bodily and mental health. Exercising means different activities and different levels of intensity. It is for everyone: the young and the elderly.

Many are discouraged because they perceive it to be a rigid sort of activity, a military-style situation that will be imposed on their life on a daily basis. But exercise can take many forms and levels of intensity. Even the simplest sport's activity can be enjoyable, as long as we turn it into a flow experience that attracts our interest, has goals, immediate results, attracts our attention, and our abilities are proportional to its difficulties. Any activity is worthwhile for the enjoyment it offers and not for other purposes, such as health, fitness, and fashion. One such enjoyable activity is to play sports. Mature persons over 65 who regularly play sports were found to be more optimistic, to have lower pressure and suffer less from anxiety and mood fluctuations. They were also more resistant to diseases, such as Alzheimer's and dementia.

Sports and exercise are not the only experiences that the body is capable of offering. A wide range of bodily activities are based on rhythmic and harmonic body movements. Among them, dance is perhaps the oldest and the most important because it is distinguished by universality and variety.

The beneficial effect on physical health

Frequent and regular aerobic exercises help to prevent and treat serious chronic somatic symptoms such as high blood pressure, obesity, heart disease, diabetes, and insomnia. According to the World Health Organization, physical inactivity contributes to about 17% of heart diseases and diabetes, 12% of the falls of the elderly, and 10% of breast, colon and intestine cancers. Physical activity is also beneficial to the functions of the brain. Specifically, it improves learning ability and reduces the risk of dementia and strokes because the flow of blood and oxygen inhalation improve, and new neurons are created in the brain.

The beneficial effect of exercise on the cardiovascular system is documented by studies and research. It has been found that lack of exercise significantly increases the risk of developing coronary heart disease. The most beneficial effects on cardiovascular performance are caused by moderate exercise. Those who begin regular exercise after a myocardial infarction significantly improve their chances of survival, while the positive effects are significant to healthy individuals as well.

Epidemiological evidence shows that moderate physical activity strengthens the immune system and reduces the risk of upper respiratory tract infections. Conversely, studies in marathon runners found that prolonged, high-intensity exercises are associated with an increased risk of infections. The functions of the immune system cells decline after prolonged and intensive exercises, so athletes who are excessively stressed run a higher risk of contracting infections.

The beneficial effect on mental health and sociability

It was found, even long ago, that exercise and sports increase the serotonin and endorphin levels in the brain which in turn render one cheerful, active, with increased self-esteem, and the ability to effectively manage one's weight. The positive effects of exercise are kept for several days afterwards, and this is why it is considered an effective natural method of treating mild depression. Exercise and sports are a very effective stress management technique. Indeed, it has been found that physical activity releases the repressed energy affected by cortisol and the other hormones that are secreted into the blood stream when we are under stress. In the opposite case, the retention of these substances in the body makes one excitable, complicates sleep, and causes a wide range of psychosomatic diseases. Also, exercise and sports reduce the accumulated rage that has been found to create phobic trends and panic, while they improve the quality of sleep and combat insomnia.

Physical exercise makes us feel satisfied with ourselves, it boosts self-confidence, and it gives a sense of control over the body and the mind. The immune system becomes less susceptible to colds and flu, and it generally decreases the fear of illness. It helps get the body fit so that we can wear the clothes we fancy, feel safe, look good, and feel happy.

Another aspect of sports is the social aspect. While many sports require one to be solitary, others require sociability. They bring people together; they offer social interaction, create pleasant feelings, and help get rid of worries and disappointments. The competitive desire to win a match in a sport that we love and enjoy gives us the opportunity to feel at ease and to feel good. During a game, attention is detached from feelings of anger, frustration or fear and focused on pleasure, performance and success.

For those leading a sedentary lifestyle, it is never too soon–and never too late–to begin to move and become more active. Walking, hiking, running, biking, swimming and many other activities have great physical and emotional benefits. These activities produce even greater benefits when they are performed with pleasure, and not in a mechanical way out of a sense of duty. Exercising in a gym is usually good, but climbing to the top of a hill near home and enjoying the sunrise or sunset is better emotionally and physically.

Movement–whether through exercise at home, in the gym, or hiking in the woods–increases vitality, enhances endurance, strengthens the heart, and produces many other beneficial results. In addition, movement reduces stress, helps fight allergy symptoms, decreases appetite, helps counteract anxiety and depression, controls blood sugar, and helps the body in its struggle against many other common ailments and conditions. Movement helps to increase a person's sense of optimism and hopefulness, self-confidence and self-image. All healthy movement increases vitality and the joy of living.

CHAPTER 20

OTHER PLEASURES

"Every pleasure is a good thing, since it has a nature akin to us."

Epicurus, *Letter to Menoeceus*

The pleasure of art

Cultures are defensive mechanisms against the uncertainties of life. They provide goals and a means to tackle the challenges of existence. However, cultures differ in the degree of opportunities they offer in the pursuit of happiness. The quality of life in certain time periods is clearly better than during others. This can be attained either by design or due to circumstances. The Athenian "polis" in classical Greece was a successful example of how culture can increase enjoyment for those who were lucky to live at that time. By contrast, in the Hellenistic Greece of Epicurus, interest in the arts was limited since Athens was under the sovereignty of the Macedonians, and people were interested more in survival than in entertainment and culture.

Epicurus enthusiastically welcomed the arts. It is said that he woke up early in the morning to go to the theater to enjoy a tragedy. Tragedy is known to combine theater and music, being more similar to operas than to Shakespearean plays.

Today we have the comfort of seeking more forms of pleasure. The arts have become one of the greatest pleasures of modern life that contribute to happiness. All research associates the arts with an increased dopamine production and activation of the frontal brain cortex. These biological changes cause feelings of pleasure, like those of romantic love. Generally speaking, when a delightful piece of artwork is displayed, the positive feelings are almost immediate. According to recent surveys, repeated satisfaction from creating or watching art can reduce depression and anxiety by stimulating the connection of the nucleus accumbens of the brain. Perhaps it is linked to what psychologists call flow, offering some of the same positive effects as meditation and yoga. To the extent that active participation in an arts program gives participants the opportunity to gain public recognition, it also improves their self-confidence and their sense of autonomy. In addition, those who undertake art psychotherapy sessions appreciate the positive role that art plays in their happiness. They find relief from the fact that through art their attention is driven away from their personal problems and focused on exploration and creation.

Dealing with art has been found to cause the so called "Mozart effect" in children. Children who listen to Mozart, or have similar artistic stimuli, have improved performance in learning. Moreover, to the extent that they are allowed to participate in the organizing of cultural activities, they acquire new skills, enhance their creativity, and improve their self-esteem.

Music is the most traditional form of art. The enjoyment of music begins with listening, it continues with the feeling of sounds, the projection of music to the brain in images, and finally it ends with the performance, the acoustics, and the comparison of performances. To enjoy music, we must devote time to listening to it, dim the lights, sit in a comfortable armchair, carefully select pieces of music and concentrate on their harmony, rhythm, and their intensity. However the most intense pleasure comes from creating music rather than listening to it. In learning to play an instrument emphasis should be given to the enjoyment of the experience rather than to the level of performance, as often happens with parents who emphasize the ability of their child over their child's enjoyment.

The pleasure of aesthetics

Becoming attuned to our senses, and ordering and shaping our life to please those senses, is integral to savoring the pleasures of being alive. Colors, textures, sounds, fragrances and flavors all combine to create the world we inhabit. And we can use them to shape a wonderfully aesthetic world that enhances the pleasures of life. An aesthetic life is not something rarefied or available only to the wealthy or the privileged. It is there for all who have the imagination. Imagination is a powerful tool that can be used to create opportunities to develop the senses to the fullest. The small pleasures of daily life can add up to great joy.

Eating combines a variety of aesthetic features. All of the senses come into play. Touch is involved in the selection and preparation of the food. Vision is involved in the preparation of the setting and the presentation of the meal. Candles and lowered lights greatly increase the enjoyment and satisfaction of a meal. The sense of smell, the most primitive and powerful of the senses, is essential to a full enjoyment of the meal. Hearing comes into play in the selection of music that can be used to enhance a meal.

It is obvious to all that a meal served with attention to aesthetics and eaten in a pleasing environment is enjoyed more on a subjective level than the same meal served under less appealing circumstances. The pleasurable environment surrounding a meal has objective benefits as well as subjective ones. For example, the body absorbs more nutrients when the meal is served in pleasurable surroundings than when the same foods are eaten in a neutral or unpleasant environment. Anyone can have fun and learn to create "pleasure recipes" that feature a great variety of different colors, aromas, flavors and textures. The psychology of eating is also a critical element. Foods must be enjoyed to be nutritious. And to be enjoyed, foods must be in harmony with each individual's personal and culturally acquired tastes.

The pleasure of humor

The healing power of humor has been recognized around the world. Humor has a powerful impact on pain. Laughter has been demonstrated to relieve pain almost immediately, and pain relief may continue for hours after the laughter has subsided. This has been of great benefit to people who suffer chronic pain from a wide range of causes. Research shows that laughter also strengthens the immune function, helps relieve tension, fights stress, minimizes panic attacks, defuses anger, counteracts depression and anxiety, and has an overall positive effect on wellness and health. There are many ways in which humor and laughter increase the pleasure of being alive, and there are many different ways to use laughter to experience a more joyful life. Humor helps bring perspective to a person's life, and perspective brings a sense of balance that is essential to good physical and emotional health.

PART THREE: WORRIES AND FEARS

CHAPTER 21

WORRIES AND FEARS: AN OVERVIEW

"Neither great riches, nor exuberant activity, nor powers, nor strength bring happiness and bliss, but non-sadness, the gentleness of feelings and moods, which recognize the limits that Nature has set."

Epicurus

The psychological approach to worries and fears

The psychodynamic analysis of Freud suggests that the origin of worries and fears develops in childhood, when the child's instincts are repressed, either due to conflicts between love and death, or due to the restrictions of the environment. However, the repressed instinctual drives are not and cannot be destroyed when they are repressed.

They continue to exist intact in the unconscious, and can give rise to the dysfunctional behavior characteristic of neuroses.

Cognitive psychology suggests that psychological distress is caused by distorted thoughts about stimuli that trigger emotional suffering: Stimulus → Thought → Emotion. Systematic errors in reasoning lead to faulty assumptions and misconceptions that are called cognitive distortions.

Existential psychology attributes worries and fears to wrong perceptions regarding the existential issues of death, freedom, isolation and meaning. Despite the universality of existential fears, human beings perceive experiences and face them in their own way. Some choose to ignore them altogether by developing defensive mechanisms, thus further aggravating the consequences. Most commonly, people choose to ignore reality and to live in illusions. For example, to face the fear of death some form the illusion that it is of no concern to them because a Savior will always be there to save them. Others, in order to withstand the responsibility that the exercise of free will entails, refrain from desiring and instead prefer to follow the desires of others, by living through them. Sometimes people adopt fatalism, accepting the view that everything is supposedly prescribed by fate and the stars and that there is no reason to want, nor try. The only way out of the vicious circle of these unsubstantiated fears is to combine scientific knowledge with a sound philosophy of life.

The physical reactive mechanism to worries and fears is the same, irrespective of the source: Worry → Risk perception → Stress → Defensive mechanism. In other words, when a stimulus is perceived by the brain, it is assessed with regard to its impact on our life. If a risk is detected, then anxiety is caused and the defense mechanism of the brain is triggered in order to protect life.

Worries and fears in the Epicurean Philosophy

Epicurus dealt extensively with both the worries that originate from going after extravagance and luxury, as well as with the existential fears that arise from the prospect of death and the punishment of the gods. He argued in his *Letter to Menoeceus* that the main source of misery in humans are the worries that stem from wrong perceptions. He claimed that we should use sober reasoning, search out the grounds for every choice and avoidance, and banish those beliefs through which the greatest tumults take possession of the soul. The worst among the faulty perceptions is the one that supports that there are higher goods than pleasure, such as wealth, honor, admiration. According to a *Vatican Saying:* "The soul neither rids itself of disturbance nor gains a worthwhile joy through the possession of greatest wealth, nor by the honor and admiration bestowed by the crowd."

A happy life requires knowing the wealth of Nature. This is our teacher who affirms that to live happily we need few and easily acquired natural pleasures. Once the necessary desires are satisfied, we experience a complete absence of worries and fears.

Simple natural desires bring peace of mind, thanks to their low cost and the ease of securing them. On the contrary, excessive desires for the acquisition of wealth and other non-natural and non-necessary means are constant sources of concerns and anxiety. Another Principal Doctrine reiterates that the wealth required by nature is limited and is simple to procure; but the wealth required by vain ideas extends to infinity. An obvious way to reduce worries is to remove the excessive desires.

In the modern world, the main sources of worries are reflected through consumerism (wealth) and politics (fame, power) to which we will turn to in the following chapters. Existential fears are diachronic. Epicurus addressed the fears of punishment by the gods and death extensively in order to ease the pains of the people. We will come to these in the following chapters.

Rounding the chapter off, modern psychology approaches worries and fears from different perspectives, attributing to them, among others, the suppression of the instincts, distortion of reasoning, existential uncertainties, and wrong perceptions. In the Epicurean Philosophy, the origin of worries is attributed to wrong perceptions and, in particular, to false opinion that there are higher goods than pleasure. The main sources of worries today are reflected through consumerism (wealth) and politics (fame, power). The existential fears remain more or less the same: death, god, and the meaning of life.

CHAPTER 22

THE WORRY OF CONSUMERISM AND WEALTH

"Do not spoil what you have
by desiring what you do not have;
but remember that what you have
now was once among the things
you only hoped for."

Epicurus, *Vatican Saying XXXV*

Experience shows that some of the conflicts among philosophies arise due to the vague meaning of some of the crucial words that define them. The need for the clarity of words was realized and emphasized by Epicurus in his letter to Herodotus: "In the first place you must understand what it is that words denote...for the primary signification of every term employed must be clearly seen, and ought to need no proving."

The problem of the misinterpretation of words started

right from the beginning of the philosophical inquiries, regarding the meaning of the word "happiness," which is often used to denote the purpose of life. For Epicurus, happiness is a psychological state—it is to feel good and not feel bad—while for Plato, Aristotle and the other idealists, ancient and modern alike, happiness means achieving goals or living according to certain principles.

We will show that this vagueness in the meaning of the word happiness has huge consequences for the lives of individuals and political systems.

The Epicurean Philosophy on consumption and wealth

To follow our feelings, as Epicurus suggests, implies to be aware of the impulses sent by our nature and nurture. These are tantamount to our natural needs and desires, just as the bodily needs are for food, shelter, health; the psychological for security, friendship; and the spiritual for knowledge. Each need has inherent limits. The upper one is reached in the removal of the pain associated with it, as Epicurus explains when he says that the magnitude of pleasure reaches its limit in the removal of all pain. When such pleasure is present, so long as it is uninterrupted, there is no pain either of body or of the mind or of both together. For example, the upper limit of satisfying hunger is a plate of food, of shelter—a home, and so on. Once the pain from the absence of food and shelter is removed, we feel fine and have no motive to add any more to it.

Along with the upper limit, there is natural lower limit too. In order to live, we have to satisfy at least our natural bodily needs and cover the necessary expenses of the public life: "There is also a limit to simple living, and he who fails to understand this, falls into an error as great as that of the man who gives way to extravagance," asserts Epicurus. Although these expenses are as low as possible, they may be high enough to some, especially when the economy is in a downturn.

In short, the necessary needs for living happily are limited in number, have limits, and are easily procured. That is to say, the cost involved in satisfying them is bounded, thus limiting consumption expenses to a restrained level. We can be happy with little money and wealth, few possessions, close family ties, friendships and pleasurable activities.

Idealistic philosophies on consumption and wealth

For the average person, the word "happiness" carries an emotional weight, and therefore it is misleading when used in the idealistic model of life. For this reason, Aristotle instead used the terms "eudaemonia" or "well-being," which combine the logical values of virtue and reason and express the state of things that a person can achieve or is willing to be. The other idealistic goals of life range from ideals to wealth–acquiring knowledge, being faithful, nationalist, successful, wealthy, powerful, famous, and so on, endlessly. Their common feature is that they have no thresholds. They can vary from zero to infinity.

The weakness of logic to set limits on thoughts renders it an easy prey of religions, official institutions, underground groups, demagogues and charlatans who use it to manipulate the preferences and the perceptions of the multitude. Consumption and wealth are examples. Driven by the influences of the environment, our reasonable desires for more constantly outstrip what we already have. Whatever we get, we will always want more. There is no point at which we can say enough is enough. The end of avarice and ambition, of the pursuit of wealth and power and preeminence is vanity, not ease or pleasure. It is vanity founded upon the belief that our being should be the object of attention and approbation.

The Consumerist philosophy

The urbanization of life over the last century cut people off from their cultural roots, traditions and family relations, causing an existential gap. To bridge it, they unconsciously turned to the easiest means that they had at their disposal, which was none other than consumption. Much research shows that this unconscious need for consumption was cultivated and boosted by the business community with the contribution of the state. Societies gradually began to adopt a new culture characterized by excessive and redundant necessities, which could never be met. The aspirations of entrepreneurs for profit, and of governments for economic growth, may have been achieved, but their effect on the psychological health of the people and the environment has been quite negative.

Advertising influences the behavior and the psychological profile of modern humans by formatting a materialist culture in which we all are perpetually consumers. To cultivate a consumerist mentality, advertisers promote the artificial image of an ideal consumerist model in which authentic human needs and desires are substituted by manufactured ones. New products are produced daily and advertisers use all of their means to create purchasing awareness for them. At first they try to degrade the capabilities of the products we own so as to provoke feelings of inadequacy and low esteem, which they reckon will provoke us to purchase their products. They know that misery and materialism are mutually complemented and reinforce each other. For many people, television is, unfortunately, their main means of contact with the outside world. Thus, TV presenters can shape political opinions; dramas and sitcoms, social values; and commercial advertising, consumer behavior. Advertisers bombard people daily with hundreds of messages to promote consumer products. They are not content with exaggerations and perversions of the truth, and they often resort to outright lies. Their strategy is based on the recipe that by frequent repetition, no matter how absurd something is, people will believe it.

The cost of the consumerist mania from a psychological, economic and social perspective has been exorbitant.

Being instilled by the consumerist culture, we try to meet all our needs through the acquisition of material goods, but in vain. Empirical findings confirm the results of research showing that the relationship between consumption and happiness is minor because the attempt to satisfy excessive consumption demands inevitably leads to overtime work, minimum free time, limited family time, less friendly and social relations, and less opportunities to enjoy ourselves. Few people have realized that they could be happier if they cut down on their consumption demands. We buy and consume in an attempt to obtain a meaningful life, claim researchers on human happiness, adding that although people insist that it is work that gives meaning to their life, they really mean consumption. The excessive pursuit of money to obtain consumer goods rarely brings satisfaction. Studies show that money has a positive effect on happiness if it is earned through joyful activities, and not if it is used as a means to other ends. Besides, experience shows us that we rarely manage to earn money if we start with this purpose in mind, while if we do something because we love and enjoy it, we will do it with passion and enthusiasm, and we will most probably succeed in it and earn money.

Positive psychology argues that people are prone to consumption because it is the easiest way to feel happy. It is the road that requires minor effort. But the satisfaction they get does not lead to continuous happiness because its effects are transient, and they diminish after a short while. Instead, psychologists support that genuine happiness, is achieved by pursuing intangible pleasures, such as those that come from family relations, friendships and enjoyable activities. These seem hard to pursue if we are nurtured with the prototype of materialistic welfare.

Compared to a few years ago, today we have many more cars, and we go out more often. But, are we happier?

Recent research has shown that today we have products and services of all sorts, big-screen TVs, microwaves, and wireless handsets at our disposal. But we are not happier than people in the past, and we may be less happy. Compared to our grandparents, we've grown up with much more prosperity, but less happiness and a much greater risk of depression.

Research shows that the wealth gained in recent decades was not accompanied by any increase in personal well-being. It seems that the relationship between mood and materialism is complex, as researchers are still trying to determine if materialism is the thing that causes misery or the other way round.

Those who maintain that materialism is the root of unhappiness argue that to satisfy our excessive consumption desires, we are forced to work more. Thus, the free time left for activities contributing to happiness is minimal. Likewise, we hold high materialistic goals that require structuring our whole life toward the success of our goals, showing no interest in other activities more conducive to happiness. Furthermore, we have high materialistic expectations that are mostly infeasible to attain, and they often cause feelings of inadequacy, guilt, and anxiety. We also use materialism as a measure of success and buy anything that passes through our minds in order to acquire the symbols of wealth and power to prove to ourselves and others that we have achieved our goals and are successful.

On the other hand, some studies show that material goods are neither bad nor good. It all depends on the role and position they have in our lives. The key is to find a workable balance so as to enjoy material goods, but not at the expense of what really matters for happiness.

Given that we all have the same consumerist culture, why do some people develop highly materialistic values while others do not? Research has shown that financial and emotional insecurity is at the heart of intense consumer desires. People become more materialistic so that they can cope with the bad things that happen in their lives when they are brought up in difficult social conditions, or live in poverty or under the threat of death. Additionally, the adolescents who reported having high materialistic values were poorer and had had less care from their mothers than those who expressed less materialistic values. Similarly, youths whose parents had divorced or had been in constant conflict were more prone to materialism than other young people who grew up under normal family conditions.

Does wealth bring about happiness? Psychologists and sociologists alike argue that wealth does not ensure happiness.

No matter how wealthy we are, wealth seems musty when it remains static for some time. The inherent tendency for adjustment makes it soon appear as average or even poor. An impulse urges us to seek something bigger, better or exceptional. People quickly get used to it and, frustrated with the current level of their wealth, set new goals, which when fulfilled, are followed by new, higher ones. They finally get caught in the vicious trap of their ever increasing expectations. The paradox of "growth expectations" precludes happiness because it endlessly shifts happiness to the future. People do not enjoy the pleasure of today with the expectation of enjoying more in the future.

The second reason that wealth does not guarantee happiness is the trend to compare our wealth to others', preferably to those who have more. Psychologists call this feeling "relative deprivation," meaning that we are worse off than others with whom we compare ourselves. As long as we compare ourselves with people who have more, no matter how much we have, the more likely it is that we feel we are lagging behind, and perhaps that we have basic shortages.

Some psychologists highlight an additional reason. They argue that the capitalist system offers consumers a wide variety of choices related to brand names and prices that create embarrassment and anxiety. An additional source of frustration is that any choice has, as an automatic consequence, the rejection of the rest, which creates both anxiety for the correctness of our choice and a sense of loss for the remaining neglected choices. This embarrassing feeling is the price we pay for the possibility of choosing. The more available choices, the greater the emotional cost will be. Researchers support that these feelings of embarrassment last for as long as it takes to create our personal "consumerist identity."

Last but not least, studies claim that people could live happier if, instead of focusing on the accumulation of wealth, they were concerned more with their internal culture. Unbridled selfishness has limited the development of happiness to such a degree that despite the fact that the real average income in the last fifty years has more than doubled, people are not happier. The probability of suffering from clinical depression is now ten times greater than a century ago. People are getting richer externally and more miserable internally.

Rich or poor, more or less materialistic, we are all nevertheless consumers. We buy food to eat, clothes to dress in, we go out to concerts, to watch movies, to have lunch, or to take art classes. Which of these expenses, though, contribute more to happiness? All research shows that the most positive effect on happiness is achieved when two conditions are taken into account. Firstly, to remain within our financial means, and secondly, to have many small experiences. In contrast, expenditure on consumer goods offers only temporary satisfaction.

In conclusion, in the Epicurean Philosophy, consumption has a maximum level that is associated with the pleasure we feel when the pain of the natural and necessary needs is removed. We can be happy with very little wealth and few possessions. In the idealistic philosophies, consumption has no limit because the "wants" of logic are limitless. For whatever we get, we will always want more. There is no point at which we can say enough is enough. The end point for this endless wanting is vanity. Advertisers work subtly to make us unhappy and unsatisfied. Wealth does not guarantee happiness, and this is supported by the syndromes of "growth expectations," "relative deprivation," and "consumerist identity." Everything works against us and leads us into a perpetual cycle of materialism. Many argue that they see work as a source of happiness, but this is not confirmed by experience because work has replaced traditional social activities and is closely linked to the desire of acquiring material goods. To enjoy the most positive effect that happiness can have on us means taking part in enjoyable experiences. Happiness is not an elusive butterfly. For the people who are trapped in consumerism and materialism though, it is often an unattainable goal.

CHAPTER 23

WORRIES ABOUT POLITICS, FAME
AND POWER

*"If you want to save the peace (of
your mind) and your humanity, stay
away from politics. Make your own
state, which will give you what the
official cannot."*

Epicurus

All the theories that refer to civic participation in politics,
from Aristotle to Rousseau and to the contemporary Sen,
highlight the feeling of pleasure that the participants in
public affairs enjoy. The empirical evidence of the Athenian
participatory democracy and of the subsequent participatory processes at a local level confirm these theoretical
analyses. In addition, personal participatory experiences
in professional and social activities support the view that

political participation has positive effects on prosperity. And yet, the findings of surveys at a European level suggest that the participation of European citizens in politics is minimal. How is this discrepancy between theory and practice explained? Why do European citizens show such a limited interest in public affairs?

Political participation in Ancient Greece

The concept of politics that had been forged in Ancient Greece was marked by the historical appearance of the independent city-state and the diversity of constitutions that prevailed in them. The city was connected with the cutting edge of human civilization and was the primary location for the integration of human pursuits. It was the place that gave people the possibility to cooperate in the search for the "good life," but it was also a place of confrontation, when their aspirations conflicted. The philosophies of the time dealt extensively with politics, with arguments concerning its usefulness, on who could participate in it and why—arguments that were used in the debates for ideological and material dominance and control.

These conflicts centered around the idea of justice, as it had evolved from the archaic period through the works of Homer. Justice was conceived by poets, legislators and philosophers as an advantageous structure for all categories of citizens, rich and poor, strong and weak, because it excludes the possibility of exploitation of man by man. So justice was considered the prerequisite for the equality of citizens, and it was believed to be the condition by which human political systems could be accepted by the gods. Politics evolved on the foundation of justice and allowed for the search for happiness and success, which in turn allowed for competition within the city walls. Justice addressed citizens as equals. However, the concept of equality was a major political issue that differentiated the democratic from the oligarchic regimes. The oligarchic regimes considered only those who belonged to the rich elite as equals. Those considered equal in democratic constitutions were all the men that were natives and free.

But slaves had no rights in any scheme, and neither did women. The exclusion of the Athenian women from active citizenship was a noticeable distinction that was a source of inspiration for stories of female domination acted out in comedies and tragedies. Among the equals, no matter how they were defined, there existed a political space for participation in counseling, decision-making and action. This invention was the hallmark of the classical Greek world. Citizens, the few, usually the rich, or the many, including the poorer, participated in the exercise of public affairs.

All modern discussions that consider political participation a good action, are attributed directly or not to Aristotle. In his analyses of politics, he stressed that "a state is not a simple society that lives in a common place, founded on crime prevention and for the sake of mutual exchange," but rather a community of families united in prosperity, for the sake of a perfect and self-sufficient life. Aristotle appreciated political participation only to the extent that it was an expression of virtue. Without it, participation in politics was assessed on the basis of expediencies. In his work on politics, he wrote that man is by nature an animal intended to live in a city. He then added that the aim of the city is to ensure the good quality of character of its members and also that all those included in this are free from injustice and from any form of evil. Hence, any true city must be dedicated to the purpose of encouraging goodness.

According to Aristotle, by living according to the laws of a good state, the citizens help the development of justice, kindness and the good quality of their characters. Aristotle proposed active participation in politics purely for its own sake. The description of the citizen, as debating and judging and participating in turn in the administration of the state by taking into account the interests of others, set the basis for later thinkers to construct a theory for the educational value of participation in political processes. In other parts of his work on politics, Aristotle supported that the participation of the many in decision-making improves the quality and the effectiveness of the decisions. Then he asked the excruciating question: "Which way of life is more desirable to anyone: to join the other citizens and take a share in the activities of the city, or to live in it as a stranger, free from the ties of civil society?" Aristotle also put into the intellectual agenda of the Western world the idea that the government's aim is to develop the character of the people. His views followed the Greek conception of man being formed by the city, developing his full potential, with joint responsibility for the laws under which he lives.

The philosophical views of Plato for an ideal state and government had significant social impact. Some of his most famous doctrines are contained in *The Republic*, the *Laws* and the *Statesman*. Plato, through the words of Socrates, argued that societies have a tripartite class structure, symbolizing the corresponding social classes, the productive, the protective and the administrative. The productive class includes the working men, the workers, carpenters, plumbers, masons, merchants, farmers, and stockbreeders, which are represented by the belly and the "appetite." The protective class includes the warriors and guards who are bold, strong and brave, and are represented by the chest and correspond to the "spirit." The administrative class are the rulers or the philosopher kings, who are intelligent, rational, autonomous, in love with wisdom, suitable for decision-making. These are few and are represented by the head, corresponding to "logic." Relying on this model, Plato rejected the principles of the Athenian democracy because he argued that the many, who participate in the democratic administration, do not have the ability to rule. Few people have the capacity for administration. The "philosopher kings" combine logic and wisdom. Plato argued that until philosophers govern as kings, or those who are now kings learn to philosophize, that is, until politics and philosophy coincide absolutely, cities will have no rest from evils, and neither will the human race.

In the context of the Hellenistic kingdoms created under the dominion of the Macedonians and Romans, significant negative developments were encountered in classical political thought and practice. The cynical philosophers totally denied the role of the city, the Epicureans avoided political involvement, and the skeptical philosophers did not take sides. Only the Stoics approved of participation in political life, combining cynical and platonic ideas. According to the Stoics, a city is a system among humans that has a stronger association than that required by law. This compound is determined by logic which provides the standard of right or wrong–suggesting to natural political animals the things to be done and the discarding of things they should not do. However this has not happened, nor will it ever be in human societies. According to this statement, we would assume that the Stoics would hold a negative attitude towards active citizenship. On the contrary, the Stoic Roman philosopher Seneca tells us that Zeno, the founder of the Stoa argued that a wise man will participate in politics, unless something prevents him. Both Zeno and later Chrysippus wrote that human behavior should be harmonized with the idea of a natural law generally expressed amid a commitment to law and order.

The political anchoritism of Epicureans

The Epicureans were characterized as anti-political thinkers, although their position was a more complex assessment of the origin and nature of politics. Politics for them was not a part of the good life or a means for the fulfillment of human nature, as it was for Aristotle. Instead of politics they respected justice because it serves utility. Justice for the Epicurean is desirable because it ensures protection and security, indispensable qualities for the peace of the soul that the city has to offer to the people.

Epicurus did not condemn the holding of public office; what he did condemn was making a career of it because it meant studying rhetoric and learning other unimportant subjects, placing our happiness at the mercy of others, making false friends, and trying to please the multitude. He used to say that he never wished to cater to the crowd; for what he knew, they did not approve of, and what they approved of, he did not know. However he also added that those who are aflame with desire and ambition, and cannot do otherwise, should follow their natural momentum for politics, asserting that doing nothing will upset and hurt them more than doing what they lust for.

The Epicurean wise man lives unnoticed, he does not deal with politics, except if a good reason arises, because he believes that the insecurities of life are better served by creating a group of friends. The Epicurean man will make no compromises to satisfy his aspirations, neither will he make false friendships, nor will he flatter the public, sacrificing the truth. He will be involved in politics only when critical conditions require doing so and when he cannot ensure his mental peace otherwise. Unfortunately, the books of

Epicurus on politics have not survived, and we learn about his opinion from third-party sources, such as from the militant attacks on his philosophy by Plutarch, the historian of the 1st century AD. He blamed Epicurus for irresponsibility and a complacent attitude toward politics. The Epicureans responded that their philosophy, the organizational structure of the Garden, and their exemplary behavior offer an alternative model of social organization that inspires people and supports the values of justice, friendship, wisdom and financial solidarity.

Epicurus was not the first philosopher who avoided the fury of political engagement. The cynical philosopher, the so called "Dog," Diogenes, preceded him. He had adopted a primitive life, far removed from the social and political conventions. These excesses, though, were repellent to Epicurus, who believed that a form of government was necessary to safeguard justice and security. At the same time, he also rejected the views of Protagoras, Plato and Aristotle, that the state was the father, and the laws the teachers. Epicurus was more attracted by the idea of the Hippocratic medical fraternity. This is what he referred to when he said that as medicine is useful because it heals the wounds of the body, so is philosophy helpful because it heals the wounds of the soul. Accordingly, he believed that, as medicine offers its services to all who have physical pains without bothering about their political expediency, so philosophy must address all of mankind without getting involved in political considerations.

First among philosophers, it was Epicurus who embraced all humans by showing the natural way to happiness. He started his mission with his own paradigm, which he meant to spread to friends and acquaintances in every house, village, and city. According to Nietzsche, Epicurus' philosophy presented similarities to the Christianity of the first centuries because both addressed the poor and the frightened. The purpose of the Epicurean Philosophy of healing the soul enfolded all people, men and women of all ages, rich and poor alike. His humanistic approach was described by one of his students when he claimed that the whole Earth is one country, the home of all, and all the world is a family. The same perspective is expressed by his poet friend Menander: "I am a man. I think that anything concerning mankind concerns me." Epicurus saw citizens as free individuals in a society beyond the local political boundaries of the city-state.

Using Nature as a measure for a happy life required equality, purity, honesty and empathy. Thus, Epicurus valued good company and set friendship as a condition for happiness. The need for good friends, in turn, gave increased importance to the virtues of moderation, kindness and solidarity.

According to Epicurus, the ideal model government was the minimum one that could ensure justice and the security of its citizens. This view was brought back after many centuries by John Locke, and later by the renowned Epicurean politician, Thomas Jefferson, who set the notions of security and happiness as key targets of the government in the Declaration of Independence of The United States of America.

The political affiliations of the Epicurean and idealistic philosophies

The preceding analysis on consumption and wealth presents convincing arguments that explain the political affiliations of the two rival philosophies. We see that on the one hand, the Epicurean Philosophy aims at feeling good at an affordable cost, and on the other hand, the idealistic philosophies aim at self-fulfillment and success. Therefore, in the Natural Philosophy of Epicurus, the "needs and wants" have natural limits that are set by the emotions, while in the idealistic philosophies there are no internal stop mechanisms set on logic. Therefore, the idealistic "needs and wants" are boundless and inevitably lead to a competitive, stressful life, suitable to ambitious people, eager for power, wealth and fame.

The Epicurean philosophical model suggests a life of pleasure, achievable by all. Pleasure opens to a world of delights and human relationships we may not yet even have dreamed of. This is a joyful life combining friendship, self-reliance and optimism.

The differences in lifestyle of the two major philosophies define, to a large extent, their political affiliations and justify the kinship of the status quo to the idealistic philosophies, and the polemic against the Epicurean

Natural Philosophy. Unfortunately the status quo managed to pass the perceptions that serve its interest to the majority of people, who act thereafter against their own interests without realizing it. This explains why people are well off and, at the same time, dissatisfied and anxious. Epicurus realized the intentions and practices of the status quo of the time and proclaimed that we must free ourselves from the prison of public education and politics.

Politics is in the jurisdiction of god

The dominance of Christianity imposed the view that the issue of human rights is the responsibility of the Church and god. In the Christian tradition, the notion of justice requires inner moral transformation and no political interference.

The social contract of Rousseau

After the lapse of many dark centuries of religious domination, politics and participation reappeared in the 18th century through Rousseau. He had to restep back to ancient Greece to revive the long forgotten notions of civic involvement in public affairs. He revived the claims of Aristotle that the job of politics is to make individuals fair, and that the political system of a country affects the character of its citizens. Rousseau added that the habit of acting in accordance with the common interest should be engraved in the citizens' hearts. To do this, we need good laws, a political philosophy that promotes social unity, and for the citizens to love their duty and to be bound by some unity of origin, interest or contract. Moreover, for Rousseau, citizens must be relatively equal. No citizen should be rich enough to buy another, and none poor enough to be forced to sell him.

For Rousseau, through the sincere acceptance of the priority of the public over the individual good, people get a new identity, become members of a larger whole, and realize the fulfillment of the law, not as a constraint, but as a spontaneous expression of themselves. According to Rousseau, only politics can bring justice to humanity, allowing people to act, not compassionately, but morally. However justice is intertwined with private property; private property implies inequality; inequality causes burdensome comparison; and burdensome comparison degrades the quality of humanity. To counter this, he argued that citizens had to reach the point of wanting the public good. Only when they place public interest above their own can the degradation associated with the political life be combated to fulfill its moral promise. Rousseau formed his political ideals not only from Athens and Rome, but also from Geneva and the Swiss communities, which in his days made decisions democratically through direct popular meetings. Having seen the people of Geneva and of the rural areas of Switzerland in local assemblies, Rousseau argued that it was unlikely that these people would be fooled by demagogic tricks and external influences. He added that as long as they understood and acted in accordance with their real interests, and were protected by the laws and the constitution, the smooth functioning of the participatory processes was guaranteed.

The positive effects of political participation

After Rousseau came the French political thinker and historian Alexis de Tocqueville who argued that participation in making democratic decisions develops the character of the individual. Alexis de Tocqueville was one of the greatest political thinkers of the 19th century, and one of the most authentic and profound exponents of the liberal tradition. His position was a reflection of the intellectual currents of his time, but also of his experiences of the town meetings of New England, where he had the same experience of face-to-face democracy that Rousseau had in Switzerland. The town meetings, De Tocqueville wrote, were for freedom what primary schools were for science. He believed the same for the involvement of lay jurors in courts, one of the most explicit forms of participation: "I do not know if a jury is useful for the parties; but I am certain it is highly beneficial to those who decide the litigation; and I look upon it as one of the most efficacious means for the education of the people which society can employ."

The British philosopher and economist John Stuart Mill embraced and supported the arguments of Alexis de Tocqueville, highlighting the positive effects of political participation on a person's character. Mill argued that political participation promotes all three forms of individual development, namely virtue, intellectual stimulation and motivation. Individual development has to do with caring about public interest and not the selfish interests of the individual; intellectual development has to do with originality and intellectual stimulation and motivation with the courage to take initiatives. He argued that the ideal form of government is one in which citizens have a voice that reaches the government and are, at least occasionally, invited to participate actively in governance by personally fulfilling a public function, locally or generally.

The way in which John Stuart Mill raised the issue of political participation in one of his essays on Alexis de Tocqueville is worth mentioning in detail: "It has often been said, and requires to be repeated still more often, that books and discourse alone are not education; that life is a problem, not a theorem: that action can only be learnt in action. A child learns to write its name only by a succession of trials; and is a man to be taught to use his mind and guide his conduct by mere precept? What can be learnt in schools is important, but not all-important. The main branch of the education of human beings is their habitual employment; which must be either their individual vocation, or some matter of general concern, in which they are called to take part. The private money-getting occupation of almost everyone is more or less a mechanical routine; it brings but few of his faculties into action, while its exclusive pursuit tends to fasten his attention and interest exclusively upon himself, and upon his family as an appendage of himself; making him indifferent to the public, to the more generous objects and the nobler interests, and, in his inordinate regard for his personal comforts, selfish and cowardly. Balance these tendencies by contrary ones; give him something to do for the public, whether as a vestryman, a juryman, or an elector; and, in that degree, his ideas and feelings are taken out of this narrow circle. He becomes acquainted with more varied business and a larger range of considerations. He is made to feel that besides the interests which separate him from his fellow-citizens, he has interests which connect him to them that not only the common weal is his weal, but that it partly depends upon his exertions."

The proponents of the idea of political participation argue that people are not only interested in the final results of the decisions affecting them, but also in the way they are taken. Participation in decisions gives the participants a sense of freedom, autonomy, equality, justice. It boosts self-esteem. It gives identity. It indicates that they belong somewhere, that they are members of a real community united by affinity and ties of kinship.

The Indian economist and philosopher Amartya Sen argues that the participation in decision-making that affects the lives of the participants as well as of other people, is fundamental to the welfare of society. Being able to achieve something important through political action is one of the few freedoms of the people that produce value in life, says Sen. As an example of such participatory practices, he mentions the decisions that are taken at a local level in Brazil that enable the distribution of public funds to disadvantaged poor areas.

The indifference of Europeans for political participation

Although theoretical literature presents a number of reasons as to why political participation increases the happiness of individuals, research does not confirm these estimates. It leaves serious doubts as to whether the standard forms of participation, as provided for in a modern representative democracy, have a positive impact on life satisfaction. The citizens of the European Union rank political participation low on the list of social relations that they consider important in their lives. Family relationships are their first priority, followed by work, friends, volunteering and religion. According to the 2006 survey on Political Participation in the European Union, 79% of respondents reported that they vote, 13% participate in political meetings and 9% communicate with relevant government agencies on policy issues. Thus, the average European citizen is a voter, but has little active policy participation.

The exercise of politics in modern democracies belongs to the exclusive competence of the government. Citizens have no opportunities to participate in governance and therefore, they have neither the power to promote their economic prosperity in a direct way, nor any chance to feel the enjoyment of active citizenship. In the constitutions of the modern world, people pin their fortunes on the government, for a period of four or five years, blankly, without any control, no matter what happens. Their participation in public life begins and ends with voting for the government. It is a purely passive form of participation, for which both the theoretical analyses and research show that instead of joy, it often leads to disappointment and embarrassment. The first reason for this is that the citizens realize that no matter what government is elected, the financially strong hold on or expand their wealth, at the expense of the poor, in the name of economic growth. The second reason is the violation of election commitments from the parties upon taking office. When a citizen sees that his party fails to be elected or, when it is elected, acts contrary to campaign promises or against his interests, he is actually less satisfied than someone who did not vote. He feels embarrassed and frustrated for the time and energy he spent in the political processes. This negative effect of participation is more pronounced in the developing world and in the emerging democracies, where the party elected to government changes its policies a short time after the elections, implementing a completely different policy than that for which the citizens have struggled.

The above considerations lead to the conclusion that citizens often refrain from active engagement in politics because there are hardly any such available provisions in the parliamentary constitutions, and also because the political parties, when elected, forget the policies they had proclaimed before the elections.

In summary, the implementation of participatory processes started in classical Athens and culminated in the era of Pericles. The administrative mode of the city-state favored the application of participatory practices, but under the domination of the Macedonians and the Romans, this was not feasible. With the advent of Christianity and the prevalence of theocratic views on social and political life, the concept of political participation was forgotten for many centuries and reappeared after the Renaissance. Although the theoretical analyses support the benefits of political participation, both for citizens and the state, research does not confirm it. Citizens refrain from active participation in politics, and this is explained by the fact that participation is hardly foreseen by the constitution of a parliamentary democracy and also by the experience of parties elected to government that violate their electoral commitments. Passive participation in politics in the form of voting for the government deprives citizens of both the enjoyment provided by the participatory processes, and the ability to promote their prosperity in a direct way. The Epicurean wise man does not deal with politics, except if a good reason arises.

CHAPTER 24

THE FEAR OF DEATH

"Death is nothing to us; for that which has been dissolved into its elements experiences no sensations, and that which has no sensation is nothing to us."

Epicurus, *Principal Doctrine II*

Of all the fears that oppress humans, none compare to the fear of death. Its prospect causes panic attacks even to those who do not face an immediate danger of death. By instinct, we believe that we will continue to live forever. If we did not see people dying around us, we would never come to the realization of the existence of death. Reality makes us face it in order to provide a way out of the terror that is caused by the prospect of the end of life.

The idealistic and religious approaches to death

Seeking an illusion to overcome death, people have sought legacy–by having children, for example, in order to live through their offspring. The richest ones erected monuments as a testimony of their life. The lure of eternal life was projected as a fair reward to the faithful for their religious devotion. And yet, there are those who wait for a drug discovery to conquer eternal youth. Another category of people cultivates the idea of the immortality of the soul, arguing that the soul does not follow the body in death and disintegration but continues to exist after life. The idea of a perishable material body and an immaterial soul has its roots in the Orphic faith. Subsequently, it was adopted by Pythagoras and Plato, who connected the immortality of the soul to reincarnation. Of interest is the narration of a story in *The Republic* of Plato, according to which, as if by magic on the twelfth day after his death, the son of Arminius returned to life and recounted the secrets of the other world. He described how after he had died, he went with others to the place of Judgment and saw the souls returning from heaven. The souls went together to a place where a new life was chosen for both humans and animals. There he saw the soul of Orpheus going into a swan, of Tamyras into a nightingale, and the soul of Atalanta into an athlete. He saw men turning into animals, wild and tamed animals converted into each other. After selecting the souls, they drank the waters of Lethe and flew away like stars to be born.

Aristotle argued that what is immaterial and immortal in man is the mind. He argued that unlike other organs, the mind does not have an established place in the body, because if it did, it would also be sensitive to a small number of stimuli like the eye, which due to its nature is sensitive to light but not to sound, and the ear, which is sensitive to sound but not to light. The mind, however, is different.

The Christian view of death is based on the dualism of the soul and body, according to which the soul is different from the body, but inseparably connected to it. The vast majority of Christians believe in some kind of heaven in which believers will enjoy the presence of god, the absence of suffering and eternal peace. A smaller proportion of Christians believe in the existence of hell, where the unbelievers and sinners are punished. Opinions differ as to whether hell is eternal, and punishment is mental or physical. Some Christians reject this idea completely. Catholics also believe in purgatory, a place of temporary punishment for Christians that die with sins they have not confessed to.

Islam, like Christianity, teaches the continued existence of the soul after death in a transformed physical existence. Muslims believe that there will be a Day of Judgment when all people will be divided between the eternal destinations of paradise and hell. A central tenet of the Koran is the day on which the world will be destroyed, and Allah will resurrect all people to be judged. The resurrection will take place on the last day and god will recreate the rotten body. The Koran mentions two exceptions to the general rule:

the "warriors" who die in god's name, who immediately enter his protection, and the "enemies of Islam," who are immediately sentenced to hell.

Buddhism sees death as an awakening or rebirth, a pass in the sphere of the flowering of the final nature of the mind. A Buddhist considers death as the breaking of the material of which the body is comprised. Death and regeneration are likened to the flame of a candle that lights another. When the flame of the burning candle touches the wick of a non-burning one, the light passes from the first candle to the next, and although the actual flame of the first candle is not transferred to the second, it is responsible for its lighting. Buddhism emphasizes that beyond the variations of this life all are, and still remain, alive.

During the Renaissance, this view of dualism continued to hold. The most modern versions came from the *Meditations on First Philosophy* of Rene Descartes, wherein the idea that there are two kinds of substances is developed: the mass that is present in space and the mind that thinks and is intangible and immortal.

The realistic and scientific view of death

According to modern psychology, death is the most obvious ultimate concern as it is obvious to everyone that it will come, and there is no escape from it. To cope with the terror of death, people usually use two types of defense mechanisms. The first is an absurd belief in the "personal specificity" of each person's death that is determined by the will of god, and the second is an "irrational faith" in the existence of an "Absolute Savior." In the first mechanism, despite the fact that people recognize the folly of this belief, they unconsciously believe that the simple laws of biology do not apply to them, and they will never die. This defense is an illusion, a groundless and irrational belief that when weakened gives its place to clinical syndromes, like those of a narcissistic character or compulsive workaholic, in search of glory and paranoia. The other important defense mechanism is based on faith in the existence of a "Savior", of a personal, omnipotent, servant friend, who protects one's welfare eternally, who even when one reaches the brink will keep the believer from falling. Immoderate use of this mechanism results in a character with elements of passiveness, dependence and servility. Often these individuals dedicate their lives to locating the distal rescuer, who may be god, the Virgin, or the saints. It is an ideology of life that precedes and paves the way for clinical depression. These people are well adapted to life when they feel the presence of the dominant "Other," but they collapse abruptly when they lose it.

The pragmatic view accepts death as a fact in the existence of living organisms that marks the definitive end of life. Death causes permanent cessation of the biological functions of the body, and its organic components are decomposed by microorganisms. The residues left are recycled and return to the food chain for reuse.

The Darwinian theory of the survival of the fittest sees

death as an important part of the process of natural selection. It considers that the organisms less adapted to the environment die sooner than the more adjustable ones, and therefore, they run a greater risk of extinction. This theory also argues that the rate of reproduction and the number of children born play an equally important role to the survival of the species. According to Darwin's criteria, an organism that dies young but leaves numerous offspring has much greater survivability than a long-lived organism leaving only one descendant.

In recent years the theory of dualism put forward by religions was challenged by the American philosopher John R. Searle who argued that the mind and body are not separate substances, as claimed by Rene Descartes. They both have a biological texture, and therefore, both are mortal. Afterwards, the neuroscientists Joseph E. LeDoux and Antonio Damazio experimentally demonstrated the single physical nature of the body and soul, and thereby confirmed their mortality. In its vast majority, the scientific community nowadays accepts the final end of physical and mental life as death.

The Epicurean view of death

Epicurus proposed, as one of his main tasks, to redeem people from the fear of death. His position was that life flows within us without thinking of ever stopping. If at any time it stops, we are indifferent because we ourselves will not feel it. He claimed that when we die, we will be as we were before we were born. According to Epicurus, the definitive end of life by death was a consequence of the physical nature of the body and soul. For that reason, he argued it would be better if we recognize aging as the normal course of life and not as a curse, and also, if we recognize and explicitly accept mortality. Anyone who denies the reality of death also denies himself the ability to live well. It is much better to accept that it is not feasible to add years to our life and to try to add life to our years.

The acceptance of the reality of death led the Epicureans to try to lighten the fears that the expectation of death creates. They put forth a series of logical arguments to support that if we enjoy the pleasures of life while we live and avoid pain, we will have nothing to fear. Epicurus wrote that death is nothing to us, saying that which has been dissolved into its elements experiences no sensations, and that which has no sensation is nothing to us. It is known that the Roman Epicureans wore rings and pendants with the image of Epicurus on which they had engraved the words "death is nothing to us." Moreover, an Epicurean epigram wrote: "I was not, I was, I am not, I do not care." Another one added that we have been born once and cannot be born a second time; for all eternity we shall no longer exist, claiming also that although we are not in control of tomorrow, we postpone our happiness. Life is wasted by delaying, and each person dies amid worries. Yet another one said not to surrender as hostages to fortune or to any other circumstance; but when it is time to go, we would spit contempt on both vain life and those who cling to it. We will leave life singing aloud a glorious triumph-song saying how nicely we experienced it.

The Roman poet Lucretius gives an integrated view of death. His reference on death in his book *De Rerum Natura*, is considered a masterpiece, not only as a literary work, but also for a range of interrelated evidence that give a clear picture of death. Asks Lucretius:

"What hast thou: o mortal, so much at heart, that thou goest such lengths in sickly sorrows? Why bemoan and bewail death? For say thy life past and gone has been welcome to thee and thy blessings have not all, as if they were poured into a perforated vessel, run through and been lost without avail? Why not then take thy departure like a guest filled with life, and with resignation, thou fool, enter upon untroubled rest? But if all that thou hast enjoyed has been squandered and lost, and life is a grievance, why seek to make any addition, to be wasted perversely in its turn and lost utterly without avail? Why not rather make an end of life and travail? For there is nothing more which I can contrive and discover for thee to give pleasure: all things are ever the same... If however one of greater age and more advanced in years should complain and lament, poor wretch, his death more than is right, would she not with greater cause raise her voice and rally him in sharp accents: away from this time forth with thy tears, rascal; a truce to thy complaining: thou decayest after full enjoyment of all the prizes of life. But because thou ever yearnest for what is not present, and despisest what is, life has slipped from thy grasp unfinished and unsatisfying, and or ever thou thoughtest, death has taken his stand at thy pillow, before thou canst take thy departure sated and filled with good things. Now however resign all things unsuited to thy age, and with a good grace up and greatly go: thou must."

Epicurus in confronting death

Historical accounts attest to the exemplary attitude of the Epicureans before death. Diogenes Laertius describes how Epicurus fared well at the end of his life in his seventieth year, dying with the same peace that he had lived. Ermarchos announced that he died of a stone that caused urinary retention, after an illness that lasted a fortnight. And finally, he joined the brass tub with warm water, he asked to drink a little neat wine, urged his friends to remember his teaching and after that, he took his last breath telling everyone to rejoice and remember the doctrines. Elsewhere Diogenes Laertius quotes an excerpt of the letter sent by Epicurus to his friend Idomeneus, saying that his last day was happy, and even though the constant pains from dysuria and dysentery had surpassed all previous records, he encountered them with the joy he felt in his soul in recalling a discussion they'd had.

The death of loved ones

No matter how prepared we are to face the possibility of our own death, we need greater courage when we find ourselves in front of the death of our beloved ones. But no matter how painful the feeling of mourning is, Epicurus tried to address it by recalling that the gifts of love and friendship do not end with death because the pleasant feelings find their way after death through memories. And indeed, the Epicureans had established ceremonies in memory of loved ones that had left life; in place of melancholy memorials were cheerful celebrations, that praised the life of the deceased.

Using memories as a means to address the pain of difficult circumstances in life first appears in Epicurus. Through proper training of the mind, we can achieve vivid recollections of old and pleasant moments and get the feeling that we are reliving those experiences and the happiness that came with them. The implementation of this idea in modern times is described in the book *Man's search for meaning* by the Viennese psychiatrist Viktor Frankl, who spent four years in several concentration camps. Frankl writes that one of the few things that were able to give him a sense of happiness was to recall the image of his beloved wife and engage in an imaginary conversation with her, saying that his mind clung to his wife's image, imagining it with an uncanny acuteness. He claimed to have heard her answering him; saw her smile, her frank and encouraging look. He said that real or not, her look then was more luminous than the sun that was beginning to rise.

On suicide

There is another delicate issue associated with death, that of suicide. The ancient Epicureans defied death as being nothing, and they were not reluctant to part with life, if that was the only way of relief from an intolerable situation. In the case of a patient who was in his last days and an intentional death would shorten an unbearable pain, the Epicurean ethic would not exclude it. Conversely, the Epicureans categorically opposed putting an end to life out of frustration and sadness when there is still enough life to live for, claiming that however many the many legitimate reasons may be to terminate one's life, it would still not be enough to justify suicide. A very unpleasant situation could be reversed in the future, and it may also be the right time to rethink what has gone wrong and learn from the mistakes so as not to repeat them in the future. All people face crises and disappointments and sometimes they may be surprised by the unexpected turn of events, finding themselves trapped in the mistakes they have made. But that is life. Pain is the teacher that Nature gave us, so instead of remaining immersed in the past, we should rather learn to avoid similar mistakes in the future.

Conclusively, death is the second, after birth, most important event in life. Its prospect fills people with fear and insecurity, no matter if they pretend to have accepted it as the natural end of life. Religious views about a perishable material body and an immaterial imperishable soul have dominated human history, but they have not been confirmed by science and experience. Although the vast majority of people logically accept mortality, they maintain emotional inhibitions to accepting the mortality of the soul. The Epicurean view on the final end of life urges us, as best as possible, to exploit the limited time we have to live and additionally, to daily examine if by our own actions, we are seeking happiness. This is very eloquently expressed by the Epicurean Roman poet Horace in his odes when he says to be wise, strain the wine; and since life is brief, prune back far-reaching hopes! Even as we speak, envious time has passed; pluck the day, putting as little trust as possible in tomorrow.

CHAPTER 25

THE FEAR OF GOD

"It is pointless for a man to pray to the gods for that which he has the power to obtain by himself."

Epicurus, *Vatican Saying LXV*

The gods in antiquity

At the dawn of philosophy the Greek philosophers of Miletus in Ionia, Thales, Anaximander and Anaximenes tried to explain the nature of the world in physical terms. Later Heraclitus claimed that everything changes and nothing remains stable, while to Parmenides, god was a material being that extended to infinity. The Stoics believed that god was not a separate Being who created the world, but Nature itself. It was a living organism in which people were the cells. Each cell in this body realizes a specific purpose, determined by the Nature and logic.

Plato believed in a transcendental, unearthly god to

whom logic and the soul should be harmonized. For Plato, beyond the variable earthly world, there is a constant immutable world that has its headquarters in heaven, with the characteristics of superiority, nobility and perfection. The earthly world is an imperfect imitation of the heavenly. This assertion of Plato laid the foundations for the idealist philosophy and religions.

Aristotle recognized that everything in the world is in a state of flux, and behind every move, there is a chain of events that cause it. He argued that this chain of events should lead to something which moves them, but the same is also immovable. This is the driving power of all actions. It is a being with eternal life, god. This driving force causes the movement of others, acting on them not as a means, for example by giving a boost, but as an objective, as the teleology of motion. Aristotle thought that this driving power forces things to move by attraction, almost like a saucer with milk attracts a cat. Milk attracts the cat, but we cannot say that it moves it. Aristotle made god passively responsible for the changes in the world in the sense that all things seek divine perfection. God infuses all things with an aim and purpose, which lays open its divine presence. God, the highest being, is concerned only with himself. Consequently he neither knows the world nor does he care at all for it, being an immovable mover. This perfect and unchanging god is the culmination of existence and knowledge. God's activity is the thought of himself, because nothing else concerns him.

According to the new Platonic philosopher Plotinus, god is the source of the universe, which is flooded with the divine spirit. Through this overflow, the universe was created by god in a historical process and was not created at once. God is impersonal. It can be described only as to what it is not. This negative way of describing god (the via negativa) survived until the Middle Ages. As god cannot be conceived mentally, for Plotinus the union with the divine is ecstatic and mystical.

Traditional, human existential issues have been tackled both in antiquity and also today by religion. Especially from the 4th to the 8th century, religions like Christianity in Europe, Islam in the Middle East, and Buddhism in Asia provided satisfactory life goals for people, but these are no longer credible in the era of scientific rationalism. Those who continue to seek solace in religion have unconsciously accepted ignoring the scientific discoveries that explain the creation and operation of the world in physical terms.

The religious evidence for the existence of god

Knowledge about the existence and attributes of god are based on three pieces of evidence: experiences, revelations and logic. Experiences are associated with the realization of the perfection and harmony of Nature and life. They start from the awe caused by the contemplation of the starry sky and end in the miracle of life to show that the perfection and harmony of the universe professes the existence of a superpower, god, who created and sustains the world. The experiences that are accompanied by visions are called revelations. They are purely subjective, and their reliability is strongly contested.

The third piece of evidence arises from knowledge, insights and experiences that lead to the logical conclusion of god's existence. However this logical reasoning is also purely subjective and cannot be confirmed.

Christianity, which has its roots in Judaism, expresses the view that god created the matter of the universe out of nothing (ex nihilo). Saint Augustine, the foremost exponent of Christian beliefs, considered god to be omniscient, omnipotent, omnipresent, morally good, and creator and promoter of the universe. His main views are borrowed from Aristotle, with the difference that while Aristotle considered god as a passive being who simply thinks of himself, Saint Augustine gave him the properties of the creator and sustainer of the cosmos, who is capable of intervening in and defining people's lives. On the question of the existence of the human will, that is, how people can be free and responsible when everything is ultimately determined by god, John Calvin was forced to invent a new theory. He stood by the view that god's will has two forms, the "irresistible" and the "resistible." The first form of will allows some human choices to conflict with the perfect irresistible will of god when it comes to serving a higher divine purpose. This theory allows both the absolute sovereignty of god, and the ability of people to define their life.

Rene Descartes tried to support the knowledge concerning god through thought and inner search. The correctness of his thought was decisively dependent on the goodness of god. He argued that he could never be deceived; saying that every clear and distinct conception is without doubt something, and hence cannot derive its origin from what is nought, but must of necessity have god as its author. God, he said, being supremely perfect, cannot be the cause of any error; and consequently we must conclude that such a conception is true.

Emmanuel Kant argued that the existence of god cannot be proven at all, but neither can it be denied. However, he supported that there is a need for moral order in the universe, and this need for "morality" in conjunction with "practical reason" leads to the conclusion of the existence of god. Kant argued that the goal of humanity is to achieve perfect happiness and virtue (the summum bonum) and as this is not often so in this life, we can rightly say that there is a life in another realm beyond our own where justice is awarded, and that god must exist in order to provide this. He claimed that the idea of god creates significant moral values, according to which, those who do good will be rewarded in the afterlife. For Kant, god exists to ensure the connection between virtue and happiness in the universe.

The realistic and scientific views of god

As faith in the existence of god moved away from the realm of reality, some bright spirits of the Renaissance looked into the ancient Greek world for the revelation of knowledge, rationality and experience. The interest in this life and the world we live in resurfaced, leading to the development of the sciences and the formulation of natural laws that interpret the functioning of the universe. The findings of scientists like Newton and Kepler show mathematical regularities in Nature, claiming a perfectly arranged universe and thus, a very reasonable god. The Newtonian universe had mechanical precision and predictability and left no margin for foreign interference, let alone divine. So, as belief about god's qualities was minimized, the religious side had to invent the theory of "theism." According to it, the source of knowing about god is not experience and revelations, but logic. Theism says that god made Nature and life, but since then he does not interfere. Therefore prayers and miracles are unnecessary, as the wisdom of god was proclaimed in the larger plan of creation. God is best known through generality and abstraction, rather than through daily intervention in the universe.

John Locke accepted that logic has to judge the truth of god's revelation. The alleged revelations about god that came solely from intuition could be accepted as true only if they were explained by logic. David Hume, the 18th century philosopher, claimed that while it may be rationally possible to believe that a god exists, it is highly improbable or unlikely that he does. We have evidence of so much evil that is seemingly pointless and of such horrendous intensity. For what valid reason would a good and powerful god allow the amount and kinds of evil that we see around us? It is logically impossible, he argued, to believe that both an evil and a good and powerful god exist in the same reality, for such a god certainly could and would destroy evil. Hume inquired about god, "Is he willing to prevent evil, but not able? Then he is impotent. Is he able, but not willing? Then he is malevolent. Is he both able and willing? Whence then is evil?"

Karl Marx named religions the products and tools of repression, the "opium of the people." People, he argued, created religions in response to the suffering caused by the injustice of society. But religions have the same properties as a drug that on the one hand, soothes pain and on the other, renders people unable to take care of the causes of suffering.

Friedrich Nietzsche rejected faith in god as weak and untenable. He believed that his era confirmed that "the god is dead," but feared the consequences. In modern societies, he argued, god has no reason for existence.

Sigmund Freud saw god as a projection of the mind, a product of "wishful thinking." He argued that when humanity accepts the scientific explanation of the universe, these beliefs about the existence of god will be rejected.

The astrophysicist Stephen Hawking rejected the need for a creator god on the basis of scientific research, claiming that because there is a law, such as gravity, the universe can be created by itself from nothing.

In the early 20th century, logical positivism maintained that only the views that are verified by the experience of life can be accepted as true or false. Based on this theory, Ludwig Wittgenstein argued that knowledge of god is not supported by experience, so it only has a social dimension. Those who claim to know god are not aware of the existence and properties of a metaphysical Being, but the use of the term god as a social life style.

The Epicurean views on gods

In a purely materialistic philosophical system like that of Epicurus, we would expect an outright denial of the gods. But Epicurus was faithful to the traditions; he participated in religious ceremonies and the celebrations that followed. He said that there are gods, and the knowledge of them is manifest, but that they are not as the multitude believe. The faith of Epicurus in the existence of the gods was based on his deep commitment to the truthfulness both of the dreams and the senses. Dreams were considered true in antiquity, and this was the reason why the patients of the time used to visit the temple of Asclepius at Olympia. By paying a fee, they could sleep in the sanctuary of the temple in the belief that a god will appear in their sleep to heal or to indicate treatment. So in line with established beliefs, Epicurus accepted the truthfulness of dreams, and consequently the existence of the gods, since he used to see them in his sleep. However, contrary to the public belief, he considered that they do not mix in the affairs of men. They are undisturbed and carefree, away from the Earth and humans; enjoying absolute peace and happiness. He also claimed that neither is it the concern of the gods the movement of the sky or stars because these pull their way according to physical laws.

Lucretius poetically presented the truthful Epicurean perception of the gods, saying that at that time, mortals, more in their sleep but also while awake, looked up to the shape of the gods' great and admirable physiques. They attributed the senses to the gods because they seemed to move their limbs and speak in wonderful voices, worthy of their immense power and their brilliant looks. The people thought that the gods had eternal life, that their look remained unchanged, and their face constantly rejuvenated. They thought that it was impossible for such robust beings to be easily defeated by any power, that the happiness of the gods was unsurpassed, because none of them felt the fear of death, and yet, people saw them doing wonders in their sleep, without any toil. People raised their gaze to the celestial regions, and they reflected on the sun and the orbits of the moon. They wondered whether they are facing a huge divine power, which causes the various movements of the stars, and maybe there was an initial birth and, likewise there will be an end. They believed in the gods and demons and the infernal torments that kept man in fear and ignorance.

Lucretius claimed that it was not piety to stand up with the head covered or kneel facing a stone and visit all the altars, nor to fall onto the soil and raise the hand to the holy gods, nor is plash their altars with the blood of sacrificial animals or knit prayers one after the other, but to face everything with an undisturbed mind. He topped his claim with the question: "Oh miserable human race to ascribe such acts to the gods and believe in their terrible wrath!

How many lamentations did men cause by them, how many wounds to us, and how many tears for our descendants?"

Lucretius supported that if people do not remove these ideas from their minds and do not persecute beliefs that are unworthy of the gods, their divine nature, underrated by the people, would often hurt them, not because they are thirsty for revenge, but because people imagine that the peaceful gods roll big waves of anger straight at them. He also said that religion, showing from the heights of heaven its terrible facet, made man creep on the ground, cowardly and shrunken. Like children who tremble in the dark, we fear much lower dangers, although we stand in the light.

In the Epicurean philosophical system, judgments are based on evidence procured by the senses. However, in the case of the gods, Epicurus allowed for an exception to the rule by assuming that due to their airy nature, gods are perceived not by the eyes but by the mind. To justify it, Epicurus makes use of his physics on vision, according to which, objects emanate atoms from their surface in the form of images (eidola) which preserve the characteristics of the objects. When the eidola reach the eyes we can see the objects. As an exception to the rule, the "eidola" of the gods are, instead, only comprehensible to the mind when the senses are at rest, which is in dreams during sleep. This happens because the structure of the gods is not solid but very thin and subtle, and the eidola they emanate are similarly thin, not visible by the eyes, but only perceived by the mind. This conclusion turned out to be false because the theory of vision on which it was based has been disqualified by modern physics. It is a known fact that vision is due to the reflection of light by the objects and not to the emanation of "eidola" from their surface.

Fortunately, this development had no impact on the truthfulness and effectiveness of the Epicurean Philosophy because what really matters is not the assertion of the existence of gods themselves, but of their attributes. And these were clearly defined by Epicurus when he acknowledged that the blissful and incorruptible god neither knows trouble itself nor occasions to trouble another, and is consequently immune to either anger or gratitude, for all such emotions reside in a weak creature. In other words, the Epicurean gods exert no influence on humans; judging by their properties they have no resemblance to the god proclaimed by the contemporary religions. This confrontation holds true from the very beginning of Christianity. According to historical sources, the Epicureans and the Christians were in constant conflict over the properties of the supernatural, creator, divine and providential god.

All in all in the Epicurean scheme, neither any ancient god nor any modern god created the world or affects human life in any way and this renders the metaphysical issue indifferent to the pursuit of happiness. This claim expresses the true outlook of the Epicureans because it is fully compatible with the natural character of the Epicurean philosophy.

What conclusions can we draw from this chapter, then? According to most religions, god is the creator of the universe, and through divine providence, interferes daily in human life. A variation on the initial religious conception of god is the theory of theism, whereby the wisdom of god was expressed through the creation of the universe and humans, but since then, god does not interfere with daily life. Opposite views completely reject the existence of god claiming that there is no evidence and empirical data to substantiate god's actual existence. Epicurus accepted the existence of gods, but maintained that they lived in bliss and happiness; they did not create the world and people, nor did they interfere in their daily lives. Epicurus' belief in the existence of gods proved false, but the properties he attributed to them are strong and valid, even today. The properties that the current religions attribute to god, as being divine, the creator, the sustainer, and providential are contrary to the Epicurean Philosophy, which instead praises the physical nature and function of the world.

CHAPTER 26

THE FEAR OF NATURAL DISASTERS

"It is impossible for someone to dispel his fears about the most important matters if he does not know the nature of the universe, but still gives some credence to myths. So without the study of Nature there is no enjoyment of pure pleasure."

Epicurus, *Principal Doctrine XII*

The vastness of the universe, the unexplained movements of the Earth, sun, and stars, as well as the risks arising from natural phenomena, provoked curiosity and the need for people to look for the causes that lie behind them. The questions that occupied people for centuries have nowadays found convincing answers through science and technology. Well-documented knowledge explains the current state of the cosmos, its function, and subsequently the real magnitude of the risks we run from it. The notions of Epicurus on the nature of the cosmos, of natural phenomena and their impact on the tranquility of the mind found full vindication through the discoveries of modern science. The exaggerated fears about natural phenomena turned out to be due to prejudice and ignorance. As a starting point, they usually have the false view that they are used by god to punish those who show disrespect to him.

The theocentric view of the universe

In Christianity, god is the Great Architect of the universe, a view supported by Saint Thomas Aquinas in the *Summa Theologica:* "God, who is the first principle of all things, may be compared to things created as the architect is to things designed (ut artifex ad artificiata)." Commentators have pointed out that the assertion that the Grand Architect of the universe is the Christian god is not evident on the basis of natural theology alone but requires an additional "leap of faith" based on the revelation of the Bible. John Calvin, in his *Institutes of the Christian Religion* in 1536 AD, repeatedly calls the Christian god "the Architect of the universe" or the "Great Architect." The theocentric view of the cosmos supported the geocentric theories formulated by the ancient Greek philosophers, according to which the Earth was the center of the universe, around which the Moon, the Sun, the stars and the five known planets, Mercury, Venus, Mars, Jupiter and Saturn, revolved. This opinion about the functioning of the universe was called geocentric cosmology.

At a time when telescopes had not yet been invented the ancient Greeks argued that the planets emitted light as did all the other stars. However unlike the stars, they changed location from night to night, so they were called "planets" meaning "wandering stars." The ancient astrologists also saw that the planets did not always move in the same direction, but sometimes they slowed down, stopped, or moved to the west for a short time before resuming their usual course to the east. To explain this motion of the planets the astronomer Hipparchus of Rhodes, in the 2nd century BC, said that the planets simultaneously made two moves, a small circular motion around an imaginary center, named the "epicycle," and a large one around the Earth. Ptolemy, one of the last, great, ancient astronomers, drew the movements of the epicycles in detail, and his cosmology dominated until the Renaissance.

The physical aspect of the universe

In antiquity, opposing views on the creation and operation of the universe also appeared, such as those of Heraclitus, who argued that there were reasons behind each change and that the world emerged from chaos based on some pre-existing data. Leucippus and Democritus argued that all things and humans alike are made of atoms that move with strictly prescribed physical laws. Furthermore, at about 300 BC, the pioneer astronomer, Aristarchus of Samos, argued that the center of the universe was the sun, and not the Earth.

In medieval times, the Polish astronomer Nicholas Copernicus confirmed by research the views of Aristarchus about a heliocentric system consisting of the Earth as one of the planets, Mercury and Venus closer to the Sun than the Earth and Mars, and with Jupiter and Saturn farther away. This same view was verified later by the telescopic observations of Galileo Galilei. Meanwhile, the astronomer Johannes Kepler argued that the planetary orbits were not circular, but elliptical. Finally, the discoveries of the astronomer-mathematician Isaac Newton about motion, gravity and light confirmed the natural function of the universe that made the need for a divine intervention needless.

The modern theory of the solar system

Scientific progress in astronomy led to the realization that the solar system is embedded in a galaxy composed of billions of stars, called the Milky Way, and additionally, there are other galaxies as far away as astronomical instruments can reach. According to the prevailing scientific model of the creation of the universe, known as the "Big Bang," the universe expanded from an extremely hot, dense phase, named "Planck time." At that time, all the matter and energy of the observable universe was concentrated to an infinite degree, to the size of no more than a grain of sand. The explosion that followed expanded the universe to its present form in an infinitesimal period of time, estimated at less than 10-32 seconds. Recent observations indicate that this expansion of the cosmos is not only continuing, but is accelerating due to the black holes that cover most of the universe. According to Einstein's theory of general relativity, space expands faster than the speed of light and as we cannot observe movements that exceed the boundaries of the speed of light, we are unable to determine whether the universe is finite or infinite.

Observations by astronomical instruments show that the age of the universe is about 13.6 billion years old and that for the most of it, the universe has been governed by the uniform laws of Nature. Various theories suggest that the universe we see is one of the many universes that exist. It has been found that the solar system was formed by a large rotating cloud of interstellar dust and gas that was in orbit around the center of the Milky Way. It consisted of hydrogen and helium and was created a few years after the Big Bang. About 4.6 billion years ago, this rotating solar nebula had begun to contract, to develop extremely high temperatures that led to the nuclear fusion of hydrogen into helium and gradually to the creation of the sun.

Meanwhile, dust particles and the rest of the rocks that were not incorporated into the sun drew away in formations of rotating rings that by conflicting with one another, they were either dissolved or coalesced into larger bodies, creating the currently known protoplanets. One of these was the Earth. Thus, according to the prevailing theory of the creation of the universe after the Big Bang, our planet initiated its formation about 4.6 billion years ago and finalized it in 10 to 20 million years.

The details of the origin of life may be unknown, but its basic principles are known. There are two approaches for the origin of life. One argues that the organic ingredients that created life fell on the Earth from space, and the other, that they were created on the Earth. If life began on the Earth, it is estimated that this could have happened 3.5-4 billion years ago. Due to repeated disasters that happened on the Earth by being constantly bombarded by asteroids, life on our planet might have been created more than once. In any case, all theories agree that life on the Earth was created through the natural process of "abiogenesis", in which life may arise from non-living things. Researchers argue that the building blocks of life are amino acids. According to experimental studies, these could be synthesized from the minerals that were formed in the early life of the Earth with the help of lightning and solar radiation. Researchers also suggest that in the energetic chemistry of the premature Earth, an organic molecule acquired a copier that could make copies of it. This initial copyist gradually evolved into what is nowadays the DNA, by using a small portion of cell membrane as a genetic code. It is believed that from the plurality of protocells, only a single row survived, the LUCA cell, which is nowadays considered the original ancestor of life on Earth. The gradual incorporation of smaller cells to larger ones resulted in the creation of complex cells, which are known today as eukaryotic cells. From these, all life was gradually created on the Earth's surface. Scientists believe that life was created at least 3.5 billion years ago when the Earth's surface acquired a crust. This view was reinforced by the recent discovery of fossilized cyanobacteria microbes in Western Australia, dated 3.5 billion years old, which are believed to be the first real signs of life on Earth. The belief in the spontaneous creation of certain forms of life out of inorganic substances originated from Aristotle, who argued that the aphids, a common plant parasite, sprang out of the dew that falls on plants, the mice from dirty hay, and the crocodiles from rotting logs at the bottom of stagnant water.

Evidence was found in the 1960's about a severe glacial action 580-750 million years ago that covered much of the planet with ice forcing many living organisms into extinction. The global warming that followed revived the frozen fossils and led to a blast of new living species, known as the Cambrian Explosion. However evidence shows that five other major mass extinctions have occurred since, the latest of which is dated back to 65 million years ago when an asteroid crashed onto Earth starting a huge fire that caused the extinction of dinosaurs and other large reptiles. Some small animals, including mammals, were spared from that fire because they lived underground for the fear of large animals. During the course of these last 65 million years, the characteristics of mammals have evolved according to the Darwinian theory of the evolution of beings and the survival of the fittest. A hallmark in the evolutionary process occurred 2-3 million years ago when an African monkey acquired the capacity to stand on its two feet. This allowed the use of tools, encouraged communication, and gradually caused the development of a larger brain known today as the rational brain. This third stage of brain in living beings, after the reptile and the mammal, marked the development of the human race.

Today we are in a glacial period that began about 40 million years ago and culminated 3 million years ago, during the Pleistocene period. Since then, many areas of the Earth go through minor glacier and thawing cycles that are repeated every 40,000 to 100,000 years.

The theory of Darwinian evolution

By the concept of "evolution" and more specifically with that of biological or organic evolution, we mean the change over time of one or more inherited characteristics. The change can be effected either by the influence of the outside population, or by the mutation of the DNA in the same population. For Charles Darwin, human beings emerged through the evolutionary process of "endogeny," according to which, a species is split into two or more different species. Endogeny was found in anatomical, genetic and other similarities observed in fossils, but also in the genetic changes that occurred in living organisms over many generations.

So according to Darwin, from the war of Nature, from famine and death, the most exalted objects that we are capable of conceiving—namely, the production of higher animals—directly follows. There is grandeur in this view of life, with its several powers having been originally breathed into a few forms or into one; and whilst this planet has gone cycling on according to the fixed law of gravity, from so simple a beginning, endless forms, most beautiful and most wonderful, have been, and are being, evolved.

Endogeny and evolution of populations generally occurs in many ways, either slowly, steadily and gradually over time, or suddenly, from one static state to another. The scientific study of the evolution of the species began in about the middle of the 19th century, when the research on fossils and living organisms convinced most scientists that the species evolve. The mechanisms that drive the changes remained unclear until the theory of natural selection was formulated by Charles Darwin in 1858.

The Epicurean cosmology

The Epicurean cosmology and physics were based on the earlier invention of the atomic theory by Democritus. Epicurus developed and modified it in order to allow for the existence of free will in people, by introducing the concept of the "swerve" of atoms, as Lucretius poetically explains: "This point too, herein we wish you to apprehend: when bodies are borne downwards through sheer void by their own weights, at quite uncertain times and uncertain spots they push themselves a little from their course: you just and only just can call it a change of inclination. If they were not used to swerve, they would all fall down, like drops of rain, through the deep void, and no clashing would have been begotten nor blow produced among the first beginnings: thus nature never would have produced aught."

Following the Ionian tradition and Democritus, Epicurus postulated that everything in the universe has been created by natural causes and is governed by natural laws. He said that the gods had no involvement in the creation of the world, nor did they participate in its functioning. Matter can neither be created nor destroyed. The sum of things is always the same, as Lucretius says, claiming that when we shall have seen that nothing can be produced from nothing, we shall then more correctly ascertain that which we are seeking, both the elements out of which everything can be produced, and the manner in which all things are done without the hand of the gods. If things came from nothing, any kind might be born of anything, nothing would require seed...but no force can change the sum of things; for there is nothing outside; nothing into which any kind of matter can escape out of the universe, nor out of which a new supply can arise and burst into the universe, changing the nature of all things and altering their motions.

Also in his *Letter to Herodotus,* Epicurus says: "Nay more: we are bound to believe that in the sky, revolutions, solstices, eclipses, risings and settings, and the like, take place without ministration or command, either now or in the future, of any Being who at the same time enjoys perfect bliss along with immortality... Hence, where we find phenomena invariably recurring, the invariability of the recurrence must be ascribed to the original interception and conglomeration of atoms whereby the world was formed." He also adds that there are infinite worlds, some like this world, and others unlike it.

Surprisingly, the Darwinian theory of evolution and survival of the fittest has its origin in the Epicurean Philosophy. Lucretius poetically describes the birth, survival and development of beings, saying that as feathers and hairs and bristles are first born on the limbs of four-footed beasts and the bodies of the strong of wing, thus the new Earth first put forth grass and bushes, and next gave birth to the races of mortal creatures springing up many in number, in many ways after diverse fashions; for no living creatures can have dropped from heaven, nor can those belonging to the land have come out of salt pools. He also stated that it follows with good reason that the Earth has got the name of mother since all things have been produced out of the Earth. And many living creatures, even now, spring out of the Earth, taking form by rains and the heat of the sun.

Wrapping this chapter up, people, amazed and terrified by the vastness of the universe and unexplained natural phenomena, attributed everything to the gods. The early Greek philosophers tried to give natural explanations to the creation and operation of the universe. The key issues that troubled them were the fear of punishment by the gods and the scientific opinion that questioned the existence of free will in humans. Epicurus recognized the negative impacts of these beliefs on the pursuit of happiness and formulated a new cosmology in which he attributes the creation of the universe and life to natural processes. The adoption of this perception shattered the unsubstantiated concerns and fears about the nature of death and god's influence in our life. Theories about the universe were initially geocentric and were based on religious beliefs about the creation of the world and man by god. These views were subsequently refuted by the observations of Copernicus, Kepler and Galileo, which prove that the universe is heliocentric. According to the prevailing scientific view, the universe was created from natural causes, it expands, has dark matter and is governed by natural laws. According to theory, the sun and the Earth were created out of the great explosion of the Big Bang. Life appeared through the processes of active chemistry and has been developing according to the theories of natural selection and the survival of the fittest expressed by Epicurus and Darwin. Human beings emerged through this evolutionary process.

PART FOUR: DECISIONS

CHAPTER 27

NEEDS, WANTS AND DESIRES

*"Of our desires, some are natural
and necessary, others are natural but
not necessary; and others are neither
natural nor necessary, but are due to
groundless opinion."*

Epicurus, *Principal Doctrine XXIX*

Needs, wants and desires: an overview

Human needs from an ontological point of view (stemming
from the condition of being human), are constant throughout all human cultures and across historical time periods;
what changes in them over time and between cultures is
the strategy by which these needs are satisfied. Along with
them, each of us has his own specific needs due to his own
individual nature. Hence, our needs are the sum of the
common human needs and our personal needs.

In the Epicurean model, the needs are branded as natural and necessary. They are limited and classified to body (food, shelter, health), psychology (safety, friends) and intellect (knowledge).

The "wants" are distinguished from the "needs" in that they are unnecessary to happiness. In the Epicurean model, for example, they are referred to as natural and unnecessary and neither natural nor necessary. The pleasure that satisfies the natural and unnecessary wants, such as luxurious meals, does not get rid of any pain, but it varies in the personal level of pleasure, while the pleasure that satisfies the non-natural and non-necessary wants, such as wealth, arises from false opinions.

"Desire" is an emotion associated with a need or a want. It expresses the strong feeling of needing or wanting to have something. It is an intimate cousin of pleasure and an opponent to fear and pain.

Thomas Hobbes, in the 17th century proposed the concept of "psychological hedonism," which asserts that the "fundamental motivation of all human action is the desire for pleasure." Later in the same line, David Hume claimed that desires are not cognitive, but automatic bodily responses, and argued that reasoning is capable only of devising a means to an end set by bodily desire. Baruch Spinoza, in the 17th century, saw natural desires as a form of bondage that is not chosen by people out of their own free will.

On the other side of the philosophical spectrum, Plato, in *The Republic*, argues that individual desires must be postponed in the name of a higher ideal. Later, Immanuel Kant called any action based on desires a hypothetical imperative, meaning by this that it is a command of reason that applies only if we desire the goal in question.

Within Christianity, a "desire" is seen as something that can either lead a person towards god and destiny or away from him. It is considered to be a powerful force within the human being that, once submitted to the Lordship of Christ, can become a tool for good, for advancement, and for abundant living.

Within the teachings of Buddhism, craving is thought to be the cause of all suffering that we experience in human existence. The eradication of craving leads us to ultimate happiness, or Nirvana. However, desire for wholesome things is seen as liberating and enhancing. While the stream of desire for sense-pleasures must eventually be cut, a practitioner on the path to liberation is encouraged by the Buddha to generate desire for the fostering of skillful qualities and the abandoning of unskillful ones.

In the Epicurean Philosophy, desires are considered a hardwired capacity of the human mind acting as Nature's automatic guide in everyday life. They emerge from the mechanical functions of the mind such as the sensations, the emotions and the anticipations. Out of these desires, only those that are associated with the necessary natural needs contribute to happiness. The rest either give a variety to happiness or are quite unnecessary.

The novelty of the Epicurean Philosophy was the rejection of logic as a means of conveying true desires because it has no direct contact with reality, and it necessarily uses the senses, emotions and anticipations to come into contact with the world. Logic, which contributes to the instant feedback it gets, alters the truth. Its natural role is instead constrained to evaluating the natural desires, and making decisions on which of these to satisfy.

For the pioneer, existential psychologist Rollo May, "desire is the first step of the function of will. It is the fantasy of the probability of something happening in the future." He also claims that desires differ from needs at a very important point. They contain meaning. They do not simply reflect the mechanical inner impulses, but their interpretation by means of the perceptions of the individual. For example, if one has an instinctive desire for sex, this does not mean that he will satisfy it with any partner, but with someone he finds attractive or sexually appealing, according to his perceptions. If we have no preferences at all, then something wrong is going on, psychologists argue. Either we are under extreme oppression, as happens with soldiers and prisoners, or we exhibit psychopathological symptoms.

Freud distinguished between the unconscious and conscious desires. The strongest desires, he said, are those in the unconscious that we do not perceive. They emanate from the instincts; they have not been altered, either willingly or by the influence of third parties, so they are genuine. The conscious desires instead are created or changed by the intervention of logic or the environment, and therefore cease to be genuine and true.

Psychologists nowadays emphasize the importance and influence of experiences and perceptions on desires. Existential psychologists, for example, claim that the strongest desires are related to the search for meaning in life, the management of freedom, the fear of isolation and the fear of death. This position shifts the focus of desires, from the instincts to experiences and perceptions.

Research has shown that desires are largely affected by individual psychology. People with blocked feelings are usually introverted and have difficulty in expressing desires, and when they do, their desires usually originate from thoughts or external influences, instead of the inner mind.

From this chapter, we can therefore conclude that a desire is an emotion associated with a specific need or want. The desires associated with the natural and necessary human needs are good enough for happiness, according to the Epicurean Philosophy. The natural and unnecessary give simply variety to it, while the non-natural and non-necessary are harmful.

CHAPTER 28

CHOICES

*"Necessity is an evil; but there
is no necessity for continuing to
live with necessity."*
Epicurus, *Vatican Saying IX*

The determinants of choices

The available options in life depend primarily on self-knowledge in as much as the way we see life is subjective. Our
choices depend on our capacities, but also on the way we
perceive ourself and the world around us. In this respect,
self-knowledge is a prerequisite in evaluating the opportunities and the risks we confront in everyday life.

Knowing ourself bears inherent difficulties.

We usually avoid dealing with ourselves, seeing it as
painful and time consuming. Some intuitively assume that
they know themselves, and there is no need to look into

it further. However, emotions and capacities are hidden in the unconscious mind, and we are unaware of them. On top of this, we are partial in judging ourselves. We overestimate our virtues and underestimate our shortcomings to ward off negative feelings or boost self-esteem. Lack of information is another barrier, as it is hard to observe our own capacities and traits. Other people have a more accurate view of some of our traits, and this makes it necessary to turn to intimate friends who, as a mirror, will reflect back our true Self.

Referring to the concept of self-knowledge, the realization of our financial capacity and the estimation of its prospects in a volatile economic environment is also included. We often undertake long term financial obligations based solely on our current financial position, and this is one of the reasons why we find ourselves trapped in high leverage situations once the economic environment is reversed. We should give serious consideration when we are to make decisions with long term consequences.

The external environment is the other determinant of the accessible choices. This is defined by the political, economic, social and cultural conditions prevailing in society. Our experience confirms great discrepancies among various parts of the world, with the majority of human beings living below the poverty level, in famine, sickness, illiteracy, oppression, religious obsession, violence and wars. Under these conditions, it is meaningless to raise delicate issues such as the pursuit of individual happiness; this requires some minimum conditions of subsistence, education, safety, and openness of mind. Unfortunately, such considerations are the privilege of a minority of human beings who are lucky enough to live in the so-called affluent societies.

Surprisingly, over the last few decades, anxiety and resentment have been accelerating in societies of relative or high economic welfare. As research shows, happiness and economic welfare move in opposite directions when a certain economic level is reached. This finding lays open the inherent shortcomings of the free market economy and the prevalent philosophy of life. What then is the reason behind this odd at first-sight development? The answer is simply that the prevailing idealistic philosophies of life (consumerist, religious) by definition, do not aim at happiness, but in achieving goals. In other words, the aims of modern people by and large have to do with some concepts of logic or logical perceptions that are unrelated to feelings. It is known, though, that reason and emotion are two discreet and independent functions of the mind, and their products, such as success and feeling respectively, are therefore, uncorrelated. We may be very successful and unhappy at the same time and vice versa, while the co-existence of success and happiness is a rare coincidence that arises under very special circumstances. The discontent of people in affluent societies is due to the false priorities that they set in their life. They aim at success in order to get to happiness, instead of aiming directly for happiness.

Loneliness and brainwashing as side effects of idealism

A major consequence of the popular, false idealistic philosophies is loneliness, isolation, and lack of friends.

It is well known now that strong and lasting bonds are developed through feelings and not through logical means, in that emotions are biologically long-term, while thoughts are short term. This explains why long-term professional relations last as long as this relation is in place. They are simply motivated by a common interest, and when this comes to an end, so does the relationship. It is of no surprise then, that the widespread philosophies of thought give rise to loneliness and isolation. Indeed, all research shows that people suffer losses in the quality and quantity of close friendships, the average number of confidants has dropped dramatically, and a significant percentage of people have no close confidants at all.

Technological advancement has also been blamed for the decline in friendships. Longer hours of work and a great deal of online communication take away from personal communication, making it harder to make friends. Social media has also led to a decrease in the amount of personal communication experienced in everyday life, and serve to make emotional attachments more difficult to achieve. Face-to-face chatting is giving way to texting and messaging; people even prefer these electronic exchanges to simply talking on the phone. Small circles of friends are being replaced by social media acquaintances numbered in the hundreds.

Amid these trends, growing research suggests we could be entering a period of crisis for the entire concept of friendship. Where is all this leading modern-day society to? It is, perhaps, leading to a dark future, one where electronic stimuli will replace the joys of human contact. People realize they are living well, in a lonelier society, and while they would like to live closer to their families and friends, social trends force them to live farther apart. Even more discouraging is the data that show that these trends hold true on a broader scale, well beyond the urban jungle.

People nowadays find themselves working hard to support an imposed way of life that, at the end of the day, leaves them empty and disappointed, and at the same time, lonely and with no friends to turn to. Their obvious reaction is exactly what experience and research show. They turn to the easiest means of comfort; shopping, churches, substances, violence, gambling and so on, instead of taking responsibility for their life in their own hands. The realization of the problem is the first step in cutting away from the influences of the environment. Next is to get rid of the vain ideas of logic and follow the solid guidance of Nature. The Philosophy of Epicurus will help us to re-discover the natural patterns of human existence. It recommends a pleasant, easy-going way of life with our family and friends.

The second most important negative consequence of the common idealistic model of life is that it renders people vulnerable to external influences. Logic, through brainwashing, adopts conventional trends that submit to serving the interests of the political, economic, religious and underground status quo. It comes as no surprise then, that this mighty system of power sponsors logical and not emotional goals of life. It is glaringly obvious that it is not interested in people's happiness, but in commanding their minds to support their interests. They usually succeed in their efforts by means of well-developed techniques, delicately designed to influence the preferences and the perceptions of people. We work overtime and increase leveraging to support our artificial wants instead of pursuing happiness. But all these unfounded pleasures offer temporary satisfaction, and in the long run, they lead to frustration and disappointment.

Most people regard multiple, consumer choices as a good thing. Though a severely limited or artificially restricted choice can lead to discomfort in choosing, and possibly to an unsatisfactory outcome, in contrast, a choice with excessively numerous options may lead to confusion and regret. One reason is that the large number of choices imposes a cognitive burden on the individual, and a second is the regret we experience from the possibility of having made a sub-optimal choice.

In conclusion, the choices in our life are closely related to self-knowledge because the way we see life is subjective. People's choices are restrained by the false recommendations of the prevailing idealistic philosophies of life. Logic makes our thoughts vulnerable to harmful external influences and therefore, it is unreliable. A secondary effect of the idealistic way of life is alienation and lack of friends, a main cause of misery and unhappiness. Despite the rising level of income, the level of happiness is declining, as people are not directly interested in happiness but in achieving goals. The way out of idealistic traps is to take responsibility for our life, to reject the conceptual aims of life and to introduce the natural.

CHAPTER 29

DECISIONS

"While, therefore, all pleasure because it is naturally akin to us is good, not all pleasure should be chosen, just as all pain is an evil and yet, not all pain is to be shunned. It is, however, by measuring one against another, and by looking at the conveniences and inconveniences, that all these matters must be judged. Sometimes we treat the good as an evil, and the evil, on the contrary, as a good."

Epicurus, *Letter to Menoeceus*

In the Epicurean context, decisions are made consciously through logic. Logic is the mind's filter of our desires on the one hand, and the limitations of ourself and the restrictions and opportunities of the environment on the other. It has the hard task of matching our inner impulses to the capacities of the Self and the available choices of the environment. Therefore, the act of making a decision is the final stage of a process that originates in the inner parts of the brain, under the influence of heredity and nurture, and ends up in the front part of it in our consciousness.

The automatic functions of the mind disclose our needs and wants, which in turn take their biological path to consciousness in order for us to gain satisfaction. By entering consciousness, they are first realized by the neurons of will, which are either activated to empower the stimuli to continue their journey into logic or they stay inert, declining to support their satisfaction.

In the case where the stimuli do reach logic, the latter examines if they are true, and then it classifies them according to what kind they are and to their priority. At the same time, logic acknowledges the emotions that are associated with them by observing their bodily manifestation. It carries out a quick test of self-knowledge and investigates the restrictions and the opportunities of the environment. As a rule, it subsequently rejects all the needs and wants that are associated with unpleasant feelings and holds the pleasurable ones for further investigation and cost-benefit analysis.

Experience and research show that emotions are actively involved in decision-making. A classic example is the brain's reaction to unexpected danger. When we are in danger, the mind unconsciously reacts with the emotion of fear, which in turn activates the defense mechanism of the autonomous nervous system in order to deal with the risk. Conventional reactions include instinctive physical manifestations, such as an increased heart rate, increased blood pressure, sweating and so on. When these reactions are perceived by our conscious mind, it estimates the possible consequences to our life, and in this way causes a second set of feelings of fear, usually of greater intensity than the original. The effects of the secondary, conscious emotional reactions are crucial in determining the final attitude that logic will take toward the risk. So logic has the opportunity to exaggerate or reduce the size of the original emotional reactions, and this makes the role of positive or negative thinking in life important. The latter is the major source of anxiety and panic in modern societies.

Generally, it is impossible to make logical decisions without an emotional boost. This position is completely different from the view declared by Plato and Descartes, according to whom logic is the best and perhaps the only driver for decision-making, and therefore, feelings should be kept away. For them, people ideally carry out a cost-benefit analysis for every available option and eventually choose the solution that has the maximum anticipated usefulness. But research does not confirm these hypotheses. Instead it shows that emotions are essential to thought to the same extent as they are necessary in art and culture. Consideration of the emotional reactions to a stimulus usually leads to correct and effective decisions. Also, emotions are particularly useful in the evaluation of interpersonal and social relations.

The determinants of decision-making

To make decisions and plan for the future, self-knowledge is essential. We need to make use of the Delphic inscription that advises us to know ourselves–to be aware of our inclinations, deficiencies, and capacities in order to make valid and effective judgments. Of course, self-consciousness has to come with self-acceptability and self-esteem.

Recognizing our needs and wants is also vital in decision-making. We know that they are formed through the mechanical functions of the inner brain and take meaning through our perceptions about life. Some are natural and necessary, others natural and unnecessary, while others neither natural nor necessary.

Emotions act as the green or red light in decision-making. They are automatically set in motion by our needs and wants, and make themselves visible through their bodily manifestations. In decision-making, logic rejects, as a rule, all the needs and wants that are tied to unpleasant emotions and reflects on the rest. In idealistic philosophies, on the other hand, emotions are entirely neglected in decision-making.

Decision-making is meaningful when more than one option is at our disposal. By and large, we do have multiple choices and are able to choose the best among them. In exceptional cases however, such as those when a person is in an oppressive and coercive situation or experiences drug dependence, unemployment or economic deprivation, hardly any choices exist and we are forced to follow the trend.

Supposing we have choices available, it still takes a strong will to fuel decision-making. Will is that function of the mind that equips it with the ability to "swerve"; to revise, in other words, the course of events prescheduled by heredity, habits and the environment, in order to shape its own authentic way in life. Despite the great contribution of will in prosperity, we often avoid exercising it.

Under the influence of habits, we do not often decide on using our own will and therefore, life is not entirely ours. However to realize our objectives, we need to take control of our attention in order to channel our energy into accomplishing them. But we cannot succeed in this with inaction or indifference. It takes effort, determination and discipline to put the forces of nature and nurture under our own control. It is necessary to discover and develop our virtues in order to effectively utilize them in fulfilling our aims.

Knowledge also plays a significant role in making effective decisions. In ancient philosophies, the theory of knowledge often ended up verbose, overlapping the essence of philosophy. Epicurus eased the mind from unnecessary knowledge, definitions and dialectical tricks. He said that these do not help in the pursuit of happiness and often disorient it. This is the reason he avoided technical terminology, bizarre expressions and sterile logical games. He also emphasized the separation of the real from the imaginary through the application of the Canon of Truth, by rejecting idealistic, vague talk, and bringing the wandering mind back to the solid human base in the search for the true nature of the world. The Canon of Truth introduces the senses, emotions and anticipations as criteria for the knowledge that contributes to happiness, and it uses science as a tool to the extent that it contributes to the peace of the soul. As Epicurus says: "Through the knowledge of the truth we can discover the limitations of Nature and ourselves in order to define the framework for wise decision-making."

Perceptions are particularly important in decision-making. Before embarking on an evaluation of specific issues, the students in the Garden learned well the Principles of the Epicurean Philosophy regarding the vital issues of the time. Among the significant ones were death and the gods, pleasure and pain, doom and fortune, politics, wealth, fame, friendship, food, and so on. *The Principle Doctrines* recommend for politics, to avoid it; for glory, to ignore it; and for friendship, to take care of it as the greatest wealth of the wise man. Another important principle concerns to our attitudes about today, yesterday and tomorrow. The Epicurean principles recommend considering the past unchangeable, and to cherish to this with feelings of gratitude and satisfaction, and to consider the future uncontrollable; to be prepared, and face it with hope and optimism. They presume that we only have the ability to control and enjoy the present.

Regarding the existence of freedom of choice and free will, they postulate that "life inside us knows no boss," meaning that we have freedom of choice in our inner world. As for the environment, they consider that we have a limited capacity to affect it. For luck, they propose that we cultivate foresight to avoid its adverse junctures. For the passion of anger, they claim that the right attitude is to consider it an outbreak, a brief madness. The wrong perception is to believe that satisfaction may result from revenge. Anger stirs the soul and, therefore, disturbs equanimity. Moreover, angry reactions cause reprisals that further disturb peace and safety. Finally, the most fundamental Principle Doctrine states that some desires are natural and necessary, others are natural but not necessary; and yet others are neither natural nor necessary, but are born from empty ideas.

The criteria for decision-making: Virtues

In the Epicurean Philosophy, the criteria for decision-making are the virtues of phronesis (logic, reason, and wisdom), temperance, courage and justice. Unlike the Aristotelian and Stoic philosophies, these virtues are appreciated, not for the delight they offer in themselves, but because they contribute to better decisions and, thereby, to increasing pleasure.

The Epicurean interlocutor of Cicero in his *de Finibus* treatise articulates the role of virtues in the Epicurean Philosophy when he says that those who identify the highest value solely by virtue have been misled by the brilliance of a word and do not understand the true requirements of Nature. If they agree to obey Epicurus, they will rid themselves of the most slapstick fallacy; virtues are worthy if they bring pleasure. Otherwise, who considers them desirable?

In order to liberate ourselves from the slavery of the erroneous opinion and make every action a product of our choice we need reason (phronesis). This investigates the reliability of knowledge by rejecting unsupported ideas and by seeking more evidence for that which is in doubt. It then weighs the advantages against the disadvantages in order to make the best choices.

By choosing phronesis as a criterion, Epicurus meant to differentiate himself from Plato, who used wisdom as a criterion. In Plato's thought, wisdom acquired heavenly meaning; it was identified with pure and divine reason. Moreover, it was the prerogative of the few who had the power to impose it on the uneducated many. Epicurus despised classifications, considering all people equal regarding their need to be free from false opinions, concerns and fears. That is why he declared the practical sense, phronesis, the starting point of all virtues. The method followed by phronesis was to weigh the advantages against the disadvantages before taking any action. In this way, we can control our lives and not rely on the favors of fortune.

Some critics accuse Epicurus of underestimating logic, while others accuse him of the opposite. What is certain though is that he redefined the traditional role that Plato and the religions attributed to it, namely that logic clarifies the true desires of human nature. Bacon, Locke and other thinkers later identified with the Epicurean view by expressing their disdain for dialectic logic; they especially renounced the complex paths it takes trying to impose itself on events. The webs of logic trap the mind, but whoever is in the open air of experience may despise its tricks, Bacon said.

In the Epicurean Philosophy, logic evaluates every desire by first identifying whether it is reliable, then by classifying it in one of the categories of the Epicurean desires. Then it examines its priority towards other natural desires, studies its long term effects, investigates our ability to meet its cost, and calculates the benefits against the costs.

The poet Lucretius praised phronesis in a miraculous way: "It is sweet to look upon the mighty struggles of war arrayed along the plains without taking part yourself in the danger. But nothing is more welcome than to hold the lofty and serene positions, well-fortified by the learning of the wise, from which you may look down upon others and see them wandering all abroad and going astray in their search for the path of life, see the contest of intellect among them, the rivalry of birth, the striving night and day with surpassing effort to struggle up to the summit of power and be masters of the world. O miserable minds of men! O blind hearts! In what darkness of life and in what great dangers is passed this term of life whatever its duration! Not choosing to see that nature craves for herself no more than this, that pain hold aloof from the body, and that the mind enjoys a feeling of pleasure exempt from care and fear? Therefore we see that for the body's nature few things are needed at all, such and such only as take away pain."

The second fundamental virtue is temperance, because it makes us rulers over our passions, capable of bringing harmony and peace of mind. The beautiful facets of pleasure may challenge our attention and imprison it in their passions, without reflecting on the consequences. Resistance to pleasure may fade away as soon as pleasure appears in front of our eyes. We need our dispassionate judgment and strength. For the sake of a small and unnecessary pleasure that we could secure otherwise, or renounce altogether without any pain, we can suffer a serious illness, or loss of property, or suffer punishments.

On the other hand, when we enjoy pleasure by avoiding any painful consequences, we are reaping a higher pleasure. The same holds true when we endure pain in order not to expose ourselves to worse. This proves that temperance is desired, not because it renounces pleasure, but because it ensures greater pleasure to come. The Roman poet Lucretius wrote 2,000 years ago that it is sweet, when on the great sea the winds trouble its waters, to behold from land another's deep distress; not that it is a pleasure and delight that any should be afflicted, but because it is sweet to see from what evils you are yourself exempt.

The third fundamental virtue is courage, which is the bravery to face difficulties whenever the path of bliss is blocked without betraying our principles for the sake of convenience or micro considerations. We reaffirm the ethical course we have set and that we have an authentic sense of purpose. Epicurus appreciated natural courage, not as a virtue in political and military life, but as an element of social behavior and moral attitude. Courage is identical with the lack of cowardice and servility. It promotes honest behavior and respect for others to the same degree that we claim them for ourself. It declares our commitment to realize and make up for our mistakes, instead of indulging in masking acts. Bravery may lead us to assume painful or even dangerous tasks, if these are the last way out from an acute or lasting pain. It may urge us to choose to die with honor than to live as hostages of an authoritarian regime or of an incurable disease.

Cicero says in *de Finibus* that the performance of labors and the endurance of pain are not attractive in and of themselves. Neither is patience, industry, watchfulness, or that much-praised virtue, perseverance, or even courage itself, worthy of praise apart from that which they produce. Instead, we aim for these virtues in order to live without anxiety and fear, and in so far as possible, to be free from the pain of mind and body.

As the fourth virtue, the Epicureans recognized justice. Like the other virtues, it is not considered an absolute good, but a means to ensure happiness. Justice is a product of convention, founded on the promise not to harm our fellow humans and not let unjust actions go unpunished. Throughout history, it has proven beneficial for people to embrace this agreement. Epicurus said that the Just life is marked by the greatest quietude, but the unjust overflows with the greatest unrest. When we live in conditions of legal order and protection we are free from the burden of anxiety that we may fall victims of crime, or when this happens, we have confidence that we can find justice. On the other hand, when we transgress the social contract by committing crimes or behaving dishonestly, we get upset from worrying about being exposed and suffer the consequences of our acts or omissions. According to Epicurus, there has never been such a thing as absolute justice, only agreements made in mutual dealings among men in various places and times to provide against infliction or suffering from harm. In the Epicurean context, an unjust action is not an evil in itself. What causes harm is the fear of a possible revelation and punishment, for no one who violates the legitimate will ever feel secure that they will remain unnoticed, even though they have escaped a thousand times.

The decision-making process

In the Epicurean Philosophy, decisions emanate from the human mind and they do not arise from such abstract ideas as the logic of the universe, or of some unknown mind expressing eternal ideas, perfect moves and harmonious relations. The Epicurean Philosophy is interested in life on Earth; it is anthropocentric and opposes the theocentric view that the universe is ruled by the divine and immaterial reason. For Epicurus, decisions contribute to happiness if they are harnessed to the data of Nature. Without the testimony of Nature, any decision is worthless, maintained the biographer of the lives of the eminent philosophers, Diogenes Laertius who advocated that we must start from plain facts when we draw inferences about the unknown. He added that all our notions are derived from perceptions, either by actual contact or by analogy, or resemblance, or composition, with some slight aid from reasoning.

The simple reflection of our natural desires, with no involvement of reason, is called "spontaneous decision." The processing of them by reason renders the decisions "sober."

Often our decisions are a spontaneous expression of our desires that are automatically formed under the guidance of heredity and nurture. If we adopt the Epicurean principles, these desires emanate from the senses, emotions and anticipations. Although the spontaneous decisions are true and natural, they are not always reliable because they do not take into account the limitations of ourselves and the environment. These are known only to the conscious mind and the participation of reason is necessary in the final stage of decision-making.

Sober decisions, on the other hand, are the result of the processing of spontaneous decisions by the conscious mind and especially by logic. By the criterion of logic, Epicurus ranked the unconscious desires by the extent to which they contribute to the pursuit of happiness. He suggested satisfying the natural and necessary desires, the natural and unnecessary if they are not harmful, and rejecting the rest. In the evaluation of desires, logic combines the knowledge that is stored in the mind as experiences, the reliable testimonies of other sources, and the methods of reasoning, such as analogy, comparison, synthesis, abstraction, deduction, and induction.

Epicurus called for sober judgment, sober calculation, practical reason, saying that sober calculation, which investigates the reasons for every choice and avoidance, is the one that expels false opinions, which are the chief cause of turmoil that can take possession of the souls of men.

Logic is akin to a judge, before whom the sensations, emotions and anticipations, present their testimonies and ask to be accepted. The judge accepts the valid evidence, makes a distinction between mere opinion and knowledge, between the idea waiting to be confirmed by additional evidence and that which is already true, between the close clear image and the distant, misleading one, between the counterfeit and genuine desires, and between the mistaken and correct views. If logic is unable to cope with these requirements, the agitation in the soul will continue. In this case, there is the risk of indecision, something that has more negative effects on happiness than a wrong decision.

The desires of the unconscious mind prescribe the outline of the final decision, the "mood" in the jargon of the Epicurean Philosophy. But the final choice lies in the expediency of free will. Even though internal and external forces compete to get the upper hand and enforce their interests in our life, Nature has endowed us with the capacity to take conscious decisions that bear our personal stamp.

We are the ones solely responsible for our decisions and the quality of our life. We cannot evade them or attribute them to others. Under the most stifling conditions, we still have the option of taking decisions. As long as we are able to think, we can discover or create options and make choices. And although our conscious decisions are generally in line with the unconscious recommendations of the mind, in exceptional cases they may be contrary. For example, while our general attitude to pain is to consider it bad and avoid it, in the specific case of a necessary surgery, we choose to suffer for a while in the expectation of a greater good. Accordingly, while the right attitude to diet is to prefer the simple diet, when the opportunity arises, we overcome the limits and give in to food, drink, and entertainment.

Examples of decision-making

The purchase of a house is a natural, necessary desire. It springs from the instinct of survival. We cannot live without shelter, so it is a naturally true and necessary desire that we have to satisfy. The decision, however, is to be made through logic by weighing a number of factors. First of all, logic will consider the quality of our emotions. Our feelings are triggered automatically by the stimulus of the need for a house and our perceptions that interpret it. Our perceptions prescribe the outline of the house we would like to buy; they express our outlook toward purchasing a house.

This stimulus, of the house we need and want, follows its biological path to consciousness to demand its satisfaction. In parallel, our conscious mind, through logic, is aware of the feelings associated with it by observing the bodily manifestations of the emotions. If we feel joyful, logic proceeds to the next phase of the cost benefit analysis. Feelings are Nature's guide to life, and researchers find they are the best guide we have at our disposal, by far outweighing reason. This is the fundamental distinction between the Epicurean Philosophy and the rest. In the idealistic philosophies, everything begins and ends with logical thoughts. There is no place for feelings because by definition, idealists consider reason superior to feelings.

In the case where we feel good about our desire, logic proceeds with an evaluation of the pros and cons, and it makes a final decision. On the other hand, when we feel uneasy, that is a sign that something is worrying us, and we should try to find the reasons behind it. Our feelings are characterized by intuition; they preconceive the dangers or the opportunities in order to react before the danger makes itself evident. Based on pleasurable feelings, logic proceeds with a cost-benefit analysis, and carefully examines whether the cost is within our financial capabilities, and if there remain enough resources to fund the rest of the natural and necessary pleasures, not to mention some unnecessary ones, like entertainment. Also, logic considers whether we can afford the concomitant charges, such as taxes, maintenance, and utilities, and recommends avoiding borrowing or restricting this to the minimum, so as not to relinquish the major pleasure of self-sufficiency. If logic is unable or unwilling to go through all these considerations, the consequences may outweigh the pleasure of the purchase.

In the case where logic advises us to make adjustments to our plans, a second round of enquiry may be required to reach a decision.

The purchase of a car, on the other hand, is a natural desire in as much as it satisfies the need for transportation and the want for recreation, but it is not necessary for happiness; we can live without a car. In Epicurus, it is classified as an unnecessary desire that we may satisfy, if we can afford it, though not at the expense of the natural and necessary desires. Our evaluation follows the same course of decision-making as the previous, first taking into account our feelings about buying a car. Once we feel joyful about the prospect of buying a car, we use our logic to weigh the advantages and disadvantages of buying the type of car we love the most. Finally, we will go on with the purchase of the car we fancy and can afford. In addition, Epicurus would advise us to not provoke envy among our social environment in order to avoid harmful reactions.

Another natural, unnecessary desire is choosing a sexual partner. It expresses a natural want, which Epicurus argued is not necessary for happiness. We can live without sex, he suggested, but for those that have a strong sexual drive, he advised them to follow their drive as long as they do not harm themselves. Nowadays though, social conditions, habits, health care and other considerations allow for a more loose interpretation of the ancient Epicurean recommendation and approach to sexual relations, as a potential love affair may lead to creating a family. Let us consider this desire in the current social context, following the natural way of the Epicurean Philosophy.

In the classical version, sexual acquaintance begins by visual contact, which stimulates the inner functions of the mind and gives rise to sexual desire. This need and the associated emotions are realized by the conscious mind, initially by the free will, which acts as a boosting force for the realization of the desire. If the will is strong enough then logic takes over its double role: to examine on the one hand the related feelings, and on the other, the restrictions of the Self and the environment. If the feelings are positive and the conditions favorable, logic decides to satisfy the desire.

In the case that the sexual drive is strong but the feelings are negative, the Epicurean scheme would advise us to avoid the sexual contact because our primary concern is to feel pleasant. For the sake of the discussion, let us assume that the feelings grow and a relationship is established.

How long will we stay in this? We will go on for as long as we have a pleasant feeling. We will always follow our feelings. In the case that our feelings subside, the Epicurean model would suggest to disengage–the sooner the better. We often stay in a stagnant relationship out of insecurity, which means that we indirectly change our purpose in life from happiness to simply survival. Maintaining such a relationship for a long time will cause boredom, anxiety, and inevitably, psychosomatic symptoms. The best course of action is to go away and calm down.

What about the prospect of having a family? Well in this case, along with the present considerations, we need to estimate the long-term prospects of the relationship. Are we happy at present? Does the relationship contribute to meeting our objectives? Does it fit within our meaning of life? Do we have evidence for serious concerns? Certainly there are many unpredictable factors that hinder our estimates. Luck also plays its games and necessity can force us to play by its rules. While we accept that anything can occur and that we may fall out of our estimates, we firmly believe that we are the ones responsible for our life. We can design our future and prepare for it. This is the central message of the Epicurean life philosophy.

One unnatural desire is the need to be the focus of attention and admiration. In the Epicurean model, this desire is classified as neither natural nor necessary and is rejected. Normally it should not be included in the desires of the unconscious mind. If it has, nevertheless, crept into it, this is due to the perceptions of logic that suggest that fame contributes to well-being.

According to the Epicurean Philosophy, such a desire over the long-run turns painful because the continuous effort to remain at the center of attention causes stress and anxiety. Nevertheless, for those people that enjoy publicity, Epicurus would advise them to follow their natural inclination for as long as they feel happy. If, on the other hand, the associated feelings are embarrassing, logic rejects the desire and recommends the adjustment of the perceptions to the suggestions of the Natural Philosophy.

One natural existential fear is the fear of god's wrath. This fear relates to existential insecurities, and therefore, it originates out of the instinct of survival and takes shape in accordance with our perceptions about god. When the feeling of fear is realized by consciousness, logic evaluates it and finds out that it arises from our perception on the nature and properties of god. These usually proclaim the existence of an afterlife where god will judge people to live in eternal happiness or pain. So logic recommends replacing these fearful perceptions with the Epicurean, which reject the religious claims as arbitrary and unfounded.

An everyday worry is whether we will get a job after graduation. Work is associated with the acquisition of the financial means to support our lives, and therefore it is a means to satisfy our needs for survival. When our worry gets the attention of consciousness, logic steps in to appraise it and to realize that the cause of it is this stressful perception about securing the future. Logic then advises us to revise this worrisome perception and introduce a more flexible and relaxing one, such as the Epicurean. This suggests that life is a dynamic process and everyone has to constantly fight to support our survival and happiness. There are no guarantees regarding the future. The best course of action is to enjoy everyday life as much as possible and be prepared and optimistic about the future.

Some worries are both unnatural and unnecessary, for instance, worrying about whether or not one will do well in school or athletics or be promoted at work. These concerns usually come out of a desire for fame and prestige, which in turn originate from groundless perceptions about what really matters in life. Perceptions that emphasize the importance of being successful put the mind on constant alert, causing stress and worries. The Epicurean Philosophy suggests instead that what matters in life is not success but to feel good, and the latter is a result of enjoying the pleasures of life. The cure to these worries is the adoption of the natural conceptions of life.

Concluding this passage, we see that decision-making in the Epicurean context includes two phases: an unconscious automatic and a conscious volitional. The automatic functions of the inner mind witness our needs and wants and the associated emotions. The volitional decide through logic which of the desires will be satisfied given the restrictions within ourself and the environment. The primary criterion of choice is feelings. Logic takes into account those needs and wants that are pleasant and rejects the rest. In exceptional cases, reason may opt for painful experiences if the returns will be higher in the future.

PART FIVE: IMPLEMENTATION

CHAPTER 30

THE PURSUIT OF HAPPINESS
IN MODERN LIFE

> *"The wise man who has become*
> *accustomed to necessities knows better*
> *how to share with others than how to*
> *take from them, so great a treasure of*
> *self-sufficiency has he found."*
> Epicurus, *Vatican Saying XLIV*

The philosophy of Epicurus is psychological. It is the counterpart to medicine. As medicine is worthwhile so long as it expels the diseases of the body, so is philosophy worthwhile as long as it expels the maladies of the soul. Albeit though the symptoms of the diseases are visible, it is often hard to detect whether their source is of a biological or psychological nature. Human existence is uniformly corporeal, and any stimulus affects both the soul and the body regardless of which part of it is affected first. So to treat any disease we need to examine for both physical and emotional causes.

By nature, our mind follows the pleasant emotions and avoids the painful. This is our genetically-given perception to live happily. In order to cope with the pressures and the complexities of everyday life the mind needs additional guidance. This is the role that our upbringing undertakes through learning and experience, which in the course of time, shapes our perceptions on the general issues of life, the diatheses, in ancient terms. Epicurus took the safe side in developing the perceptions of his philosophy. He kept the emotions as the criterion for choice and avoidance, and supported the mind with perceptions harmonized to and supportive of its physical traits. The respect and the compliance of Epicurus to the functions and the traits of human nature have established his philosophy as the Natural Philosophy.

What, then, are the natural needs of human beings? What are the fundamental Epicurean perceptions for a happy life? What are their implications?

Reality, Truth, Happiness

Is there reality?

For Epicurus there is a reality, consisting of both the external world and us. The reality of the outer world is detected through the senses and scientific instruments, and abides by the natural laws governing the universe. The physical existence of our body and mind makes up the reality of ourselves, and also complies with the same laws.

The reality of our mind is substantiated through the guidance of nature and nurture in the neurons and synapses of the brain. Both are known to constitute our personality, or anticipations and prolepses in the Epicurean jargon. In them our genetic dispositions and experiences, as well as their interpretation, are encoded. By the latter function, the mind instantaneously applies meaning to them to facilitate and accelerate evaluation and decision-making.

The functions of the senses and emotions, alongside with anticipations and perceptions, disclose the outer and inner reality of our daily experiences, comprising conjointly the Epicurean Canon of Truth. As soon as realities become conscious, logic steps in to check out their reliability. It is through this function of reason that the realities of our life are classified as true or false, reliable or fraudulent. In plain English, finding truth involves reasoning. Only then is reality enriched to knowledge.

How does reality and truth relate to the quest for happiness?

Body language and facial expressions are the genuine indicators of happiness. Bodily postures combined with the gaze of our eyes, a pale or bright face, laughter or sadness, a diathesis to enjoy life or to be apathetic, grumble and worry, are bodily manifestations of emotions that we are used to calling mood and temper. They are unconscious, emotional reactions to experiences and the meanings we attach to them. The latter is an inherent aspect of the mind through which it is able to instantaneously distinguish good from bad and danger from opportunity, in order to either protect the Self or unleash its energy in pursuing creativity and joy. Perceptions exert a compelling leverage on mood; according to Epicurus, they are "the chief cause of the turmoil that takes possession of the souls of men." He argued that by changing our perceptions on the fundamental issues of life, we can affect changes in our mood and improve the quality of our life.

In idealism, logic is king. Emotions, senses, instincts and experiences are envisaged as either misleading or inferior in comprehending reality as compared to reason. This claim, though unsupported by convincing evidence, has drawn overwhelming approval through its propagation by religion and public education. We are shaped by the imperatives of reason to neglect and repress our natural desires. For Epicurus, anxiety and unhappiness are the punishment of Nature for showing contempt to its calls.

The natural needs of human beings

According to Epicurus, only two things are needed for complete happiness: bodily health and peace of mind. Nothing else is necessary to produce the greatest joy of life. The desire for bodily health and peace of mind is natural and necessary, as are the activities and things that support the body and soul (health, food and drink, shelter, clothing, safety, friendship and knowledge). The desire for anything more is either unnecessary or entirely artificial. Gaining such "additions" do not increase our joy in living, they only vary it.

Epicurus did think that life is simple, and happiness is easy. He praised blessed Nature that has made what is necessary handy, and what is not easy to get, unnecessary. By necessary, he meant that its lack causes pain, whereas if it doesn't, then it is superfluous and unnecessary. He also advised us not to blame the body for the greatest evils, nor to attribute our troubles to mere circumstance. Instead, we should seek their cause within the soul by giving up every groundless and fleeting desire. As Lucretius put it, the natural goal of life is often to set a limit to desire and an end to fear.

Epicurus had a deep reverence for life; he felt joy in being alive and in enjoying its simple pleasures. To him, everything above the necessary was merely an embellishment. He supported that as long as we are alive and healthy, and not threatened by cold or worried about where our next meal will come from, we feel perfectly happy because the very fact of being alive is precious and beautiful. If we cannot enjoy the simple pleasure of taking a deep breath or the taste of our morning coffee or the joy of listening to birds singing or the sight of trees changing colors in autumn, we are missing the natural rhythms of being alive. In a real sense, all we have is the present moment; let us relax and enjoy it; let us be thankful we do not have an ache or turmoil in the mind; there is so much pleasure available to our five senses and intellect. It is simply a matter of developing the habit of awareness and appreciation.

The key Epicurean perceptions

Epicurus holds that autarkeia (autonomy, self-reliance) is vital to living happily. If we limit our desires to what is natural and necessary then we will be fearless and self-reliant, and we will have great natural wealth and personal freedom. If our desires are groundless and unlimited then we will be fearful and dependent, and we will live in true poverty and servitude. The study of what is natural shows that we have to be self-reliant and value our own good qualities rather than the good things that have come to us from external circumstances. As Epicurus put it: "Self-reliance is a great good, not so that we will always have only a few things, but so that if we do not have much, we will rejoice in the few things we have, firmly persuaded that those who need luxury the least enjoy it the most, and that everything natural is easily obtained whereas everything groundless is hard to get."

Epicurus suggested taking responsibility for what is within our control and putting aside the forces outside of our control, such as god, fate, astrology luck, culture or environment, and society. Instead of following the herd or being brainwashed by the culture around us, let us pay attention to Nature which teaches us to think nothing of what prosperity fortune may bring and stand ready for its seeming evils. Nature claims that the wise man is not swayed by the winds of fortune or driven by chance events, but instead directs his life by his own power. Also, Epicurus recommended becoming familiar with what is possible and what is not. By perceiving the limits of life, we can be aware of how uncomplicated it is to expel the pain produced by the lack of a necessary good, and how needless are the things that are achieved through struggle. By acting within our limits we will be happy with what we have and what we are, and there will be no need to be envious of other people. He stated also that we must envy no one; for the good do not deserve envy, and as for the bad, the more they prosper, the more they ruin it for themselves.

Epicurus considered optimism a prerequisite to happiness, saying that to those who are able to reason it out, the highest and surest joy is found in the stable health of the body and a firm confidence in keeping it. His whole philosophy is centered at establishing a favorable attitude towards life; to live happily, he claims, we need to satisfy only a few natural and necessary desires, readily procured. Pessimism and misery owe to unnecessary desires that arise from groundless perceptions. Once these are replaced by the Epicurean perceptions, optimism and joy will follow.

A common, groundless desire is for immortality, which results in a fear of death. If instead, we accept our own mortality, we will have a love and appreciation for life instead of a fear of death. The desire for immortality is considered by Epicurus a kind of disease of the soul, which can be cured through the ministrations of philosophy. The desire for luxury (fancy things, exciting experiences, and such) owes to the fear of being perceived as ordinary; though there is no need to show off, but being in active engagement with the world around us. The fear of insecurity leads to the desire of acquiring wealth and living extravagantly, following the herd, being ungrateful for what we have, and seeking to impress other people. These things are outside of our control; whether we have them or not is a matter of good fortune, not of our own actions. In Epicurus' words: "The ignoble soul is inflated by good fortune and deflated by misfortune."

Epicurus said that there is no need to live in fear, neither in the present nor in anticipation of future, unfortunate developments. Our fear of what could happen takes us out of the pleasure we can experience right here and now. Nothing spoils our tranquility more than being anxious, continually worrying, fretting and fidgeting over the future. We have dealt with pain up to this moment, and we can deal with any future pain even more effectively, now that we are committed and dedicated to philosophy. The ups and downs, pleasure and pain are part of Nature. Fortunately for us, there is a lot more pleasure than pain. Instead of worrying about future pains, let us focus on the pleasure of what is happening around us. The physical pleasures through our senses and the mental pleasures through our mind are an endless ocean. All we need to do is become more attentive to the present and not allow ourselves to be pulled out of our on-going pleasure by fear of future pain. So, as Epicurus argued, the choice is fairly stark: if we give in to groundless desires for things that are unnatural or unnecessary, we will live a life of pain and fear. By contrast, if we stay focused on what is natural and necessary then we will experience joy and a confidence in our ability to live.

The practical implications of the Epicurean perceptions

Epicurus was in favor of living simply and opposed to the pursuit of extravagance and luxury. He enjoyed living on bread and water, and rejoiced in the pleasure of a little vessel of cheese, that he could feast on whenever he pleased. He preferred to lie serene upon a bed of straw than be full of troubles on a golden chair at an overflowing table. Instead of always wanting what we do not have, he recommended being grateful for and satisfied with what we have, because what we have now are the things we once did wish for. Ingratitude makes us greedy and never satisfied. We can be happy with few things. Few things are more pleasurable than listening to or playing music, taking a walk in Nature, or cultivating and enjoying the beauty of colors, an intimate touch, tastes, and smells. We will surprise ourselves at how much our senses will give us, if we really open up to them. Concentrating our thoughts and energies on what is natural and necessary makes us calm and grounded. However, if we are always chasing after those embellishments beyond the necessary, then we will be of many minds, torn between conflicting desires that make us troubled and confused. For most people, to be quiet is to be numb and to be active is to be frenzied. For such people, Epicurus offers the possibility of combining mindful serenity and flowing activity. Those who claim that Epicurus counseled laziness and indolence are far from the truth.

Epicurus was not in favor of science for the sake of science as some people might be nowadays; the point of knowing about Nature is to experience undiluted enjoyment of life. His philosophy also acts as a deterrent to struggling in the public arena or making ourselves slaves to mass opinion or authorities. He suggested freeing ourselves from the prison of public affairs and living unnoticed. Living pleasantly for Epicurus means living without agitation, anxiety and fear, being comfortable and confident with who we are, far removed from repression or violence or greed for wealth, fame, status and political advantage. Without these burdens we are free to think in a calm and clear way. Rather than reacting, we interact and respond sensitively to others and the world around us. A life lived wisely, honorably and justly, is one in which we are kind, courteous, honest, considerate and full of good will. A kind and gentle man has no place for irony or feigned ignorance, for being snide or sarcastic, or lashing out with a sharp tongue. We degrade ourselves when we are condescending to others.

How do we square the Epicurean perceptions with modern life? By focusing on work and earning power and getting ahead? Is it possible to drop out of the rat race?

It is certainly difficult to apply ancient ideas in today's world because our modern existence is so different from how people lived back then. Nowadays we are forced to continually refine our skills, seek new opportunities and ways to thrive in the free market economy. Although that kind of dynamic was missing from ancient society, that does not mean we need to indulge in groundless desires for more and more material possessions, as many people do today. Unless we really love the work we do and can do it with a measure of tranquility, we must take steps to avoid being stuck in a bad work situation, surrounded by narrow-minded people or overbearing bosses. We would do well to do whatever is necessary to extract ourselves from such a suffocating world of anxiety.

Epicurus was also a hard-working person; he founded a philosophy, taught, and wrote many books—though his motive was not the acquisition of wealth, power and fame, but rather the pleasure of spreading his philosophy in a friendly environment.

Living within a community nowadays is inconsistent with the contemporary life, and that hinders the implementation of an Epicurean way of life, especially as it concerns friendship. Indeed, urban life is not conducive to intimate friendships. We have to systematically cultivate socializing and developing intimate acquaintances to enjoy the benefits of the Epicurean Philosophy.

Friendship in Epicurus runs much deeper than the superficial relation that gives pleasure or eases worries. This is eminent in how Epicurus exhorted his friend Menoeceus to practice these ideas day and night, alone and with a like-minded friend. The presence of a friend reinforces our practice of the precepts of true philosophy, and enables us to live as a god among men because friendship is an immortal good. These are certainly strong claims for the power of friendship, but Epicurus made them because the love and practice of philosophy is something we can achieve much more easily in collaboration with the people we value most deeply.

Epicurus also offered some guidelines for friendship—doing favors for our friends, making sure that they benefit from their interactions with us, and taking reasonable risks to build and maintain our friendships. He also said that a friend is not one who is constantly seeking some benefit, nor one who never connects friendship with utility; for the former trades kindness for compensation, while the latter cuts off all hope for the future.

The mainstream attitude of today suggests that by being famous we can enjoy a high social status in life: a big house, a fancy car, flashy clothes, and an enviable job. This creates a craving and endless dreams of being rich and famous. If we would like to live in inner harmony then we will quickly recognize the need to fend off the onslaught of the mass media and social culture. The desire for wealth leads to the fear of poverty and the pursuit of greed though there is no need to be rich. We only need to have enough material goods to meet our true and natural needs for food, shelter, clothing, and companionship. Joy through wealth, fame, being a celebrity, or anything else that is a result of vain ideas, will not banish emotional disturbance because all of these are outside our control. Epicurus states: "Happiness and bliss are produced not by great riches nor vast possessions nor exalted occupations nor positions of power, but rather by calmness of mind, freedom from pain, and a disposition of the soul that sets its limits in accordance with Nature."

Lucretius described how someone who seeks fame and power is like a real-life Sisyphus who is never satisfied because his goals are illusions that cannot be reached. The desire for power leads to the fear of weakness yet there is no use holding power over other people. There is only use in being effective enough to meet our own needs. Fame is also unnatural. If we have a groundless desire for fame then we will have a corresponding fear of living in obscurity. That combination of desire and fear might lead us to do things that will make us unhappy, and still, being renowned to the world is worthless. What is valuable is being connected to the people who truly matter to us. The desire for public honors leads to the fear of being disliked, yet it is useless to be the recipient of great public esteem, but important to have self-respect and to be respected by those whom we know and admire.

Epicurus' goal was to teach people to relax and enjoy life without worrying so much. His first interest was to remove the idea of the gods from the psyche of people. To Epicurus, the gods did exist, but they lived so far away from the affairs of men, in a permanent state of ataraxia, that they didn't interfere with humanity. In fact, they weren't even aware of humanity. With the removal of this fear of the gods came two advantages for the Epicureans. First, there would be no judgment after death and therefore, death shouldn't be feared. Everything is material, so whatever "soul" exists is connected to the physical body and ceases to exist upon death. Second, there would be no judgment during life. There is no way to appease a god who doesn't know you exist and doesn't care about your life. Therefore, you are free to find fulfillment in your life outside of religious rules and expectations.

The remedy of pains

What remedy does "the psychologist philosopher" Epicurus prescribe to cure the ills of the soul and the pains of the body?

Simply to align our life with what is natural and necessary. Before making a decision or implementing a desire, to question: "Will it require intense exertion to realize this desire?" and "is this a desire for something that is not really necessary for life itself, for physical health, and serenity of the soul?" If the answer to either of those questions is positive, then the desire is groundless. We can understand that the thing we desire is unnatural or unnecessary or harmful, and it is best to reject it. A key consequence of questioning our desires is that the harmony of our desires, decisions, and actions lead to peace of mind.

The remedy to painful feelings is mental training in adopting and learning the natural Epicurean perceptions of life. Epicurus counseled his followers to repeat certain phrases to themselves each day, when they were feeling troubled or when they were about to make a decision. That might account for the brief and often memorable aphorisms we find in the Principal Doctrines and Vatican Sayings. It seems to be that if we train ourselves to believe, for example, that "death is nothing to us" then we will not fear death; we will not be continually troubled by our own mortality; we will not dishonor our life. We will also not have a groundless desire to live forever, nor will we believe and do things that are driven by such a groundless desire; instead, we will face the prospect of our own extinction without fear. We will be untroubled by death in our day-to-day existence. We will honor our life and enjoy the span of days that is given to us. Notice how Epicurus says to train ourselves that death is nothing to us and how he focuses on the practices that enable us to live well and to die well.

CHAPTER 31

FREQUENT QUESTIONS

Why should we study the Epicurean Philosophy?

In the beginning out of curiosity, but later, our interest is preserved due to the usefulness of it.

What might be useful in the Epicurean Philosophy?

Despite the economic prosperity of contemporary life, people are often dissatisfied and anxious. It seems that something is missing from their lives. The Epicurean Philosophy claims to have the remedy that brings harmony between living in prosperity and feeling good. It offers the health of body in a peaceful mind.

Are the remedies of the past effective in modern life?

Certainly many things have changed in the social, political and economic environment over the 23 centuries that elapsed since Epicurus lived. Convincing answers were found to the stressful questions and worries of that era. However, the natural character of the Epicurean Philosophy renders it timeless and timely. The Epicurean Philosophy reintroduces Nature's purpose and suggests Nature's means to achieve it. Interestingly, all the goods we need are readily available, but we neglect them. We are now more privileged than ever to please ourselves and be free of worries.

Does the Epicurean Philosophy have the traits of a modern philosophy?

Surely it does. "Living pleasantly" is the end of life, "pleasure" the means to it, and "reason" the decision-making criterion.

How does it relate to other philosophies?

The Epicurean Philosophy looks for natural means to explain the natural phenomena of life and follows feeling as its guide to living happily. It was initiated by the Ionian philosopher Thales, continued by Democritus and culminated with Epicurus. In the modern era, many prominent intellectuals have expressed their sympathy and affiliation to it. Among them were Bentham, Hume, John Stuart Mill, Nietzsche, Sartre, Freud, Ray, Yalom, and Maslow. On the other hand, the philosophies of logic consider thoughts and reasoning the means to explain life and to live with

۱ most influential of them give prevalence to
۱nd becoming wealthy, as well as to living
۱ously and honourably.

..۱at role do feelings play in other philosophies?

In the non-natural philosophies reason is the prevalent tool in the quest of truth. They consider it superior to the older features of man, the emotions, senses, and instincts. These have to submit to reason and be kept under control. An exception to this comes from religious practices. These praise feelings, with love holding a central role in their teachings. But love has a particular meaning in religion. In Christianity, for example, it is referred to as "agape"; it is not a feeling, nor does it come naturally to us. It is a virtue modeled by Christ to denote the unconditional love for friends and enemies alike. Because of our fallen nature though, we are incapable of producing such a love. It can only enter our hearts through the Holy Spirit. "Agape" love is a determined act of will, and therefore unrelated to emotions.

Can everyone be happy?

Happiness is a mental state, and by nature, all of us are able to feel. It only requires us to bring harmony among our desires, thoughts, decisions, and actions and keep to satisfying only our necessary, natural needs and those of the unnecessary kind that are easily procured.

Are the Epicurean recommendations effective?

They definitely are because they simply reintroduce

Nature's means to happiness. In fact, the emergence and flourishing of psychology has been based on them. Modern psychotherapy originates in Epicurus.

What does the Epicurean philosophy advocate concerning politics?

While Epicurus discourages active participation in politics or making a career out of it, he allows for exceptions, such as when one has a natural inclination and advantage, or if it is the only means of getting away from an oppressive regime.

Can one be both religious and Epicurean?

The simple answer is no. By definition, the Epicurean Philosophy is alternative to the religious one. It suggests its own purpose of life as well as the means to realize it.

Is there empirical evidence about the application of the Epicurean Philosophy?

The empirical data that confirms the efficacy of the Epicurean Philosophy is rich. It was one of the most prevalent and long lasting philosophies of antiquity, having a major influence on Greek and Roman societies for more than seven centuries. Its teaching was violently interrupted by the introduction of Christianity as the official religion of the Byzantine Empire in the 4th century AD. Nevertheless, and despite the destruction of the texts of Epicurus, the philosophy survived through letters, fragments and indirect sources. The Epicurean Philosophy has also influenced the intellectuals of the Renaissance. The modern world, which embraced it, applied it to their lives and transmitted it to the younger generations. Up to today, it remains a source of inspiration and reflection and many Epicurean communities around the world apply and enjoy its benefits.

Is it as straightforward as it seems to apply it?

One has just to follow his feelings and to choose wisely which among them to pursue or avoid. However, things are complicated in real life because we have been brought up in a environment hostile to happiness. We are deeply influenced by the prevailing religious and mercenary culture and are forced by them to implement vital changes in our perceptions and lifestyle. Change is, by nature, difficult to bring about. One needs a strong will, patience and discipline–virtues that are hard to impose upon our life. Again, by differentiating ourselves from the dominant culture we will inevitably come into conflict with our environment. Furthermore, feelings are hard to deal with, and intimate friendships are diminishing in contemporary life.

PART SIX: APPENDICES

ANNEX 1

THE PRINCIPAL DOCTRINES
OF EPICURUS

Translated by Cyril Bailey - Oxford, 1926

1. The blessed and immortal nature knows no trouble itself nor causes trouble to any other, so that it is never constrained by anger or favour. For all such things exist only in the weak.

2. Death is nothing to us, for that which is dissolved is without sensation; and that which lacks sensation is nothing to us.

3. The limit of quantity in pleasures is the removal of all that is painful. Wherever pleasure is present, as long as it is there, there is neither pain of body nor of mind, nor of both at once.

4. Pain does not last continuously in the flesh, but the acutest pain is there for a very short time, and even that which just exceeds the pleasure in the flesh does not continue for many days at once. But chronic illnesses permit a predominance of pleasure over pain in the flesh.

5. It is not possible to live pleasantly without living prudently and honorably and justly, [nor again to live a life of prudence, honor, and Justice] without living pleasantly. And the man who does not possess the pleasant life, is not living prudently and honorably and justly, [and the man who does not possess the virtuous life], cannot possibly live pleasantly.

6. To secure protection from men, anything is a natural good by which you may be able to attain this end.

7. Some men wished to become famous and conspicuous, thinking that they would thus win for themselves safety from other men. Wherefore if the life of such men is safe, they have obtained the good which nature craves; but if it is not safe, they do not possess that for which they strove at first by the instinct of nature.

8. No pleasure is a bad thing in itself: but the means which produce some pleasures bring with them disturbances many times greater than the pleasures.

9. If every pleasure could be intensified so that it lasted and influenced the whole organism or the most essential parts of our nature, pleasures would never differ from one another.

10. If the things that produce the pleasures of profligates

could dispel the fears of the mind about the phenomena of the sky and death and its pains, and also teach the limits of desires [and of pains], we should never have cause to blame them: for they would be filling themselves full with pleasures from every source and never have pain of body or mind, which is the evil of life.

11. If we were not troubled by our suspicions of the phenomena of the sky and about death, fearing that it concerns us, and also by our failure to grasp the limits of pains and desires, we should have no need of natural science.

12. A man cannot dispel his fear about the most important matters if he does not know what the nature of the universe is, but suspects the truth of some mythical story. So that without natural science it is not possible to attain our pleasures unalloyed.

13. There is no profit in securing protection in relation to men, if things above and things beneath the Earth and indeed all in the boundless universe remain matters of suspicion.

14. The most unalloyed source of protection from men, which is secured to some extent by a certain force of expulsion, is in fact the immunity which results from a quiet life and the retirement from the world.

15. The wealth demanded by nature is both limited and easily procured; that demanded by idle imaginings stretches on to infinity.

16. In but few things chance hinders a wise man, but the

greatest and most important matters reason has ordained and throughout the whole period of life does and will ordain.

17. The just man is most free from trouble, the unjust most full of trouble.

18. The pleasure in the flesh is not increased, when once the pain due to want is removed, but is only varied: and the limit as regards pleasure in the mind is begotten by the reasoned understanding of these very pleasures and of the emotions akin to them, which used to cause the greatest fear to the mind.

19. Infinite time contains no greater pleasure than limited time, if one measures by reason the limits of pleasure.

20. The flesh perceives the limits of pleasure as unlimited, and unlimited time is required to supply it. But the mind, having attained a reasoned understanding of the ultimate good of the flesh and its limits and having dissipated the fears concerning the time to come, supplies us with the complete life, and we have no further need of infinite time: but neither does the mind shun pleasure, nor, when circumstances begin to bring about the departure from life, does it approach its end as though it fell short in any way of the best life.

21. He who has learned the limits of life knows that that which removes the pain due to want and makes the whole of life complete is readily procured, so that there is no need of actions which involve competition.

22. We must consider both the real purpose and all the evidence of direct perception, to which we always refer the conclusions of opinion; otherwise, all will be full of doubt and confusion.

23. If you fight against all sensations, you will have no standard by which to judge even those of them which you say are false.

24. If you reject any single sensation and fail to distinguish between the conclusion of opinion as to the appearance awaiting confirmation and that which is actually given by the sensation or feeling, or each intuitive apprehension of the mind, you will confound all other sensations as well with the same groundless opinion, so that you will reject every standard of judgment. And if among the mental images created by your opinion you affirm both that which awaits confirmation and that which does not, you will not escape error; since you will have preserved the whole cause of doubt in every judgment between what is right and what is wrong.

25. If on each occasion, instead of referring your actions to the end of nature, you turn to some other nearer standard when you are making a choice or an avoidance, your actions will not be consistent with your principles.

26. Of desires, all that do not lead to a sense of pain, if they are not satisfied, are not necessary, but involve a craving which is easily dispelled, when the object is hard to procure or they seem likely to produce harm.

27. Of all the things which wisdom acquires to produce the blessedness of the complete life, far the greatest is the possession of friendship.

28. The same conviction which has given us confidence that there is nothing terrible that lasts forever or even for long, has also seen the protection of friendship most fully completed in the limited evils of this life.

29. Among desires, some are natural [and necessary, some natural] but not necessary, and others neither natural nor necessary, but due to idle imagination.

30. Wherever in the case of desires which are physical, but do not lead to a sense of pain, if they are not fulfilled, the effort is intense, such pleasures are due to idle imagination, and it is not owing to their own nature that they fail to be dispelled, but owing to the empty imaginings of the man.

31. The justice which arises from nature is a pledge of mutual advantage to restrain men from harming one another and save them from being harmed.

32. For all living things which have not been able to make compacts not to harm one another or be harmed, nothing ever is either just or unjust; and likewise too for all tribes of men which have been unable or unwilling to make compacts not to harm or be harmed.

33. Justice never is anything in itself, but in the dealings of men with one another in any place whatever and at any time it is a kind of compact not to harm or be harmed.

34. Injustice is not an evil in itself, but only in consequence of the fear which attaches to the apprehension of being unable to escape those appointed to punish such actions.

35. It is not possible for one who acts in secret contravention of the terms of the compact not to harm or be harmed, to be confident that he will escape detection, even if at present he escapes a thousand times. For up to the time of death it cannot be certain that he will indeed escape.

36. In its general aspect justice is the same for all, for it is a kind of mutual advantage in the dealings of men with one another: but with reference to the individual peculiarities of a country or any other circumstances, the same thing does not turn out to be just for all.

37. Among actions which are sanctioned as just by law, that which is proved on examination to be of advantage in the requirements of men's dealings with one another, has the guarantee of justice, whether it is the same for all or not. But if a man makes a law and it does not turn out to lead to advantage in men's dealings with each other, then it no longer has the essential nature of justice. And even if the advantage in the matter of justice shifts from one side to the other, but for a while accords with the general concept, it is nonetheless just for that period in the eyes of those who do not confound themselves with empty sounds but look to the actual facts.

38. Where, provided the circumstances have not been altered, actions which were considered just, have been shown not to accord with the general concept in actual practice, then they are not just. But where, when circumstances have changed, the same actions which were sanctioned as just no longer lead to advantage, there they were just at the time when they were of advantage for the dealings of fellow-citizens with one another, but subsequently they are no longer just, when no longer of advantage.

39. The man who has best ordered the element of disquiet arising from external circumstances has made those things that he could akin to himself and the rest at least not alien; but with all to which he could not do even this, he has refrained from mixing, and has expelled from his life all which it was of advantage to treat thus.

40. As many as possess the power to procure complete immunity from their neighbors, these also live most pleasantly with one another, since they have the most certain pledge of security, and after they have enjoyed the fullest intimacy, they do not lament the previous departure of a dead friend, as though he were to be pitied.

ANNEX 2

THE VATICAN SAYINGS

Translated by Cyril Bailey - Oxford, 1926

This list by an unknown author was discovered in 1888 at the Vatican and is reputed to date from the fourteenth century.

1. A blessed and indestructible being has no trouble himself and brings no trouble upon any other being; so he is free from anger and partiality, for all such things imply weakness.

2. Death is nothing to us; for that which has been dissolved into its elements experiences no sensations, and that which has no sensation is nothing to us.

3. Continuous bodily pain does not last long; instead, pain, if extreme, is present a very short time, and even that degree of pain which slightly exceeds bodily pleasure

does not last for many days at once. Diseases of long duration allow an excess of bodily pleasure over pain.

4. All bodily suffering is easy to disregard: for that which causes acute pain has short duration, and that which endures long in the flesh causes but mild pain.

5. It is impossible to live a pleasant life without living wisely and honorably and justly, and it is impossible to live wisely and honorably and justly without living pleasantly. Whenever any one of these is lacking, when, for instance, the man is not able to live wisely, though he lives honorably and justly, it is impossible for him to live a pleasant life.

6. It is impossible for a man who secretly violates the terms of the agreement not to harm or be harmed to feel confident that he will remain undiscovered, even if he has already escaped ten thousand times; for until his death he is never sure that he will not be detected. [see *Principle Doctrine* 35]

7. It is hard for an evil-doer to escape detection, but to be confident that he will continue to escape detection indefinitely is impossible.

8. The wealth required by nature is limited and is easy to procure; but the wealth required by vain ideals extends to infinity. [see *Principle Doctrine* 15]

9. Necessity is an evil, but there is no necessity to live under the control of necessity.

10. Remember that you are mortal and have a limited time to live and have devoted yourself to discussions on

Nature for all time and eternity and have seen things that are now and are to come and have been.

11. For most men, rest is stagnation and activity is madness.

12. The just man is most free from disturbance, while the unjust is full of the utmost disturbance. [see *Principle Doctrine* 17]

13. Among the things held to be just by law, whatever is proved to be of advantage in men's dealings has the stamp of justice, whether or not it be the same for all; but if a man makes a law and it does not prove to be mutually advantageous, then this is no longer just. And if what is mutually advantageous varies and only for a time corresponds to our concept of justice, nevertheless for that time it is just for those who do not trouble themselves about empty words, but look simply at the facts. [see *Principle Doctrine* 37]

14. We are born once and cannot be born twice, but for all time must be no more. But you, who are not master of tomorrow, postpone your happiness. Life is wasted in procrastination, and each one of us dies without allowing himself leisure.

15. We value our characters as something peculiar to ourselves, whether they are good and we are esteemed by men or not, so ought we to value the characters of others, if they are well-disposed to us.

16. No one when he sees evil deliberately chooses it, but is enticed by it as being good in comparison with a greater evil and so pursues it.

17. It is not the young man who should be thought happy, but the old man who has lived a good life. For the young man at the height of his powers is unstable and is carried this way and that by fortune, like a headlong stream. But the old man has come to anchor in old age as though in port, and the good things for which before he hardly hoped he has brought into safe harbor in his grateful recollections.

18. If sight, association, and intercourse are removed, the passion of love is ended.

19. Forgetting the good that has been, he has become old this very day.

20. Of our desires some are natural and necessary, others are natural but not necessary; and others are neither natural nor necessary, but are due to groundless opinion. [see *Principle Doctrine* 29]

21. We must not violate nature, but obey her; and we shall obey her if we fulfill those desires that are necessary, and also those that are natural but bring no harm to us, but we must sternly reject those that are harmful.

22. Unlimited time and limited time afford an equal amount of pleasure, if we measure the limits of that pleasure by reason. [see *Principle Doctrine* 19]

23. All friendship is desirable in itself, though it starts from the need of help.

24. Dreams have neither divine character nor any prophetic force, but they originate from the influx of images.

25. Poverty, when measured by the natural purpose of life, is great wealth, but unlimited wealth is great poverty.

26. You must understand that whether the discourse is long or short it tends to the same end.

27. In all other occupations the fruit comes painfully after completion, but in philosophy pleasure goes hand in hand with knowledge; for enjoyment does not follow comprehension, but comprehension and enjoyment are simultaneous.

28. We must not approve either those who are always ready for friendship, or those who hang back, but for friendship's sake we must run risks.

29. In investigating nature I would prefer to speak openly and like an oracle to give answers serviceable to all mankind, even though no one should understand me, rather than to conform to popular opinions and so win the praise freely scattered by the mob.

30. Some men throughout their lives spend their time gathering together the means of life, for they do not see that the draught swallowed by all of us at birth is a draught of death.

31. Against all else it is possible to provide security, but as against death all of us mortals alike dwell in an unfortified city.

32. The veneration of the wise man is a great blessing to those who venerate him.

33. The flesh cries out to be saved from hunger, thirst, and

cold. For if a man possess this safety and hope to possess it, he might rival even Zeus in happiness.

34. It is not so much our friends' help that helps us as it is the confidence of their help.

35. We should not spoil what we have by desiring what we do not have, but remember that what we have too was the gift of fortune.

36. Epicurus' life, when compared to other men's in respect of gentleness and self-sufficiency, might be thought a mere legend.

37. Nature is weak toward evil, not toward good: because it is saved by pleasures, but destroyed by pains.

38. He is a little man in all respects who has many good reasons for quitting life.

39. He is no friend who is continually asking for help, nor he who never associates help with friendship. For the former barters kindly feeling for a practical return and the latter destroys the hope of good in the future.

40. The man who says that all things come to pass by necessity cannot criticize one who denies that all things come to pass by necessity: for he admits that this too happens of necessity.

41. We must laugh and philosophize at the same time and do our household duties and employ our other faculties, and never cease proclaiming the sayings of the true philosophy.

42. The same span of time embraces both the beginning and the end of the greatest good.

43. The love of money, if unjustly gained, is impious, and, if justly gained, is shameful; for it is unseemly to be parsimonious even with justice on one's side.

44. The wise man when he has accommodated himself to straits knows better how to give than to receive, so great is the treasure of self-sufficiency which he has discovered.

45. The study of nature does not make men productive of boasting or bragging nor apt to display that culture which is the object of rivalry with the many, but high-spirited and self-sufficient, taking pride in the good things of their own minds and not of their circumstances.

46. Let us utterly drive from us our bad habits as if they were evil men who have long done us great harm.

47. I have anticipated thee, Fortune, and entrenched myself against all thy secret attacks. And I will not give myself up as captive to thee or to any other circumstance; but when it is time for me to go, spitting contempt on life and on those who vainly cling to it, I will leave life crying aloud a glorious triumph-song that I have lived well.

48. We must try to make the end of the journey better than the beginning, as long as we are journeying; but when we come to the end, we must be happy and content.

49. It is impossible for someone to dispel his fears about the most important matters if he does not know the nature of the universe but still gives some credence to myths. So without the study of Nature there is no enjoyment of pure pleasure. [see *Principle Doctrine* 12]

50. No pleasure is a bad thing in itself, but the things which produce certain pleasures entail disturbances many times greater than the pleasures themselves. [see *Principle Doctrine* 8]

51. You tell me that the stimulus of the flesh makes you too prone to the pleasures of love. Provided that you do not break the laws or good customs and do not distress any of your neighbors or do harm to your body or squander your pittance, you may indulge your inclination as you please. Yet it is impossible not to come up against one or other of these barriers, for the pleasures of love never profited a man and he is lucky if they do him no harm.

52. Friendship dances around the world bidding us all to awaken to the recognition of happiness.

53. We must envy no one, for the good do not deserve envy and the bad, the more they prosper, the more they injure themselves.

54. We must not pretend to study philosophy, but study it in reality, for it is not the appearance of health that we need, but real health.

55. We must heal our misfortunes by the grateful recollec-

tion of what has been and by the recognition that it is impossible to undo that which has been done.

56. The wise man feels no more pain when being tortured himself than when his friend tortured.

57. On occasion a man will die for his friend, for if he betrays his friend, his whole life will be confounded by distrust and completely upset.

58. We must free ourselves from the prison of public education and politics.

59. It is not the stomach that is insatiable, as is generally said, but the false opinion that the stomach needs an unlimited amount to fill it.

60. Every man passes out of life as though he had just been born.

61. Most beautiful too is the sight of those near and dear to us, when our original kinship makes us of one mind; for such sight is great incitement to this end.

62. Now if parents are justly angry with their children, it is certainly useless to fight against it and not to ask for pardon; but if their anger is unjust and irrational, it is quite ridiculous to add fuel to their irrational passion by nursing one's own indignation, and not to attempt to turn aside their wrath in other ways by gentleness.

63. Frugality too has a limit, and the man who disregards it is like him who errs through excess.

64. Praise from others must come unasked, and we must concern ourselves with the healing of our own lives.

65. It is vain to ask of the gods what a man is capable of supplying for himself.

66. Let us show our feeling for our lost friends not by lamentation but by meditation.

67. A free life cannot acquire many possessions, because this is not easy to do without servility to mobs or monarchs, yet it possesses all things in unfailing abundance; and if by chance it obtains many possessions, it is easy to distribute them so as to win the gratitude of neighbors.

68. Nothing is sufficient for him to whom what is sufficient seems too little.

69. The ungrateful greed of the soul makes the creature everlastingly desire varieties in its lifestyle.

70. Let nothing be done in your life which will cause you fear if it becomes known to your neighbor.

71. Every desire must be confronted by this question: what will happen to me if the object of my desire is accomplished, and what if it is not?

72. There is no advantage to obtaining protection from other men so long as we are alarmed by events above or below the Earth or in general by whatever happens in the boundless universe.

73. The occurrence of certain bodily pains assists us in guarding against others like them.

74. In a philosophical discussion, he who is defeated gains more, since he learns more.

75. The saying, "look to the end of a long life," shows ungratefulness for past good fortune.

76. You are in your old age just such as I urge you to be, and you have seen the difference between studying philosophy for oneself and proclaiming it to Greece at large; I rejoice with you.

77. The greatest fruit of self-sufficiency is freedom.

78. The noble soul occupies itself with wisdom and friendship; of these the one is a mortal good, the other immortal.

79. The man who is serene causes no disturbance to himself or to another.

80. The first measure of security is to watch over one's youth and to guard against what makes havoc of all by means of maddening desires.

81. The disturbance of the soul cannot be ended nor true joy created either by the possession of the greatest wealth or by honor and respect in the eyes of the mob or by anything else that is associated with or caused by unlimited desire.

ANNEX 3

THE LETTER OF EPICURUS
TO MENOECEUS

Translated by Cyril Bailey, Oxford, 1926

Greeting,

Let no one when young delay to study philosophy, nor when he is old grow weary of his study. For no one can come too early or too late to secure the health of his soul. And the man who says that the age for philosophy has either not yet come or has gone by is like the man who says that the age for happiness is not yet come to him, or has passed away. Wherefore, both when young and old, a man must study philosophy, so that as he grows old he may be young in blessings through the grateful recollection of what has been, and in youth he may be old as well, since he will know no fear of what is to come. We must then meditate on the things that make our happiness, seeing that when that is with us, we have all, but when it is absent, we do all to win it.

The things which I used unceasingly to commend to you, these, do and practice, considering them to be the first principles of the good life. First of all, believe that god is a being immortal and blessed, even as the common idea of a god is engraved on men's minds, and do not assign to him anything alien to his immortality or ill-suited to his blessedness: but believe about him everything that can uphold his blessedness and immortality. For gods there are, since the knowledge of them is by clear vision. But they are not such as the many believe them to be: for indeed they do not consistently represent them as they believe them to be. And the impious man is not he who popularly denies the gods of the many, but he who attaches to the gods the beliefs of the many. For the statements of the many about the gods are not conceptions derived from sensation, but false suppositions, according to which the greatest misfortunes befall the wicked and the greatest blessings (the good) by the gift of the gods. For men, being accustomed always to their own virtues, welcome those like themselves, but regard all that is not of their nature as alien.

Become accustomed to the belief that death is nothing to us. For all good and evil consists of sensation, but death is deprivation of sensation. And therefore, a right understanding that death is nothing to us makes the mortality of life enjoyable, not because it adds to it an infinite span of time, but because it takes away the craving for immortality.

For there is nothing terrible in life for the man who has truly comprehended that there is nothing terrible in not living. So that the man speaks but idly who says that he fears death not because it will be painful when it comes, but because it is painful in anticipation. For that which gives no trouble when it comes is but an empty pain in anticipation. So death, the most terrifying of ills, is nothing to us, since so long as we exist, death is not with us; but when death comes, then we do not exist. It does not then concern either the living or the dead, since for the former it is not, and the latter are no more.

But the many at one moment shun death as the greatest of evils, at another, [yearn for it] as a respite from the [evils] in life. But the wise man neither seeks to escape life nor fears the cessation of life, for neither does life offend him nor does the absence of life seem to be any evil. And just as with food, he does not seek simply the larger share and nothing else, but rather the most pleasant, so he seeks to enjoy not the longest period of time, but the most pleasant. And he who counsels the young man to live well, but the old man to make a good end, is foolish, not merely because of the desirability of life, but also because it is the same training which teaches to live well and to die well. Yet much worse still is the man who says it is good not to be born but once born makes haste to pass the gates of Death. For if he says this from conviction why does he not pass away out of life? For it is open to him to do so, if he had firmly made up his mind to this. But if he speaks in jest, his words are idle among men who cannot receive them.

We must then bear in mind that the future is neither ours, nor yet wholly not ours, so that we may not altogether expect it as sure to come, nor abandon hope of it, as if it will certainly not come.

We must consider that of desires, some are natural, others vain; and of the natural, some are necessary and others merely natural; and of the necessary, some are necessary for happiness, others for the repose of the body, and others for very life. The right understanding of these facts enables us to refer all choice and avoidance to the health of the body and [the soul's] freedom from disturbance, since this is the aim of the life of blessedness. For it is to obtain this end that we always act, namely, to avoid pain and fear. And when this is once secured for us, all the tempest of the soul is dispersed, since the living creature has not to wander as though in search of something that is missing, and to look for some other thing by which he can fulfill the good of the soul and the good of the body. For it is then that we have need of pleasure, when we feel pain owing to the absence of pleasure; [but when we do not feel pain], we no longer need pleasure. And for this cause we call pleasure the beginning and end of the blessed life. For we recognize pleasure as the first good innate in us, and from pleasure we begin every act of choice and avoidance, and to pleasure we return again, using the feeling as the standard by which we judge every good.

And since pleasure is the first good and natural to us, for this very reason we do not choose every pleasure, but sometimes we pass over many pleasures, when greater discomfort accrues to us as the result of them: and similarly we think many pains better than pleasures, since a greater pleasure comes to us when we have endured pains for a long time. Every pleasure then because of its natural kinship to us is good, yet not every pleasure is to be chosen: even as every pain also is an evil, yet not all are always of a nature to be avoided. Yet by a scale of comparison and by the consideration of advantages and disadvantages we must form our judgment on all these matters. For the good on certain occasions we treat as bad, and conversely the bad as good.

And again independence of desire we think a great good—not that we may at all times enjoy but a few things, but that, if we do not possess many, we may enjoy the few in the genuine persuasion that those have the sweetest pleasure in luxury who least need it, and that all that is natural is easy to be obtained, but that which is superfluous is hard. And so plain savours bring us a pleasure equal to a luxurious diet, when all the pain due to want is removed; and bread and water produce the highest pleasure, when one who needs them puts them to his lips. To grow accustomed therefore to simple and not luxurious diet gives us health to the full, and makes a man alert for the needful employments of life, and when after long intervals we approach luxuries disposes us better towards them, and fits us to be fearless of fortune.

When, therefore, we maintain that pleasure is the end, we do not mean the pleasures of profligates and those that consist in sensuality, as is supposed by some who are either ignorant or disagree with us or do not understand, but freedom from pain in the body and from trouble in the mind. For it is not continuous drinkings and revelings, nor the satisfaction of lusts, nor the enjoyment of fish and other luxuries of the wealthy table, which produce a pleasant life, but sober reasoning, searching out the motives for all choice and avoidance, and banishing mere opinions, to which are due the greatest disturbance of the spirit.

Of all this, the beginning and the greatest good is prudence. Wherefore prudence is a more precious thing even than philosophy: for from prudence are sprung all the other virtues, and it teaches us that it is not possible to live pleasantly without living prudently and honourably and justly, [nor, again, to live a life of prudence, honour, and justice] without living pleasantly. For the virtues are by nature bound up with the pleasant life, and the pleasant life is inseparable from them. For indeed, who, think you, is a better man than he who holds reverent opinions concerning the gods, and is at all times free from fear of death, and has reasoned out the end ordained by nature? He understands that the limit of good things is easy to fulfill and easy to attain, whereas the course of ills is either short in time or slight in pain; he laughs at [destiny], whom some have introduced as the mistress of all things. [He thinks that with us lies the chief power in determining events, some of which happen by necessity] and some by chance, and some are within our control; for while necessity cannot be called to account, he sees that chance is inconstant, but that which is in our control is subject to no master, and to it are naturally attached praise and blame. For, indeed, it was better to follow the myths about the gods than to become a slave to the destiny of the natural philosophers: for the former suggests a hope of placating the gods by worship, whereas the latter involves a necessity which knows no placation. As to chance, he does not regard it as a god as most men do [for in a god's acts there is no disorder], nor as an uncertain cause [of all things] for he does not believe that good and evil are given by chance to man for the framing of a blessed life, but that opportunities for great good and great evil are afforded by it. He therefore thinks it better to be unfortunate in reasonable action than to prosper in unreason. For it is better in a man's actions that what is well-chosen [should fail, rather than that what is ill chosen] should be successful owing to chance.

Meditate, therefore, on these things, and things akin to them, night and day by yourself; and with a companion like to yourself, and never shall you be disturbed waking or asleep, but you shall live like a god among men. For a man who lives among immortal blessings is not like unto a mortal being.

ANNEX 4

DIOGENES LAERTIUS: EPICURUS

Diogenes Laertius (3rd century AD) is the primary source for the surviving complete letters of Epicurus and for biographical and other pertinent information about him:

Index:
Biography of Epicurus
Epicurus' followers and namesakes
Epicurus' writings
Overview of Epicureanism
Epicurean epistemology and physics
Epicurean ethics
Biography of Epicurus

Translated by Robert Drew Hicks

Epicurus, son of Neocles and Chaerestrate, was an Athenian of the Gargettus ward and the Philaidae clan, as

Metrodorus says in his book *On Noble Birth*. He is said by Heraclides (in his *Epitome of Sotion*) as well as by others, to have been brought up at Samos after the Athenians had sent colonists there and to have come to Athens at the age of eighteen, at the time when Xenocrates was head of the Academy, and Aristotle was in Chalcis. After the death of Alexander of Macedon and the expulsion of the Athenian colonists from Samos by Perdiccas, Epicurus left Athens to join his father in Colophon; for some time he stayed there and gathered students around him, then returned to Athens again during the archonship of Anaxicrates (307–306 BC).

For a while, it is said, he pursued his studies in common with other philosophers, but afterwards put forward independent views by founding the school named after him. He says himself that he first came to study philosophy at the age of fourteen, Apollodorus the Epicurean (in the first book of his *Life of Epicurus*) says that he turned to philosophy in contempt of the school teachers who could not tell him the meaning of "chaos" in Hesiod. According to Hermippus, however, he started as a school teacher, but up on coming across the works of Democritus, turned eagerly to philosophy, which accounts for Timon's allusion in the lines: "Again there is the latest and most shameless of the natural philosophers, the school teacher's son from Samos, himself the most ill-bred and undisciplined of mankind."

At his encouragement, his three brothers, Neocles, Chaeredemus, and Aristobulus, joined in his studies, as Philodemus the Epicurean relates in the tenth book of his comprehensive work *On Philosophers;* as did his slave named Mys, as stated by Myronianus in *Historical Parallels*. Diotimus the Stoic, who was very hostile to him, assailed him with bitter slanders, attributing fifty obscene letters as having been written by Epicurus; and so too did the author who ascribed to Epicurus the letters commonly attributed to Chrysippus (the Stoic). They are followed in this by Posidonius the Stoic and his school, and Nicolaus and Sotion in the twelfth of twenty-four books of his work entitled *Dioclean Refutations,* also by Dionysius of Halicarnassus. They allege that he used to go round with his mother to small cottages to perform purification rites and read charms, and assist his father in his school for a pitiful fee; further, that one of his brothers was a pimp and lived with the courtesan Leontion (Lioness); that he put forward as his own the doctrines of Democritus about atoms and of Aristippus about pleasure; that he was not a genuine Athenian, a charge brought by Timocrates and by Herodotus in a book *On the Training of Epicurus as a Cadet,* that he basely flattered Mithras, the viceroy of Lysimachus, bestowing on him in his letters Apollo's titles of *Healer* and *Lord.* They further charged that he extolled Idomeneus, Herodotus, and Timocrates, who had published his esoteric doctrines, and flattered them for that very reason. Also that in his letters he wrote to Leontion: "O Lord Apollo, my dear little Leontion, with what tumultuous applause we were inspired as we read your letter." Then again to Themista, the wife of Leonteus: "I am quite ready, if you do not come to see me, to roll around three times on my own axis and be propelled to any place that you, including

Themista, agree upon"; and to the beautiful Pythocles he wrote: "I will sit quietly and await with desire for your god-like coming" and, as Theodorus says in the fourth book of his work, *Against Epicurus,* in another letter to Themista he thinks he preaches to her. It is added that he corresponded with many courtesans, and especially with Leontion, of whom Metrodorus was also enamored. It is observed too that in his treatise, *On the Ethical End,* he writes in these terms : "I know not how to conceive the good, apart from the pleasures of taste, of sex, of sound, and the pleasures of beautiful form" and in his letter to Pythocles: "Hoist all sails, my dear boy, and steer clear of all indoctrination." Epictetus calls him preacher of effeminacy and showers abuse on him. Again there was Timocrates, the brother of Metrodorus, who was his student and then left the school. In the book *Merriment* he asserts that Epicurus vomited twice a day from over-indulgence, and goes on to say that he himself had great difficulty in escaping from that notorious midnight philosophizing and the confraternity with all its secrets; further, that Epicurus' understanding of philosophy was small and his understanding of life even smaller; that his bodily health was pitiful, so much so that for many years he was unable to rise from his chair; and that he spent a whole mina daily on his meals, as he himself says in his letter to Leontion and in that to the philosophers at Mitylene. Also that among other courtesans who consorted with him and Metrodorus were Mammarion and Hedia and Erotion and Nikidion. He alleges too that in his thirty-seven books *On Nature* Epicurus says the same things over and over again and writes largely in sheer opposition to others, especially against Nausiphanes. Here are his own words: "Nay, let them go hang: for, when laboring with an idea, he too had the sophist's off-hand boastfulness like many another servile soul." Besides, he himself in his letters says of Nausiphanes: "This so maddened him that he abused me and called me pedagogue." Epicurus used to call this Nausiphanes jellyfish, an illiterate, a fraud, and a trollop; Plato's school he called "the toadies of Dionysius," their master himself the "golden" Plato, and Aristotle a profligate who after devouring his patrimony took to soldiering and selling drugs; Protagoras, a porter and the secretary of Democritus and village school teacher; Heraclitus a muddler; Democritus Lerocritus a trifler; and Antidorus Sannidorus a flattering gift-bearer; the Cynics, enemies of Greece; the Dialecticians, consumed with envy; and Pyrrho (the Skeptic), an ignorant boor.

But these people are stark mad. For our philosopher has numerous witnesses to attest his unsurpassed goodwill to all men; his native land, which honored him with statues in bronze; his friends, so many in number that they could hardly be counted by whole cities, and indeed all who knew him, held fast as they were by the siren-charms of his doctrine, save Metrodorus of Stratonicea, who went over to Carneades, being, perhaps, burdened by his master's excessive goodness; the Garden itself which, while nearly all the others have died out, continues forever without interruption through numberless successions of one director after another; his gratitude to his parents, his generosity to his brothers, his gentleness to his servants, as evidenced by the terms of his will and by the fact that they were members of the Garden, the most eminent of them being the aforesaid Mys; and in general, his benevolence to all mankind. His piety towards the gods and his affection for his country, no words can describe. He carried his modesty to such an excess that he did not even enter public life. He spent all his life in Greece, notwithstanding the calamities which had befallen her in that era; when he did once or twice take a trip to Ionia, it was to visit his friends there. Friends, indeed, came to him from all parts and lived with him in his Garden. This is stated by Apollodorus, who also says that he purchased the Garden for eighty minae. And to the same effect, Diocles in the third book of his *Epitome* speaks of them as living a very simple and frugal life; at all events they were content with a cup of thin wine and were, for the rest, thoroughgoing water-drinkers. He further says that Epicurus did not think it right that their property should be held in common, as required by the maxim of Pythagoras about the goods of friends; such a practice in his opinion implied mistrust, and without confidence there is no friendship. In his correspondence, he himself mentions that he was content with plain bread and water. And again: "Send me a little pot of cheese that, when I like, I may fare sumptuously." Such was the man who laid down that pleasure was the end of life. And here is the epigram in which Athenaeus eulogizes him: "You toil, men, for paltry things and incessantly begin strife and war for gain; but Nature's wealth extends to a moderate bound, whereas

vain judgments have a limitless range. This lesson Neocles'
wise son heard from the Muses or from the sacred tripod
at Delphi." And, as we go on, we shall know this better
from his doctrines and his sayings. Among the early philosophers, says Diocles, his favorite was Anaxagoras, although
he occasionally disagreed with him, and Archelaus, the
teacher of Socrates. Diocles adds that he used to train his
friends in committing his treatises to memory, Apollodorus
in his *Chronology* tells us that our philosopher was a pupil
of Nausiphanes and Praxiphanes; but in his letter to Eurylochus, Epicurus himself denies it and says that he was self-
taught. Both Epicurus and Hermarchus deny the very existence of Leucippus the philosopher, though by some and
by Apollodorus the Epicurean he is said to have been the
teacher of Democritus. Demetrius the Magnesian affirms
that Epicurus also attended the lectures of Xenocrates. The
terms he used for things were the ordinary terms, and Aris-
tophanes the grammarian credits him with a very characteristic style. He was so lucid a writer that in the work *On
Rhetoric* he makes clearness the sole requisite. And in his
correspondence, he replaces the usual greeting "I wish you
joy" with wishes for welfare and right living, "May you do
well," and "Live well." Ariston says in his *Life of Epicurus*
that he derived his work, entitled *The Canon* from the *Tripod* of Nausiphanes, adding that Epicurus had been this
man's pupil as well as of the Platonist, Pamphilus, in Samos.
Further, that he began to study philosophy when he was
twelve years old, and started his own school at thirty-two.
He was born, according to Apollodorus in his *Chronology,*

in the third year of the 109th Olympiad, in the archonship of Sosigenes, on the seventh day of the month Gamelion, in the seventh year after the death of Plato (February 4, 341 BC). When he was thirty-two he founded a school of philosophy, first in Mitylene and Lampsacus, and then five years later removed to Athens, where he died in the second year of the 127th Olympiad, in the archonship of Pytharatus, at the age of seventy-two (270 BC); and Hermarchus the son of Agemortus, a Mitylenaean, took over the Garden. Epicurus died of renal calculus after an illness which lasted a fortnight; so Hermarchus tells us in his letters. Hermippus relates that he entered a bronze bath of lukewarm water and asked for unmixed wine, which he swallowed, and then, having bidden his friends to remember his doctrines, breathed his last.

Here is something of my own about him:

"Farewell, my friends; the truths I taught hold fast, thus Epicurus spoke, and breathed his last. He sat in a warm bath and neat wine quaffed, and straightway, found chill death in that same draught."

Such was the life of the sage, and such his end.

Epicurus' followers and namesakes

Among his disciples, of whom there were many, the following were eminent: Metrodorus, the son of Athenaeus (or of Timocrates) and of Sande, a citizen of Lampsacus, who from his first acquaintance with Epicurus never left him except once for six months spent on a visit to his native place, from which he returned to him again. His goodness was proved in all ways, as Epicurus testifies in the introductions to his works and in the third book of the Timocrates. Such he was: he gave his sister Batis to Idomeneus to wife, and himself took Leontion the Athenian courtesan as his concubine. He showed dauntless courage in meeting troubles and death, as Epicurus declares in the first book of his memoir.

He died, we learn, seven years before Epicurus in his fifty-third year and Epicurus himself in his *Will* already cited clearly speaks of him as departed, and enjoins upon his executors to make provision for Metrodorus' children. The above mentioned Timocrates also, the brother of Metrodorus and a giddy fellow was another of his pupils.

Metrodorus works

Against the Physicians, in three books, *On Sensations, Against Timocrates, On Magnanimity, On Epicurus' Weak Health, Against the Dialecticians, Against the Sophists,* in nine books, *The Way to Wisdom, On Change, On Wealth, Against Democritus, On Noble Birth.*

Next came Polyaenus, son of Athenodorus, a citizen of Lampsacus, a just and kindly man, as Philodemus and his pupils affirm. Next came Epicurus' successor Hermarchus, son of Agemortus, a citizen of Mitylene, the son of a poor man and at the outset a student of rhetoric. The following excellent works are in circulation by him: *Correspondence concerning Empedocles,* in twenty-two books, *On*

Mathematics, Against Plato, Against Aristotle. He died of paralysis, but not until he had given full proof of his ability.

And then there is Leonteus of Lampsacus and his wife Themista, to whom Epicurus wrote letters; further, Colotes and Idomeneus, who were also natives of Lampsacus. All these were distinguished, and with them Polystratus, the successor of Hermarchus; he was succeeded by Dionysius, and he by Basilides. Apollodorus, known as the tyrant of the Garden, who wrote over four hundred books, is also famous; and the two Ptolemaei of Alexandria, the one black and the other white; and Zeno of Sidon, the pupil of Apollodorus, a voluminous author; and Demetrius, who was called the Laconian; and Diogenes of Tarsus, who compiled the select lectures; and Orion, and others whom the genuine Epicureans call Sophists. There were three other men who bore the name of Epicurus: one the son of Leonteus and Themista; another Magnesian by birth; and a third, a drill-sergeant.

Epicurus' writings

Epicurus was a most prolific author and eclipsed all before him in the number of his writings: for they amount to about three hundred rolls, and contain not a single citation from other authors; it is Epicurus himself who speaks throughout. Chrysippus (the Stoic) tried to outdo him in authorship according to Carneades, who therefore calls him the literary parasite of Epicurus: "For every subject treated by Epicurus, Chrysippus in his contentiousness must treat at equal length; hence he has frequently repeated himself and set down the first thought that occurred to him, and in his haste has left things unrevised, and he has so many citations that they alone fill his books, nor is this unexampled in Zeno and Aristotle."

Such, then, in number and character are the writings of Epicurus, the best of which are the following: *On Nature,* thirty seven books; *On Atoms and Void; On Love; Epitome of Objections to the Physicists; Against the Megarians; Problems; Principal Doctrines; On Choice and Avoidance; On the End; On the Standard,* or *Canon; Chaeredemus; On the gods; On Piety; Hegesianax; On Human Life,* four books; *On Just Dealing; Neocles*-dedicated to Themista; *Symposium; Eurylochus*-dedicated to Metrodorus; *On Vision; On the Angle in the Atom; On Touch; On Fate; Theories of the Feelings, Against Timocrates; Discovery of the Future; Introduction to Philosophy; On Images; On Presentation; Aristobulus; On Music; On Justice and the other Virtues; On Benefits and Gratitude; Polymedes; Timocrates,* three books; *Metrodorus,* five books; *Antidorus,* two books; *Theories about Diseases and Death*-to Mithras; *Callistolas; On Kingship; Anaximenes; Correspondence.*

Overview of Epicureanism

The views expressed in these works I will try to set forth by quoting three of his letters, in which he has given an epitome of his whole system. I will also set down his *Principal Doctrines* and any other utterance of his that seems worth citing, that you may be in a position to study the philosopher on all sides and know how to judge him.

The first letter is addressed to Herodotus and deals with physics; the second to Pytbocles and deals with astronomy or meteorology; the third is addressed to Menoeceus and its subject is human life. We must begin with the first after some few preliminary remarks upon his division of philosophy.

It is divided into three parts; Canonics, Physics, Ethics. Canonics (canon=measure), hence Canonics as the measure or standard of truth, or what is now called (epistemology) forms the introduction to the system and is contained in a single work entitled *The Canon*. The physical part includes the entire theory of Nature; it is contained in the thirty-seven books of Nature and, in a summary form, in the letters. The ethical part deals with the facts of choice and aversion: this may be found in the books *On Human Life, Correspondence,* and in his treatise *On the End.*

The usual arrangement, however, is to conjoin Canonics with Physics, and the former they call the science which deals with the standard and the first principle, or the elementary part of philosophy, while physics proper, they say, deals with becoming and perishing and with Nature; ethics, on the other hand, deals with things to be sought and avoided, with human life and with the ultimate end. They reject dialectic as superfluous; holding that in their inquiries the physicists should be content to employ the ordinary terms for things.

Epicurean epistemology and physics

Now in *The Canon*, Epicurus affirms that our sensations and preconceptions and our feelings are the standards of truth; the Epicureans generally consider perceptions of mental presentations to be standard. His own statements are also to be found in the Summary addressed to Herodotus and in the *Principal Doctrines*. Every sensation, he says, is devoid of reason and incapable of memory; for neither is in itself caused nor, regarded as having an external cause, can it add anything thereto or take anything therefrom. Nor is there anything which can refute sensations or convict them of error: one sensation cannot convict another and kindred sensations, for they are equally valid; nor can one sensation refute another which is not kindred but heterogeneous, for the objects which the two senses judge not to be the same; nor again can reason refute them, for reason is wholly dependent on sensation; nor can one sense refute another, since we pay equal heed to all. And the reality of separate perceptions guarantees the truth of our senses. But seeing and hearing are just as real as feeling pain.

Hence it is from plain facts that we must start when we draw inferences about the unknown. For all our notions are derived from perceptions, either by actual contact or by analogy, or resemblance, or composition, with some slight aid from reasoning. Even the objects presented to madmen and to people in dreams are true, for they produce effects, i.e. movements in the mind; which that which is unreal never does.

By preconception, they mean a sort of apprehension or a right opinion or notion, or universal idea stored in the mind; that is, such a recollection of an external object often presented, e.g. such and such a thing is a man: for no sooner is the word man uttered than we think of his shape by an act of preconception, in which the senses take the lead. Thus, the object primarily denoted by every term is then plain and clear. And we should never have started an investigation, unless we had known what it was that we were in search of. For example: the object standing yonder is a horse or a cow. Before making this judgment, we must at some time or other have known by preconception the shape of a horse or a cow. We should not have given anything a name, if we had not first learnt its form by way of preconception. It follows, then, that preconceptions are clear. The object of a judgment is derived from something previously clear, by reference to which we frame the proposition, e.g. "How do we know that this is a man?" Opinion they also call conception or assumption, and declare it to be true and false; for it is true if it is subsequently confirmed or if it is not contradicted by evidence, and false if it is not subsequently confirmed or is contradicted by evidence. Hence the introduction of the phrase, "that which waits for" confirmation, e.g. to wait and get close to the tower and then learn what it looks like at close quarters.

They affirm that there are two states of feeling, pleasure and pain, which arise in every animate being, and that the one is favourable and the other hostile to that being, and by their means, choice and avoidance are determined; and that there are two kinds of inquiry, the one concerned with things, the other with nothing but words. So much, then, for his division and criterion in their main outline.

Epicurean ethics

But as to the conduct of life, what we ought to avoid and what to choose, he writes as follows. Before quoting his words, however, let me go into the views of Epicurus himself and his school concerning the wise man.

There are three motives to injurious acts among men: hatred, envy, and contempt; and these, the wise man overcomes by reason. Moreover, he who has once become wise never more assumes the opposite habit, not even in semblance, if he can help it. He will be more susceptible to emotion than other men; that will be no hindrance to his wisdom. However, not every bodily constitution or every nationality would permit a man to become wise.

Even on the rack, the wise man is happy. He alone will feel gratitude towards friends, present and absent alike, and show it by word and deed. When on the rack, however, he will give vent to cries and groans. As regards women, he will submit to the restrictions imposed by the law, as Diogenes says in his epitome of Epicurus' ethical doctrines. Nor will he punish his servants; rather he will pity them and make allowance on occasion for those who are of good character.

Epicureans do not suffer the wise man to fall in love; nor will he trouble himself about funeral rites; according to them, love does not come by divine inspiration. So Diogenes in his twelfth book. The wise man will not make fine speeches. No one was ever the better for sexual indulgence, and it is well if he be not the worse. Nor, again, will the wise man marry and rear a family, so Epicurus says in *Problems* and in *On Nature*. Occasionally he may marry owing to special circumstances in his life. Some too will turn aside from their purpose. Nor will he drivel, when drunken: so Epicurus says in the *Symposium*. Nor will he take part in politics, as is stated in the first book *On Life*; nor will he make himself a tyrant; nor will he turn Cynic (so the second book *On Life* tells us); nor will he be a mendicant.

But even when he has lost his sight, he will not withdraw himself from life: this is stated in the same book. The wise man will also feel grief, according to Diogenes in the fifth book of his *Epilecta*. And be will take a suit into court. He will leave written words behind him, but will not compose panegyric. He will have regard for his property and for the future. He will be fond of the country. He will be armed against fortune and will never give up a friend. He will pay just so much regard to his reputation as not to be looked down upon. He will take more delight than other men in public festivals. The wise man will set up votive images. Whether he is well off or not will be a matter of indifference to him. Only the wise man will be able to converse correctly about music and poetry, without however actually writing poems himself. One wise man does not move more wisely than another. And he will make money, but only by his wisdom, if he should be in poverty, and he will pay court to a king, if need be. He will be grateful to anyone when he is corrected.

He will found a school, but not in such a manner as to draw the crowd after him; and will give readings in public, but only by request. He will be a dogmatist but not a mere skeptic; and he will be like himself even when asleep. And he will on occasion die for a friend. The school holds that sins are not all equal; that health is in some cases a good, in others a thing indifferent; that courage is not a natural gift but comes from calculation of expediency; and that friendship is prompted by our needs. One of the friends, however, must make the first advances (just as we have to cast seed into the Earth), but it is maintained by a partnership in the enjoyment of life's pleasures.

Two sorts of happiness can be conceived, the one the highest possible, such as the gods enjoy, which cannot be augmented, the other admitting addition and subtraction of pleasures.

Elsewhere he rejects the whole of divination, as in the short epitome, and says, "No means of predicting the future really exists, and if it did, we must regard what happens according to it as nothing to us."

Such are his views on life and conduct; and he has discoursed upon them at greater length elsewhere. He differs from the Cyrenaics with regard to pleasure. They do not include under the term the pleasure which is a state of rest, but only that which consists in motion. Epicurus admits both; also pleasure of mind as well as of body, as he states in his work *On Choice and Avoidance* and in *On the Ethical End*, and in the first book of his work *On Human Life* and in the epistle to his philosopher friends in Mytilene.

So also Diogenes in the seventeenth book of his *Epilecta*, and Metrodorus in his *Timocrates*, whose actual words are: "Thus Pleasure being conceived both as that species which consists in motion and that which is a state of rest." The words of Epicurus in his work *On Choice and Avoidance* are: "Peace of mind and freedom from pain are pleasures which imply a state of rest; joy and delight are seen to consist in motion and activity."

He further disagrees with the Cyrenaics in that they hold that pains of body are worse than mental pains; in all events, evil-doers are made to suffer bodily punishment; whereas Epicurus holds the pains of the mind to be worse. At any rate, the flesh endures the storms of the present alone, the mind those of the past and future as well as the present. In this way also he holds mental pleasures to be greater than those of the body. And as proof that pleasure is the end he adduces the fact that living things, as soon as they are born, are well content with pleasure and are at enmity with pain, by the prompting of Nature and apart from reason. Left to our own feelings, then, we shun pain; as when even Heracles, devoured by the poisoned robe, cries aloud, and bites and yells, and rock to rock resounds,

Headlands of Locris and Euboean cliffs. And we choose the virtues too on account of pleasure and not for their own sake, as we take medicine for the sake of health. So too in the twentieth book of his *Epilecta,* says Diogenes, who also calls education recreation. Epicurus describes virtue as the sine qua non of pleasure, i.e. the one thing without which pleasure cannot be, everything else, food, for instance, being separable, i.e. not indispensable to pleasure.

Come, then, let me set the seal, so to say, on my entire work as well as on this philosopher's life by citing his *Principal Doctrines*, so to bring the whole work to a close and making the end of it to coincide with the beginning of happiness.

ANNEX 5

HISTORICAL BACKGROUND

By Haris Dimitriadis

The end of the city-state

There is no doubt that the Peloponnesian War marked the end of the city-state as a creative power that fulfilled the lives of the citizens. After the defeat of Athenians by the Spartans, Athenian participatory democracy lost its dominance in the Greek world. But the Spartan domination did not last long either. Full of arrogance and pride Sparta was embroiled in constant wars and was inevitably subjugated under the Macedonian yoke. The immediate cause of the collapse of classical Greece was the painful experience of a multiannual war with enormous losses in manpower, but also the brutal bleeding of financial resources. The city-state could no longer provide an acceptable standard of living for its citizens, and intellectuals began to move away from the principles of direct democracy, embracing the idea of monarchy.

The transition from the Greece of Pericles to that of Alexander the Great was more than just another bloody war experience. It caused profound changes in the mentality of the people, especially in their attitude towards politics and the state. While they used to perceive the public and private life as a single whole, they suddenly found themselves without any role in public affairs–foreign, and cut off from the management of the city. This is reflected in art, sculpture, architecture and philosophy, where the emphasis was put on individualism and introspection. While the comedies of the 5th century criticized the affairs of the city, satirizing and lampooning public figures, in the 4th century they dealt with private issues and family life. An additional factor that accelerated these changes was the transition from the small size of the city-state to the vastness of the cosmopolis of the Macedonian empire. Citizens were raised in the anonymity of the new bureaucratic kingdoms, at the mercy of the decisions of unknown bureaucrats.

Philosophy and religion

In the world of the Hellenistic period, beginning with the death of Alexander the Great in 323 BC and ending with the battle of Actium in 31 BC, philosophy was very different. The increased risks that people ran shifted the attention of philosophers from politics to ensuring people's psychological health. The dominant philosophies were the Epicurean and Stoic. Stoicism attracted those who meant to continue their efforts to bring order to the chaos of Hellenistic life. The Epicureans addressed those who had given up this effort and had turned to pursuing a simple and pleasant life in the company of friends.

But even these simple philosophical remedies proved unable to meet the concerns and needs of ordinary people. They seemed to address the higher class and not the common people, who were groaning under the weight of the cosmopolis. The simple man wanted something more concrete and practical, something less demanding than the philosophical cures that were being offered. They found what they were looking for in the mystical cults that could explain their pain in the simplest of terms. The most popular cults were those associated with a mother-goddess, like Ishtar in Sumer, Isis in Egypt or those that taught the coming of a savior, like Osiris and Mithras. The savior would come to liberate man from the forces of darkness that threatened to wipe him out. Many of these cults believed in the resurrection of the body after death. The mother-goddess taught that although her love and affection accompanies them in this life, their salvation will come after death, when they reunite with her. The mystical cults paved the way for the creation and acceptance of Christianity by the inhabitants of the Roman Empire.

Christianity addressed and expressed the insecurity, oppression and indignation of the people under the oppressive Roman yoke. While initially it was seen as another mystical cult, it spread quickly throughout the Roman

Empire and was eventually selected as its official religion. This development dealt a deadly blow to the philosophical quest of the people, and its legacy continues to affect people's thinking and way of life.

The economy

In the good times of the Athenian Republic, the life of the common citizen reached a level never before experienced. The people made their living, as artisans, judges, dancers for public holidays, or rowers. They felt safe and enjoyed their lives. The economic conditions of the time explain the fun of the Classical Athenian period and the admirable progress of a state of 40,000 adult men. The good life and the vision for better days were ruined by the Peloponnesian War. The economy, based on slaves, had no solid foundations, and as soon as they escaped and found protection by the Spartans in the fortified Dekelia, the Athenian workshops and crafts remained stagnant. Later under the Spartan occupation, the Athenian countryside lost its residents. Adult Athenians fell from 40,000 before the Peloponnesian war to 20,000 at 310 BC. In Athens, entire neighborhoods were emptied or demolished. Due to these conditions, social and economic relationships were disrupted. The monetary system thrived and the supply of money was abundant, thus causing inflation. The land fell into few hands, as also later happened in the Roman period. The Piraeus brokers bought the ruined fields and hired slaves and foreign immigrants to cultivate it. Athens not only lost its rural population, but its composition also dramatically changed. The inhabitants of Athens consisted of a small majority of wealthy citizens with a low education and a low level of humanity, and the destitute and impoverished masses.

ANNEX 6

THE BIOGRAPHY OF EPICURUS

By Haris Dimitriadis

"Epicurus, son of Neocles and Chaerestrate, was an Athenian of the Gargettus ward and the Philaidae clan, as Metrodorus says in his book *On Noble Birth*. He is said by Heraclides (in his *Epitome of Sotion*) as well as by others, to have been brought up at Samos after the Athenians had sent colonists there, and to have come to Athens at the age of eighteen, at the time when Xenocrates was head of the Academy and Aristotle was in Chalcis. After the death of Alexander of Macedon and the expulsion of the Athenian colonists from Samos by Perdiccas, Epicurus left Athens to join his father in Colophon; for some time he stayed there and gathered students around him, then returned to Athens again during the archonship of Anaxicrates." (Diogenes Laertius).

Epicurus' parents transmitted to him the democratic spirit, while his experience of the disasters that Athens suffered from the aristocracy and the militaristic regimes influenced him to see life from the point of view of the common man, in contrast with the famous aristocrat sages, Plato and Aristotle. In Samos he was taught by Nausiphanes, and the Platonic Pamphilus. As the island was under the influence of the Ionian naturalistic culture, Epicurus soon moved away from the Platonic beliefs and turned to the materialistic theories of Democritus. At the age of eighteen he was drafted into the Athenian army, where he met his intimate friend, the dramatic poet Menander.

Little is known of his life during the following fifteen years. What is known, though, is that he created his own philosophical circle in Mytilene and then in Lampsacus. He returned to Athens in around 307 BC at the age of thirty four to buy a piece of land between Athens and Piraeus, close to the present Agronomic School. There he housed his philosophical school, which he named "The Garden." Epicurus taught there for thirty-five years, following a simple life, surrounded by men, women, courtesans and slaves, who participated equally in the Epicurean Garden. He died when he was seventy-one years old, in 270 BC.

During the Hellenistic period the dominant philosophical schools were the Epicurean and the Stoic, followed by the Platonic, the Aristotelian, the Skeptics and the Cynics. The principles of the Epicurean Philosophy spread throughout the Greek and the Roman world from the Epicurean school of philosophy in Athens. Epicurus was among the most prolific philosophers in history. He authored works, developed in 300 rolls, the fate of which has been ignored ever since the proclamation of Christianity as the official religion of the Byzantine Empire. Through Diogenes Laertius, a biographer of philosophers of the 3rd century AD, three of his letters survived (to Herodotus, *On Nature*, to Pythocles, *On Celestial Bodies* and to Menoeceus, *On Ethics*), as well as his *Will* and the *Principal Doctrines*, which is a summary of his philosophy.

Ponzio Bratziolini also discovered the poem *De Rerum Natura (On the Nature of Things)* of the Roman Epicurean poet Lucretius (94-55 BC), in a German monastery, in 1414 AD. The poem is developed over six books and contains the Epicurean views on Nature. In 1884, two French archaeologists discovered the great inscription of the Epicurean Diogenes Oenoanda in Ionia, Asia Minor, which is considered a grand philosophical monument of humanity. A collection of Epicurean doctrines named *Vatican Sayings* was found at the Vatican in 1888. Opinions on the Epicurean Philosophy were identified in the works of many writers, Athenaeus, Cicero, Seneca, Sextus Empiricus, Plutarch, and so on. Also, new texts are still coming to light from the charred papyri of an ancient villa that was destroyed by the eruption of Vesuvius, close to the city of Herculaneum in Italy.

Intellectuals in the period of the Enlightenment embraced the Epicurean principles and spread them around the world. An eminent figure of world history, Thomas Jefferson (1743-1826), the third President of the USA (1801-1809) and leading author of the Declaration of

Independence, wrote in his letter to William Short: "As you say of yourself, I too am an Epicurean... Their [the Stoics] great crime was in their calumnies of Epicurus and misrepresentations of his doctrines..."

Today, both in Greece and globally, the Epicurean Philosophy is followed and spread by the modern Epicureans according to Epicurus' will: "Farewell my friends, the truths I taught hold fast." The Epicurean Philosophy laid the foundations for individual and materialist metaphysical views of the universe. It was a source of inspiration for Marx, as we can conclude from the topic of his doctoral thesis, *Difference between the Democritean and Epicurean Philosophy of Nature.* Although initially Marx applauded the Epicurean views, he later embraced the Stoic ideas of Hegel, and suggested the pursuance of duty in the context of destiny as the end of life, according to the stoic philosophy, instead of the pursuit of pleasure.

The spread of the Epicurean teaching in antiquity owes to its practical spirit, according to which philosophy is not an end in itself, but a means and an aid in achieving the objective of human life, which is happiness. Therefore Epicurus did not give any importance to extensive theoretical, grammatical, historical and mathematical research if it did not contribute to living happily. On the other hand, he attributed the malaise of the people to ignorance and superstition, and proposed the knowledge and application of the laws that govern the nature of the cosmos and human beings as a cure.

ANNEX 7

THOMAS JEFFERSON: I AM EPICUREAN

Thomas Jefferson to William Short,
October 31, 1819

Your favor of the 21st is received. My late illness, in which you are so kind as to feel an interest, was produced by a spasmodic stricture of the ilium, which came upon me on the 7th inst. The crisis was short, passed over favorably on the fourth day, and I should soon have been well but that a dose of calomel and jalap, in which there were only eight or nine grains of the former, brought on a salivation. Of this, however, nothing now remains but a little soreness of the mouth. I have been able to get on horseback for three or four days past.

As you say of yourself, I too am an Epicurean. I consider the genuine (not the imputed) doctrines of Epicurus as containing everything rational in moral philosophy which

Greece and Rome have left us. Epictetus indeed, has given us what was good of the stoics; all beyond, of their dogmas, being hypocrisy and grimace. Their great crime was in their calumnies of Epicurus and misrepresentations of his doctrines; in which we lament to see the candid character of Cicero engaging as an accomplice. Diffuse, vapid, rhetorical, but enchanting. His prototype Plato, eloquent as himself, dealing out mysticisms incomprehensible to the human mind, has been deified by certain sects usurping the name of Christians; because, in his foggy conceptions, they found a basis of impenetrable darkness whereon to rear fabrications as delirious, of their own invention. These they fathered blasphemously on him who they claimed as their founder, but who would disclaim them with the indignation which their caricatures of his religion so justly excite. Of Socrates we have nothing genuine but in the Memorabilia of Xenophon; for Plato makes him one of his Collocutors merely to cover his own whimsies under the mantle of his name; a liberty of which we are told Socrates himself complained. Seneca is indeed a fine moralist, disguising his work at times with some Stoicisms, and affecting too much of antithesis and point, yet giving us on the whole a great deal of sound and practical morality. But the greatest of all the reformers of the depraved religion of his own country, was Jesus of Nazareth. Abstracting what is really his from the rubbish in which it is buried, easily distinguished by its lustre from the dross of his biographers, and as separable from that as the diamond from the dunghill, we have the outlines of a system of the most sublime morality which has ever fallen from the lips of man; outlines which it is lamentable he did not live to fill up. Epictetus and Epicurus give laws for governing ourselves, Jesus a supplement of the duties and charities we owe to others. The establishment of the innocent and genuine character of this benevolent moralist, and the rescuing it form the imputation of imposture, which has resulted from artificial systems, invented by ultra-Christian sects, and unauthorized by a single word ever uttered by him, is a most desirable object, and one to which Priestley has successfully devoted his labors and learning. It would in time, it is to be hoped, affect a quiet euthanasia of the heresies of bigotry and fanaticism which have so long triumphed over human reason, and so generally and deeply afflicted mankind; but this work is to be begun by winnowing the grain from the chaff of the historians of his life. I have sometimes thought of translating Epictetus (for he has never been tolerably translated into English) by adding the genuine doctrines of Epicurus from the Syntagma of Gassendi, and an abstract from the Evangelists of whatever has the stamp of the eloquence and fine imagination of Jesus. The last I attempted too hastily some twelve or fifteen years ago. It was the work of two or three nights only, at Washington, after getting through the evening task of reading the letters and papers of the day. But with one foot in the grave, these are now idle projects for me. My business is to beguile the wearisomeness of declining life, as I endeavor to do, by the delights of classical reading and of mathematical truths, and by the consolations of a sound philosophy, equally indifferent to hope and fear.

I take the liberty of observing that you are not a true disciple of our master Epicurus, in indulging the indolence to which you say you are yielding. One of his canons, you know, was that "that indulgence which prevents a greater pleasure, or produces a greater pain, is to be avoided." Your love of repose will lead, in its progress, to a suspension of healthy exercise, a relaxation of mind, an indifference to everything around you, and finally to a debility of body, and hebetude of the mind, the farthest of all things from the happiness which the well-regulated indulgences of Epicurus ensure; fortitude, you know is one of his four cardinal virtues. That teaches us to meet and surmount difficulties; not to fly from them, like cowards; and to fly, too, in vain, for they will meet and arrest us at every turn of our road. Weigh this matter well; brace yourself up; take a seat with Correa, and come and see the finest portion of your country, which, if you have not forgotten, you still do not know, because it is no longer the same as when you knew it. It will add much to the happiness of my recovery to be able to receive Correa and yourself, and prove the estimation in which I hold you both. Come, too, and see your incipient University, which has advanced with great activity this year. By the end of the next, we shall have elegant accommodations for seven professors, and the year following the professors themselves. No secondary character will be received among them. It will be either the ablest which America or Europe can furnish or none at all. They will give us the selected society of a great city separated from the dissipations and levities of its ephemeral insects.

I am glad the bust of Condorcet has been saved and so well placed. His genius should be before us; while the lamentable, but singular act of ingratitude which tarnished his latter days, may be thrown behind us. I will place under this a syllabus of the doctrines of Epicurus, somewhat in the lapidary style, which I wrote some twenty years ago; a like one of the philosophy of Jesus of nearly the same age, is too long to be copied. Vale, et tibi persuade carissimum te esse mihi.

Thomas Jefferson

e. g. The immaculate conception of Jesus, his deification, the creation of the world by him, his miraculous powers, his resurrection and visible ascension, his corporeal presence in the Eucharist, the Trinity; original sin, atonement, regeneration, election, orders of Hierarchy, &c.

Syllabus of the doctrines of Epicurus

Physical -
The universe is eternal.
Its parts, great and small, interchangeable.
Matter and Void alone.
Motion–inherent in matter which is weighty and declining.
Eternal circulation of the elements of bodies.
Gods, an order of beings next superior to man, enjoying in their sphere, their own felicities; but not meddling with the concerns of the scale of beings below them.

Moral -

Happiness is the aim of life.

Virtue the foundation of happiness.

Utility the test of virtue.

Pleasure active and In-do-lent.

In-do-lence (a-tarax-ia) is the absence of pain, the true felicity.

Active, consists in agreeable motion; it is not happiness, but the means to produce it.

Thus the absence of hunger is an article of felicity; eating the means to obtain it.

The summum bonum is to be not pained in the body, nor troubled in the mind.

i.e. In-do-lence of body, tranquility of the mind.

To procure tranquility of the mind we must avoid desire and fear, the two principal diseases of the mind.

Man is a free agent.

Virtue consists in:

1) Prudence.

2) Temperance.

3} Fortitude.

4) Justice.

To which are opposed:

1) Folly.

2) Desire.

3) Fear.

4) Deceit.

THE PRINCIPAL DOCTRINES TRANSFERRED IN CONTEMPORARY TERMS

By Haris Dimitriadis

1. I philosophize on the necessities of life.

2. Everything happens according to the natural laws, without any divine intervention.

3. All creatures have sprung from within the mother Earth.

4. I obey the laws of Nature.

5. I pursue a happy life.

6. I seek pleasure; I avoid pain.

7. I make choices wisely.

8. I live a quiet life away from the crowd.

9. I cultivate friendship.

10. I enjoy the moment.

11. I recall the past with gratitude.

12. I look to the future with optimism.

The way in which we see life, our thoughts, plans and decisions depend on the perceptions that, consciously or unconsciously, have been imprinted in our minds through heredity and experiences. The most important concepts of the Epicurean Philosophy had been coded by Epicurus in a list, known as *Principal Doctrines*, which the students of the Epicurean "university" had to adopt and memorize. The *Principal Doctrines*, forty in number, constituted the core of his philosophy, out of which all other conceptions arise with a series of simple reasoning. An attempt has been made by the author to transfer these doctrines in contemporary terms by referencing original excerpts. A positive attitude towards them is a prerequisite for those who wish to enjoy the positive effects of the implementation of the Epicurean Philosophy in life.

The Contemporary Doctrines with Reference to Ancient Epicurean Excerpts

1: I philosophize on the necessities of life

"To be involved and to philosophize with the issues and needs of life and to not be wasted on marginal issues, with barren discussions and dialectical tricks."

"Vain is the philosophical suggestion, which does not cure any human passion."

"We need to ponder on what brings happiness."

"We can discover the limitations of Nature and ourselves through the knowledge of the truth."

"At the same time, we must philosophize, laugh, and manage our household and other business, while never ceasing to proclaim the words of true philosophy."

2: Everything happens according to the natural laws, without any divine intervention

"The universe has always been what it is now and it will always be the same."

"Nothing comes from nothing."

"Nothing can be dissolved into nothing."

"Apart from atoms and void, nothing is true."

"The universe is infinite."

"But even the worlds are infinite: the ones like ours and the dissimilar ones.

"Our starting point in this study of Nature is this primary observation: nothing ever comes from nothing; neither gods nor any other forces are observed to create anything from nothing."

3: All creatures have sprung from within the mother Earth

"And it must needs be that many races of living things perished and could not beget and propagate their offspring. For whatever animals you see feeding on the breath of life, either their craft or bravery, aye or their swiftness has protected and preserved their kind from the beginning of their being."

"The living beings are nothing but atoms combined in an especially appropriate manner."

"Our spirit is born as a mortal physical substance, and it is not to be left upright forever."

"The mind and the soul are held tightly to each other and constitute a single nature."

4: I obey the laws of Nature

"We must not resist Nature but submit to it. We shall satisfy it if we satisfy the necessary desires and also those bodily desires that cause us no harm, while sternly rejecting those that are harmful."

"Freedom is the greatest fruit of self-sufficiency."

"Natural wealth is both limited and easily obtained, but vanity is insatiable."

"If you arbitrarily reject any sensory experience and fail to differentiate between an opinion awaiting confirmation and what is already perceived by the senses, feelings, and every intuitive faculty of mind, you will impute trouble to all other sensory experiences, thereby rejecting every criterion."

5: I seek a happy life

"We must practice what produces happiness because when we have it, we have everything, and if we lack it, we shall do everything necessary to regain it. So I encourage you, as always, to study and practice my teachings, for they are the basic ingredients of a happy life."

"These are the root of all evil: fear of god, of death, of pain, and desire which goes beyond what Nature requires for a happy life."

"Feelings, they say, are two: pleasure and pain, which affect every living being. Pleasure is congenial to our nature, while pain is hostile to it. Thus they serve as criteria for all choice or avoidance."

6: I look for pleasure, I avoid pain

"Pleasure is the beginning and the end of the happy life because it is the primary good related to our nature."

"Pleasure, we declare, is the beginning and end of the happy life. We are endowed by nature to recognize pleasure as the greatest good. Every choice and avoidance we make is guided by pleasure as our standard for judging the goodness of everything."

"When we say that pleasure is the goal, we do not mean the pleasure of debauchery or sensuality. Despite whatever may be said by those who misunderstand, disagree with, or deliberately slander our teachings, the goal we do seek is this: freedom from pain in the body and freedom from turmoil in the soul. For it is not continuous drinking and revelry, the sexual enjoyment of women and boys, or feasting upon fish and fancy cuisine which result in a happy life. Sober reasoning is what is needed, which decides every choice and avoidance and liberates us from the false beliefs which are the greatest source of anxiety."

7: I make choices wisely

"If you do not reconcile your behavior with the goal of Nature, but instead use some other criterion in matters of choice and avoidance, then there will be a conflict between theory and practice."

"Sober reasoning is what is needed, which decides every choice and avoidance and liberates us from the false beliefs which are the greatest source of anxiety."

"Among desires some are natural and necessary, some natural but not necessary, and others neither natural nor necessary, but based on baseless opinion."

"Those natural desires which create no pain when unfulfilled, though pursued with an intense effort, are also based on baseless opinion; and if they are not dispelled, it is not because of their own nature, but because of human vanity."

"Necessity is an evil; but there is no necessity for continuing to live subjected to necessity."

"By continuously managing the most important matters of life according to the dictates of reason, the wise man or woman constructs a lifelong defense against misfortunes and troubles and seldom suffers from them."

"Wealth, power, and the like are no guarantee of happiness – only reason has power over the fear of death and other irrational fears."

"Do not reason with something based on erroneous observations of the facts of reality, or else your conclusions will also be erroneous."

"Chance has little effect upon the wise man, for his greatest and highest interests are directed by reason throughout the course of his life."

8: I live a quiet life away from the crowd

"I have never wished to cater to the crowd; for what I know they do not approve, and what they approve I do not know."

"True security is that of a quiet life and away from the crowd."

"I live unnoticed."

"We must free ourselves from the prison of private and public affairs."

9: I cultivate friendship

"Of all things that wisdom provides for living one's entire life in happiness, the greatest by far is the possession of friendship."

"Every friendship in itself is to be desired; but the initial cause for friendship is from its advantages."

"He who desires to live in tranquility with nothing to fear from other men ought to make friends. Those of whom he cannot make friends, he should at least avoid rendering enemies; and if that is not in his power, he should, as much as possible, avoid all dealings with them, and keep them aloof, insofar as it is in his interest to do so."

"The superior man more than anything is dedicated to wisdom and friendship. Of these the first is mortal good, the second immortal."

"The major motive of friendship is security. To maintain a friendship though one needs to love the friend as one loves ourself."

10: I enjoy the moment

"There is no reason to destroy that which you have.

Instead give value to the fact that what you have surpasses your expectations."

"We have been born once and there can be no second birth. For all eternity we shall no longer be. But you, although you are not master of tomorrow, are postponing your happiness. We waste away our lives in delaying, and each of us dies without having enjoyed leisure."

11: I recall the past with gratitude

"All this is encountered with the joy that I feel in my soul as I recall a discussion we had."

"We should find solace for misfortune in the happy memory

of the things that are gone, and in the knowledge that what has come to be cannot be undone."

"We show our feeling for deceased friends, not by wailing, but by pleasant recollections."

"Mental pleasure is much more important than bodily pleasure. Whereas the body can feel pleasure only at the time of the pleasurable experience, the mind has the gifts of memory and anticipation: it can mitigate or eliminate present pain by the recollection of past pleasures or the expectation of pleasures to come."

12: I look to the future with optimism

"The steady state of wellness and the certain hope that it will last longer offers more confident joy to the one who knows how to estimate correctly."

"Future days are neither wholly ours, nor wholly not ours. We must neither depend on them as they are sure to come nor despair that we will not live to see them."

"Although the mind's ability to look back and forward is exploited by the wise to their advantage, it ruins the lives of those whose attitude to past events is bitter, and whose attitude to the future is dominated by unnecessary fears, especially of the gods and of death, and unnecessary and insatiable desires, especially for wealth and power."

ΕPICURUS
& the Pleasant Life

THE ANCIENT GREEK PHILOSOPHY APPLIED IN MODERN LIFE

ATARAXIA
*NO PAIN
IN BODY AND SOUL*

OPTIMISM
*POSITIVE THINKING
POSITIVE PERCEPTIONS*

AUTONOMY
*EXERCISE OF FREE WILL
CONTROL OF INNER WORLD: DESIRES, FEELINGS, THOUGHTS
CONTROL OF EXTERNAL WORLD: SOCIAL ENVIRONMENT, POLITICS*

PLEASURES
*1. NATURAL NECESSARY:
BODILY: FOOD, HEALTH, SHELTER
PSYCHOLOGICAL: SAFETY, FRIENDSHIP
INTELLECTUAL: KNOWLEDGE
2. NATURAL NON-NECESSARY:
SEX, MARRIAGE, KIDS, ENTERTAINMENT, TRAVELING, SPORTS, ACTIVITIES IN NATURE, ETC.*

BIBLIOGRAPHY

Amicus, Cassius. *Catius' Cat and the Forty Mice.*

Anderson, Eric. *Epicurus in the 21st Century.*

Annas, Julia Elizabeth. *Virtue, Ethics and Social Psychology.*

Aquinas, Thomas. *Summa Theologica.*

Arendt, Hannah. *Responsibility and Judgment.*

Arendt, Hannah. *The Life of the Mind.*

Aristotle. *Nicomachean Ethics.*

Armstrong, David Malet. *A Materialist Theory of the Mind.*

Armstrong, Karen. *Buddha.*

Aurelius, Marcus. *Meditations.*

Averroes and Najjar, Ibrahim. *Faith and Reason in Islam: Averroes' Exposition of Religious Arguments (Great Islamic Writings).*

Avramidis, John. *Epicurean Philosophy Sources.*

Baars, Bernard. *In the Theater of Consciousness: The Workspace of the Mind.*

Bacon, Francis. *Novum Organum.*

Bailey, Cyril. *Epicurus-The Extant Remains.*

Bailey, Cyril. *The Greek Atomists and Epicurus.*

Baird, William P. *Friends with Benefits: Other Regard in Epicurean Ethics.*

Bakalis, Nikolaos. *Handbook of Greek Philosophy from Thales to the Stoics. Analysis and fragments.*

Baumeister, Roy. *Free Will in Scientific Psychology.*

Bentham, Jeremy and Mill, John Stuart. *Utilitarianism and Other Essays.*

Berkeley, George. *A Treatise Concerning the Principles of Human Knowledge.*

Bernstein, Marc. *Friends without Favoritism.*

Blackson, Thomas A. *Ancient Greek Philosophy: From the Presocratics to the Hellenistic Philosophers.*

Blanchflower, David G. and Oswald, Andrew J. *Money, Sex and Happiness: An Empirical Study.*

Blum, Lawrence. *Friendship, Altruism, and Morality.*

Botton, Alain de. *The Consolations of Philosophy.*

Brett, G. S. *The Philosophy of Gassendi.*

Brundage, Matt. *Psychological Effects of Materialism and Work on Happiness.*

Burroughs, James E. and Rindfleisch, Aric. *Materialism and Well-Being: A Conflicting Values Perspective.*

Calvin, John. *Institutes of the Christian Religion.*

Camus, Albert. *The Myth of Sisyphus.*

Camus, Albert. *The Stranger.*

Camus, Albert. *The Plague.*

Carnegie, Dale. *How to Stop Worrying and Start Living.*

Carnegie, Dale. *How to Win Friends and Influence People.*

Cartledge, Paul. *Democritus.*

Cicero, Marcus Tullius and Rackham, Harris. *On the Ends of Good and Evil: De Finibus Bonorum et Malorum.*

Cicero, Marcus Tullius. *On the Good Life.*

Clay, Diskin. *Paradosis and survival: Three Chapters in the History of Epicurean Philosophy.*

Csikszentmihalyi, Mihaly. *Creativity.*

Csikszentmihalyi, Mihaly. *Finding Flow: The Psychology of Engagement with Everyday Life.*

Csikszentmihalyi, Mihaly. *Flow: The Psychology of Optimal Experience.*

Csikszentmihalyi, Mihaly and Hunter, Jeremy. *Happiness in Everyday Life.*

Copernicus, Nicolaus. *On the Revolutions of the Heavenly Spheres.*

Crespo, Hiram. *Tending the Epicurean Garden.*

Damasio, Antonio. *Descartes' Error: Emotion, Reason and the Human Brain.*

Damasio, Antonio. *The Feeling of What Happens.*

Darwin, Charles. *On the Origin of Species.*

Darwin, Charles. *The Expression of the Emotions in Man and Animals.*

Davis, John. *Psychological Benefits of Nature Experiences: An Outline of Research and Theory with Special Reference to Transpersonal Psychology.*

Dawkins, Richard. *The God Delusion.*

DeLeire, Thomas. *Does Consumption Buy Happiness? Evidence from the US.*

Dennett, Daniel C. *Consciousness Explained.*

Derrida, Jacques. *Writing and Difference.*

Descartes, Rene. *Meditations on First Philosophy.*

Dewey, John. *How We Think.*

De Witt Hyde, William. *The Five Great Philosophies of Life.*

DeWitt, Norman. *Epicurus and His Philosophy.*

Diogenes of Oenoanda, Chilton, C.W. *Fragments: A Translation and Commentary.*

Easterlin, Richard. *Does Economic Growth Improve the Human Lot?*

Einstein, Albert. Relativity: *The Special and the General Theory.*

Einstein, Albert. *The World As I See It.*

Emerland, Neal. *Consumerism, Nature, and the Human Spirit.*

Epicurus and Usener, Hermann. *Epicurea.*

Fish, Jeffrey and Sanders, Kirk R. *Epicurus and the Epicurean Tradition.*

Flavin, Patrick. *Life Satisfaction and Political Participation: Evidence from the United States.*

Foucault, Michel. *The Archaeology of Knowledge.*

Frankl, Viktor E. *Man's Search for Meaning.*

Friedman, Mordechai A. *Friendship and Moral Growth.*

Fromm, Erich. *Man for Himself: An Inquiry into the Psychology of Ethics.*

Fromm, Erich. *The Art of Being.*

Fromm, Erich. *The Art of Loving.*

Fromm, Erich. *To Have or To Be?*

Geer, Russell. *Epicurus: Letters, Principal Doctrines and Vatican Sayings.*

Gilbert, Dan. *Why are we Happy?*

Glad, Clarence E. *Paul and Philodemus: Adaptability in Epicurean and Early Christian Psychology.*

Goleman, Daniel. *Emotional Intelligence: Why It Can Matter More than IQ.*

Goleman, Daniel. *Focus: The Hidden Driver of Excellence.*

Gordon, Pamela. *Epicurus in Lycia. The Second-Century World of Diogenes of Oenoanda.*

Gottlieb, Anthony. *The Dream of Reason. A History of Western Philosophy from the Greeks to the Renaissance.*

Gould, Josiah B. *Philosophy of Chrysippus.*

Hawking, Stephen. *A Brief History Of Time: From Big Bang to Black Holes.*

Hawking, Stephen. *The Theory of Everything: The Origin and Fate of the Universe.*

Hawking, Stephen and Mlodinow, Leonard. *The Grand Design.*

Heath, Sir Thomas. *Aristarchus of Samos: The Ancient Copernicus.*

Heidbreder, Eva G. *Civil Society Participation in EU Governance.*

Heidegger, Martin. *Being and Time.*

Heisenberg, Werner. *Philosophical Problems of Quantum Physics.*

Heisenberg, Werner and Eckart, Carl. *The Physical Principles of the Quantum Theory.*

Heraclitus and Kirk G. S. Heraclitus: *The Cosmic Fragments.*

Hibler, Richard W. Happiness. *Through Tranquillity. The school of Epicurus.*

Hicks, R. D. *Stoic and Epicurean.*

Hitchens, Christopher. *Letters to a Young Contrarian.*

Hitchens, Christopher and Graydon Carter. *God Is Not Great: How Religion Poisons Everything.*

Hitchens, Christopher. *Mortality.*

Hippocrates. *The genuine works of Hippocrates.*

Hobbes, Thomas. *Leviathan.*

Hobbes, Thomas. *Man and Citizen: (De Homine and De Cive).*

Hoffman, Eric. *Love as a Kind of Friendship.*

Horace. *The Epistles of Horace.*

Horace and Radice Betty. *The Complete Odes and Epodes.*

Hume, David. *A Treatise of Human Nature.*

Husserl, Edmund and Moran, Dermot. *Ideas: General Intro-duction to Pure Phenomenology.*

Hyde, William. *From Epicurus to Christ; a Study in the Prin-ciples of Personality.*

James, William. *The Principles of Psychology.*

James, William and Gunn, Giles. *Pragmatism and Other Writings.*

Jefferson, Thomas and Peterson, Merrill D. *Jefferson: Writ-ings.*

Jeske, Diane. *Friendship and Reasons of Intimacy.*

Jones, Howard. *The Epicurean Tradition.*

Kahn, Charles H. *Anaximander and the Origins of Greek Cosmology.*

Kahneman, Daniel. *A Survey Method for Characterizing Daily Life Experience: The Day Reconstruction Method (DRM).*

Kant, Immanuel. *Critique of Pure Reason.*

Kechagia, Eleni. *Plutarch Against Colotes: A Lesson in His-tory of Philosophy.*

Kierkegaard, Soren and Hannay, Alastair. *The Concept of Anxiety.*

Klein, Daniel. *Travels with Epicurus: A Journey to a Greek Island in Search of a Fulfilled Life.*

Konstan, David. *A Life Worthy of the Gods.*

Konstan, David and Glad, Clarence E. *Philodemus: On Frank Criticism.*

Laertius, Diogenes and Hicks, R. D. *Lives of Eminent Philosophers, Volume II, Books 6-10.*

Lane, Robert E. *The Loss of Happiness in Market Democracies.*

Layard, Richard. *Happiness: Lessons from a New Science.*

Lazarus, von Richard S. *Stress and Emotion: A New Synthesis.*

Lazarus, von Richard S. *Emotion and Adaptation.*

LeDoux, Joseph E. *Synaptic Self: How Our Brains Become Who We Are.*

LeDoux, Joseph E. *The Emotional Brain: The Mysterious Underpinnings of Emotional Life. LeDoux, Joseph E. The Self: From Soul to Brain.*

Lee, H. D. P. *Zeno of Elea.*

Locke, John. *Two Treatises of Government and a Letter Concerning Toleration.*

Loewenstein, George and Karlsson, Niklas. *Beyond Bentham: The Search for Meaning.*

Long, Anthony A. *Hellenistic Philosophy: Stoics, Epicureans, Skeptics.*

Long, Anthony A. *From Epicurus to Epictetus.*

Lucian of Samosata. *Works of Lucian of Samosata.*

Lucretius. *On the Nature of Things.*

Lyubomirsky, Sonja. *The How of Happiness.*

Mansbridge, Jane. *Does Participation Make Better Citizens?*

Marx, Karl and Mandel, Ernest. *Capital: A Critique of Political Economy.*

Maslow, Abraham. *Hierarchy of Needs.*

May, Rollo and Yalom, Irvin. *Existential Psychotherapy.*

Mcevilley, Thomas. *The Shape of Ancient Thought: Comparative Studies.*

Menander and Razavi, William. *The Complete Fragments of Menander.*

Mills, John Stuart. *On Liberty.*

Mills, John Stuart. *Utilitarianism.*

Murray, Gilbert. *The Legacy of Greek Essays.*

Myers, David. *The American Paradox: Spiritual Hunger in an Age of Plenty.*

Naiditch, Paul G. *Philodemus and Greek Papyri.*

Newton, Isaac and Motte, Andrew. *Principia: The Mathematical Principles of Natural Philosophy.*

Nichols, Shaun. *How Can Psychology Contribute to the Free Will Debate?*

Nietzsche, Friedrich Wilhelm. *Beyond Good and Evil.*

Nietzsche, Friedrich Wilhelm. *The Antichrist.*

Nietzsche, Friedrich Wilhelm. *The Dawn.*

Nietzsche, Friedrich Wilhelm. *Thus Spoke Zarathustra.*

Noll, Samantha. *The Joining of Neuroscience, Psychology, and Philosophy in a Search for the Self.*

Nozick, Robert. *Love's Bond.*

Nussbaum, Martha C. *The Fragility of Goodness: Luck and Ethics in Greek Tragedy and Philosophy.*

Nussbaum, Martha C. *The Therapy of Desire: Theory and Practice in Hellenistic Ethics.*

Oates, Whitney J. *The Stoic and Epicurean philosophers: The Complete Extant Writings of Epicurus, Epictetus, Lucretius and Marcus Aurelius.*

O'Grady, Patricia F. *Thales of Miletus: The Beginnings of Western Science and Philosophy. O'Keefe, Tim. Epicureanism.*

Palmer, John. *Parmenides and Presocratic Philosophy.*

Panichas, George Andrew. *Epicurus.*

Pert, Candace B. *Molecules of Emotion: The Science Behind Mind-Body Medicine.*

Plato. *Gorgias.*

Plato. *Symposium.*

Plato. *The Republic.*

Plato. *Timaeus.*

Plato and Anastaplo George. *Plato: Meno.*

Plato and Annas, Julia. *Plato: The Statesman.*

Plato and Sachs, Joe. *Plato: Theaetetus.*

Plato and Schofield, Malcolm. *Plato: Laws.*

Plotinus and O'Brien, Elmer S. J. *The Essential Plotinus.*

Plutarch. *Plutarch's Lives.*

Plutarch and Shilleto, A. R. *Plutarch's Morals.*

Popper, Karl R. *Objective Knowledge: An Evolutionary Approach.*

Popper, Karl R. *The Logic of Scientific Discovery.*

Ptolemy and Robbins, F. E. *Ptolemy: Tetrabiblos.*

Ptolemy and Toomer, G. J. *Ptolemy's Almagest.*

Quine, Willard Van Orman. *Pursuit of Truth.*

Radcliff, Benjamin. *Politics, Markets, and Life Satisfaction.*

Razavi, William and Menander. *The Complete Fragments of Menander.*

Rist, J.M. *Epicurus: An introduction.*

Rousseau, Jean-Jacques and Cranston, Maurice. *The Social Contract.*

Russell, Bertrand. *The Analysis of Mind.*

Russell, Bertrand and Dennett, Daniel C. *The Conquest of Happiness.*

Ryff, Carol. *Positive Health.*

Saint-Andre, Peter. *Letters on Happiness: An Epicurean Dialogue.*

Saint Anselm of Canterbury. *Cur Deus Homo: Why God Became Man.*

Saint Augustine and Foley, Michael P. *Confessions.*

Saint Augustine Hippo and Dods, Marcus. *The City of God.*

Sagan, Carl. *Cosmos.*

Sagan, Carl. *The Demon-Haunted World.*

Sagan, Carl. *The Dragons of Eden.*

Sanders, Lynn M. *The Psychological Benefits of Political Participation.*

Sartre, Jean-Paul. *Being and Nothingness.*

Sartre, Jean-Paul. *Existentialism is a Humanism.*

Sartre, Jean-Paul. *Existentialism and Human Emotions.*

Sartre, Jean-Paul. *Iron in the Soul.*

Sartre, Jean-Paul. *Truth and Existence.*

Sartre, Jean-Paul. *We Have Only This Life to Live.*

Schopenhauer, Arthur and Hollingdale, R. J. *Essays and Aphorisms.*

Schopenhauer, Arthur and Payne, E. F. J. *The World as Will and Representation.*

Schwartz, Barry. *The Paradox of Choice: Why More is Less.*

Searle, R. John. *Mind: A Brief Introduction.*

Searle, R. John. *Seeing Things as They Are: A Theory of Perception.*

Searle, R. John. *The Mystery of Consciousness.*

Searle, R. John. *Why I am not a Property Dualist.*

Seddon, Keith and Yonge, C. D. *A Summary of Stoic Philosophy: Zeno of Citium in Diogenes Laertius Book Seven.*

Seligman, Martin. *Authentic Happiness.*

Seligman, Martin. *Learned Optimism.*

Seneca, Lucius Annaeus. *Letters from a Stoic: Epistulae Morales Ad Lucilium.*

Sen, Amartya. *Collective Choice and Social Welfare.*

Sen, Amartya. *Development as Freedom.*

Sextus Empiricus and Annas, Julia. *Sextus Empiricus: Outlines of Scepticism.*

Smith, Nicholas. D. *Reason and religion in Socratic philosophy.*

Spinoza, Benedictus and Morgan, Michael L. *The Essential Spinoza: Ethics and Related Writings.*

Stocker, Michael. *The Schizophrenia of Modern Ethical Theories.*

Strozier, Robert. *Epicurus and Hellenistic Philosophy.*

Strozier, Robert. *Foucault, Subjectivity, and Identity.*

Theodoridis, Haralambos. *Epicurus, the True Face of the Ancient World.*

Thoreau, Henry David. *Walden.*

Tocqueville, Alexis de and Mansfield, Harvey C. *Democracy in America.*

Van Deurzen, Emmy. *Existential Psychotherapy.*

Voelkel, James R. *Johannes Kepler: And the New Astronomy.*

Wallace, Claire and Pichler, Florian and Hayes, Bernadette. *First European Quality of Life Survey: Participation in Civil Society. 2007. The European Foundation for the Improvement of Living and Working Conditions.*

Wallace, William. *Epicureanism.*

Warren, James. *The Cambridge Companion to Epicureanism.*

Watson, John. *Hedonistic Theories: From Aristippus to Spencer.*

Weitz-Shapiro, Rebecca and Winters, Matthew S. *Political Participation and Quality of Life.*

Whiting, Jennifer. E. *Friends and Future Selves.*

Wilkinson, Will. *In Pursuit of Happiness: Is it Reliable?*

Wittgenstein, Ludwig and Ogden, C. K. *Tractatus Logico-Philosophicus.*

Wootton, David. *Galileo: Watcher of the Skies.*

Wright, Frances and Amicus, Cassius. *A Few Days in Athens.*

Yalom, Irvin. *Lying on the Couch.*

Yalom, Irvin. *Staring at the Sun: Overcoming the Terror of Death.*

Yalom, Irvin. *The Schopenhauer Cure.*

Yalom, Irvin. *The Spinoza Problem.*

Yalom, Irvin. *When Nietzsche Wept.*

Biographical Note

Born in Greece, Haris studied Mathematics at the Aristotelian University of Thessaloniki as well as Economics at the London School of Economics. His career spanned the business and banking industries and he has now settled into retirement. Through climbing the corporate ladder, he found it brought little peace of mind, and he turned his attention to the philosophy of Epicurus. He has devoted the last decade of his life to studying, reconstructing and practicing the ancient Epicurean philosophy. Stunned by its effectiveness, he felt compelled to share his learnings with the world by publishing this very book in Greek three years ago. With the publication of this English edition, he endeavors to disseminate this healing philosophy to the world in accordance with Epicurus' own aspiration. Haris' vision is to revive people's interest in and practice of the comprehensive and practical philosophy of Epicurus and re-establish the "Epicurean Garden" in a contemporary context.

Haris lives a simple and pleasant life in Athens with his family and friends, seeking peace of mind, freed from the anxieties and fears that the established philosophies of material welfare and religious faith provoke.